W9-ABP-174

THE DRUNKEN KING

African Systems of Thought

THE DRUNKEN KING
OR
The Origin of the State

LUC DE HEUSCH

Translated and annotated by Roy Willis

INDIANA UNIVERSITY PRESS
Bloomington

Le roi ivre ou l'origine de l'État was originally published in French by Éditions Gallimard in 1972. This English translation is published by arrangement with Gallimard.

Manufactured in the United States of America

Library of Congress Cataloging in Publication Data

Heusch, Luc de.

The drunken king, or, The origin of the state.

(African systems of thought)

Translation of: Roi ivre.

Bibliography: p.

1. Legends—Africa, Central. 2. Bantus—Folklore. 3. Bantus—Religion. 4. Mythology, African. 5. Structural anthropology. 6. Bantus—Rites and ceremonies. I. Title. II. Series.

GR357.3.H4813 398.2'0967 81–47569

ISBN 0–253–31832–7 AACR2

1 2 3 4 5 86 85 84 83 82

Contents

Translator's Introduction

Le roi ivre ou l'origine de l'État appeared in 1972, at a time when anthropological structuralism as represented in the person and ideas of Claude Lévi-Strauss was already some way past its heady apogee in the mid-1960s. The messianic overtones associated with that intellectual movement, which the sibylline pronouncements of Lévi-Strauss himself did much to maintain and promote, are to a considerable extent responsible for the neglect and even obloquy into which structuralism has fallen in more recent years, now that the Promised Land of total human self-understanding seems as far away as ever. The ensuing sense of disillusionment may explain why no new figure has yet come forward to assume the prophetic mantle (although at least one repentant ex-structuralist has raised the arcane banner of Ludwig Wittgenstein, that belatedly converted apostle of extreme cultural relativism). Instead, the once solidary discipline of social anthropology has split into a variety of seemingly unrelated and mutually disdainful schools, under such labels as neo-Marxism, symbolic anthropology, and transactionalism.

Luc de Heusch remains an avowed and unashamed structuralist, a disciple and associate of Lévi-Strauss and an accomplished practitioner of the Lévi-Straussian semiological technique of myth analysis. His extraordinary book reminds us that it is high time to recognize the full scale and purport of the achievement of Claude Lévi-Strauss, who, in laying the foundations of a comparative and universal science of man, has succeeded in a task that ultimately defeated James George Frazer, the only comparably gigantic figure in twentieth-century anthropology. It is sometimes said, by those who have not understood his argument, that Lévi-Strauss's method of myth analysis is unscientific, because unfalsifiable. The charge of "unfalsifiability" springs from a mistaken application of the logic of Western scientific discourse to the qualitatively different logic of mythical thought, a mistake that some of Lévi-Strauss's own comments on the significance of his findings have unfortunately helped to encourage. What de Heusch has achieved by his brilliant application of Lévi-Strauss's technique to a neglected body of Central African mythology is at once to prove the power and validity of the conceptual system that produced the four-volume study of Amerindian myth, the *Mythologiques*, and to confront that system with a theoretical challenge that must compel its development in a new and fruitful direction, toward "structural history." And that is precisely what constitutes scientific progress.

Although mythical thought is not "scientific" in the strict sense (in a characteristically ambiguous formulation Lévi-Strauss has referred to "the science of the concrete"), it *is* comprehensible, and it *does* convey knowledge. The proof is that through a systematic investigation of its operations as objectified in those collective and symbolic products called "myths," de Heusch has, in *Le roi ivre*, completely transformed our understanding of the thought-world of a vast aggregate of Central African peoples. The mental operations revealed in myth by structural analysis happen to be describable in terms of certain concepts employed in modern mathematics, particularly group theory, set theory, and Boolean algebra. The deep significance of this fact is related to the relatively recent development of these mathematical ideas to account for the intellectual operations involved in such apparently simple mathematical feats as counting, adding, and subtracting. What has thereby been revealed of the elementary procedures of human conceptualization strongly suggests the existence of a "universal logic," which no doubt has its simpler analogues in the mental processes of all the higher animals. It was Lévi-Strauss who discovered and demonstrated through an astonishingly vast range of material that the structures of myths, like those of mathematical groups, consist of *systems of transformations*, which is to say that they possess the properties of wholeness, transformation, and self-regulation.*

In *Le roi ivre* de Heusch makes skillful use of the Lévi-Straussian concepts of inversion, opposition, and transformation to discover law-governed relations between the mythical ideas of widely separated and culturally distinct savanna peoples such as the Luba and Kuba, and

*Cf. Piaget, 1971:5.

shows that personages such as the Luban "drunken king" Nkongolo and the tragic heroine Lueji of the Lunda are combinations of structural elements within a common mythical group and constitute inverse transformations of each other.

But de Heusch does much more than expose the abstract, quasi-mathematical forms hidden beneath the exotic myth narratives. By an extraordinary feat of empathy—extraordinary because he is working entirely through secondhand materials—he introduces the reader to human worlds of beauty and terror in which, as C. C. Wrigley has noted in a finely perceptive review,

> the chaos of human experience is transformed into an immense but orderly design, into a dance in which kings and planets, storms and sisters' sons, civet-cats and birds of dawning all have their significant movements to perform.†

The total of 33 myths analyzed by de Heusch in constructing this splendidly panoramic overview of Central African Bantu society is admittedly but a small fraction of the massive total of 813 Amerindian narratives drawn on by Lévi-Strauss in the *Mythologiques*. De Heusch believes that the relative poverty of myths in the savanna societies is in large measure a reflection of a cultural difference between the Amerindian and Central African regions, as V. W. Turner has suggested; but to compensate for this comparative dearth of mythical material he has drawn on rich accounts of the symbolism of initiation ritual among the Kuba and Lunda peoples, showing conclusively that the symbolic ideas informing these rituals are also common to the myths emanating from these two culture areas; in itself this is a discovery of considerable import.*

Another major difference between the mythical systems of the two continents (there are some strikingly unexpected parallels in detail) is that the Bantu myths convey a political ideology centered on the polar concepts of celestial (divine) and terrestrial kingship (respec-

†Wrigley, 1974:135. Wrigley's article unfortunately misconstrues what de Heusch has to say about divine ("sacral") kingship and the meaning of the rainbow symbol.

*This treatment of myth and ritual as structured by a common set of conceptual elements is at variance with the idiosyncratic and misleading account of ritual proffered by Lévi-Strauss in *L'Homme Nu* (Lévi-Strauss, 1971:600–610), according to which ritual attempts to negate the schematization imposed on the world by mythical thought by reestablishing a mindless continuity. De Heusch has rightly qualified these pages as "astounding" (de Heusch, 1975:371).

tively *bulopwe* and *bufumu* among the Luba). In this respect the Bantu myths differ from the politically innocent Amerindian myths but offer some interesting parallels with Indo-European myths of dual sovereignty, as described by Georges Dumézil. The absence of a political motif in the Amerindian corpus clearly relates to the fact that most Amerindian societies† are what Lévi-Strauss has termed "cold," with a minimum of social stratification and an inbuilt tendency to suppress perception of change in the interests of preserving an atemporal, synchronic structure. Such normatively unchanging, "cold" societies are contrasted with the stratified "hot" societies of Europe, driven by an internal dynamism to undergo continual change. The latter are societies with history, the former are history-less.*

Most of the material on myth and ritual symbolism in *Le roi ivre* comes from societies with indigenous state systems, and indigenous histories. In these societies, as the myths and rituals clearly show, an overriding structural logic coordinates perceptions of space, time, and institutional organization; yet these perceptions are subject to a historical evolution from simpler to more complex formation. A question then arises, one that Lévi-Strauss, because of the ahistorical nature of his Amerindian societies, did not have to face: What relation is there between the (as yet largely unknown) precolonial histories of these African societies and their myths and ritual symbols? Near the end of *Le roi ivre* de Heusch offers a surprising and indeed unacceptable answer to this question: The ethnohistorians, notably Jan Vansina and David Birmingham, who have interpreted the symbolic figures of Central African myth as real persons with chronological attributes, are right after all! There was a real Lunda princess called Lweji (or Lueji) who married a real Chibinda Ilunga, son of a real Kalala Ilunga of Luba country, a little before the year 1600. Some of Chibinda's followers founded the Bemba state in present-day Zambia, while Lweji's brother Chinguli went west and either he or his successor met the Portuguese in Angola (see pp. 228–29). This amicable conclusion to a long, involved, and often acrimonious debate† between exponents of literalist and symbolist readings of African historical narratives did not remain long unchallenged. Ironically, it was an Africanist historian

†It happens that Lévi-Strauss's Amerindian myths all come from stateless societies. It would be surprising if the myths of, for example, the Mayan Indians were similarly lacking in political content.

*Lévi-Strauss, 1973:40–41.

†Cf. Willis, 1980.

and a student of Vansina, Joseph C. Miller, who in 1972, the publication year of *Le roi ivre*, substantially demolished the literalist interpretation of Central African history propounded by Vansina and Birmingham and gratuitously endorsed by de Heusch (Miller, 1972). He did so by showing that *Kinguri* (rendered as *Chinguli* in this book) was not a historical individual but the name of a titled office transmitted down the generations by a common Central African procedure known to anthropologists as "positional succession." Consequently, there was no basis for Vansina's dating of the Lunda state's foundation to "just before 1600" (a date produced by projection backward from Kinguri's recorded seventeenth-century meeting with the Portuguese).*

De Heusch's 1972 statement on the historical significance of his Central African myths actually marks a regression from an earlier theoretical position in which he had envisaged

> the existence of a structural history made unknowingly (*à leur insu*) by men and engendering, in the "cold" societies with little regard for a cumulative economy, certain limited combinations. . . . This hypothesis, which should be taken further, offers the advantage of an escape from the historical nominalism to which Lévi-Strauss sometimes seems tempted to condemn social anthropology.†

De Heusch has also considered the possibility, in an African context, of analyzing "structures of subordination" (i.e., indigenous states) in a structural and transformational perspective which will offer a "third outcome" of historical change in "cold" societies in addition to the stark Lévi-Straussian alternatives of social catastrophe or total absorption of the event by synchronic structure.* Africa, de Heusch also tells us, "has rejected the history we call great, and which is studded with atrocious crimes . . . thus have been preserved human values that cumulative history has denied in order to become movement and permanent disturbance."†

These insights are all the more relevant in view of the grand perspective afforded by de Heusch's magistral achievement in *Le roi ivre*. The task of explicating and making operational the portentous concept

*Miller, 1972.

†De Heusch, 1971:31. This passage originally appeared in an article in the journal *Critique* in 1965 (Nos. 219–220:687–717).

*De Heusch, 1971:135.

†Ibid, 150.

of "structural history" is now urgent and imperative. The early savanna kingdoms developed through personal interaction and transaction conducted and constrained by and through shared cosmological (or religious) ideas and values. That is why, in the myths that record early socioeconomic change and transformation, as Lévi-Strauss has observed for his Amerindian corpus:

> At whatever level the myths situate themselves, whether cosmic, meteorological, sociological, or botanical, technical, economic, sexual, social, etc., the ideas of sharing, exchange, and transaction are dominant.*

The true history of Central Africa which will replace the old, externally imposed "history" of tribal migration and conquest is one in which decisive social changes, transformations of productive base and related political forms, were initiated and carried through in terms of a continuing and all-absorbing social dialogue or, as Maurice Bloch has well expressed it, "a long conversation."† Myth and ritual, in this perspective, represent the social consensus, constantly changing in accordance with the laws of mythical thought, on what that "conversation" is and has been all about, its form and content.* In the Central African myth we find social functions and combinations of functions being represented as symbolic personages such as the drunken and incestuous Rainbow King of the Luba and his antagonist the lunar Prince of the Night; these personages undergo dramatic changes as the myth-story unfolds; the changes culminate in a new and more complex combination of the cosmic elements constituting the personages, and new relations are established among their constituent elements. Far-reaching social changes such as those attending the emergence of a "divine" (celestial) kingship in polar opposition to an aboriginal, terrestrial authority are symbolized in these mythical dramas. Such changes always implicate the cosmological (or, as de Heusch has it, "cosmogonic") attributes of the mythically personified social functions, such as the succession of the seasons, the alternation of day and night, life and death. Thus, as de Heusch shows, the myths always tend to engage profound philosophic and religious issues.

*Lévi-Strauss, 1971:287. In Central Africa, as de Heusch has shown, the "political" has a distinctive place among these various "levels" of mythical thought.

†Bloch, 1977:278. Bloch attributes this view of society to Malinowski.

*This view makes it unnecessary to postulate, as Bloch does, a dichotomy between "ritual" and "mundane" systems of cognition (Bloch, 1977:287).

The study of Central African history, and eventually the history of adjoining and related cultural regions, has to be approached from two convergent and complementary directions. The study of transformative processes in the evolution of small-scale, nonindustrial societies is one of these directions, and one in which some Marxist anthropologists have recently made significant advances. For instance, J. Friedman and M. J. Rowlands have shown, in the course of a pioneering survey of such processes, that the emergence of polar sovereignty, which is the subject of the Luba epic myth, is characteristic of a fairly advanced phase in the evolution of a widely distributed pre-state social formation generally known as the "conical clan."† The other direction is through the analysis and interpretation of the symbolic products, particularly myth and ritual symbolism, in which important social transformations have been recorded.*

This enormous prospect has been opened up by Luc de Heusch in this groundbreaking and beautifully sensitive exploration of Central African social philosophy and experience.

Roy Willis
Edinburgh, 1980.

†Friedman and Rowlands, 1977:226–27. Positional succession, which occurs widely in Central Africa (cf. Miller, 1972), is also characteristic of the "conical clan" phase of social evolution.

*An important and indispensable theoretical tool for the eliciting of historical information from myths is Terence S. Turner's development of the concept of "diachronic structure" in myth (Turner, in Spencer, 1969:26–68. Also Turner, 1977). For an application of a similar model to the sovereignty myth of a people bordering on the Central African savanna region see Willis, 1981.

REFERENCES

Bloch, Maurice. 1977. "The past and the present in the present" (the 1976 Malinowski Memorial Lecture), *Man*, n.s., 12:278–292.

Friedman, J., and Rowlands, M. J. 1977. "Notes towards an epigenetic model of the evolution of 'civilisation,'" in J. Friedman and M. J. Rowlands, (eds.), *The Evolution of Social Systems*, London: Duckworth.

de Heusch, Luc. 1971. *Pourquoi l'épouser? et autres essais*, Paris: Gallimard.

———. 1975. "What Shall We Do With the Drunken King?" *Africa*, 45, 4:363–372.

Lévi-Strauss, Claude. 1971. *Mythologiques IV: L'Homme Nu*, Paris: Plon.

———. 1973. *Anthropologie structurale deux*, Paris: Plon.
Miller, J. C. 1972. "The Imbangala and the chronology of early Central African history," *Journal of African History*, XIII, 4:549–574.
Piaget, Jean. 1971. *Structuralism* (translated by Chaninah Maschler), London: Routledge and Kegan Paul.
Turner, Terence S. 1969. "Oedipus: Time and structure in narrative form," in Robert F. Spencer, (ed.), *Forms of Symbolic Action*, University of Washington Press.
———. 1977. "Narrative structure and mythopoesis: A critique and reformulation of structuralist concepts of myth, narrative and poetics," *Arethusa*, 10, 1:103–163.
Willis, R. G. 1980. "The literalist fallacy and the problem of oral tradition," *Social Analysis*, 4: 28–37.
———. 1981. *A State in the Making: Myth, History and Social Transformation in Pre-colonial Ufipa*, Bloomington: Indiana University Press.
Wrigley, C. C. 1974. "Myths of the savanna," *Journal of African History*, XV, 1:131–135.

THE DRUNKEN KING

Le soleil ne s'éteint jamais au coeur des songes.
Fernand Verhesen,
Franchir la nuit.

Introduction

This book is concerned with understanding African symbolic thought. No new attempt is made in it to justify the theoretical foundations of structuralism.[1] The latter should be judged by its results, by the degree to which it restores the semantic texture of a highly variegated fabric of myths and rituals emanating from a single culture area, that of the savanna civilizations to the south of the great Congo forest. This pioneering endeavor brings together, as portions of a common heritage, the oral traditions about the origins of the traditional kingdoms of the Kuba, Luba, and Lunda of Zaïre, and of the Bemba of Zambia. These ostensibly historical narratives should be treated as myths, comparable, *mutatis mutandis*, with the epic accounts of the founding of ancient Rome. Here we would like to evoke the thought of Georges Dumézil, even though our work relates more directly, but on another continent, to that of Claude Lévi-Strauss. A dual indebtedness is thus acknowledged to these two founders of modern comparative mythology.

Without prejudice to the ultimate results, this first volume seeks to discover the conceptual structure peculiar to Bantu representations of the world. The work of Guthrie, Greenberg, and Meeussen* has made it apparent that the languages spoken by the diverse and numerous

*Of these three linguists, A. E. Meeussen is mainly known for his work on the Bantu languages of Zaïre, and the late Malcolm Guthrie for his global surveys of the Bantu language family. Joseph Greenberg has built on the earlier studies of Westermann to demonstrate the genetic relations between Bantu and the Western Sudanic languages of West Africa, as well as the so-called Semi-Bantu languages of Nigeria, giving the name "Niger-Congo" to this vast and newly discovered language family. The unity of the Niger-Congo group was contested by Guthrie, but Greenberg's classificatory schema is now widely accepted by linguists. (R.W.)

Bantu peoples belong to the same family and are related to the language groups of central Cameroon and eastern Nigeria. The affinities between the languages originating from this region [Cameroon and Nigeria] are such that it is reasonable to assume a progressive occupation by the Bantu peoples, within the relatively short time span of two millennia, of the vast expanses of forest, savanna, and upland which they inhabit today, and which include the greater part of central and eastern Africa. The pioneers of this historic achievement mastered the art of ironworking. In Black Africa, the oldest relics of this highly specialized technology have been discovered on the central Nigerian plateau and dated to about the middle of the first millennium B.C.[2] People of the Iron Age, the Bantu were probably also the first to clear the land of southern Africa for cultivation. Until then this territory had been the preserve of humble hunter-gatherers, whose only remaining descendants are the Pygmies and the Bushmen. The first iron-using civilization developed in the Zambezi valley from about the beginning of the Christian era.[3]

The founders of the great Kongo kingdoms were the highly evolved heirs of this ancient Bantu culture which had become extremely diversified. Although our linguist colleagues have made considerable progress toward reconstructing the original Bantu tongue, this extraordinary cultural diversity, equally apparent in the domains of kinship, religion, and political organization, defeats any attempt at reconstituting the original body of myths, which has dissolved into a multitude of conceptual systems. The structuralist method nevertheless enables us to undertake a basic and decisive operation, that of laying bare the outlines of one of the great semiological complexes derived from this lost mythical kernel. If the dominant ideological function of this complex was to validate the more or less recent emergence of divine kingship, the ensuing anthropo-cosmogonic discourse is manifestly antecedent to the historical facts whose origin it purports to explain. History is ensnared by myth, which imposes its own sovereignty on the kings. Only later research in neighboring Bantu societies will determine whether the different symbolic systems elaborated by these related peoples can be reintegrated, by dint of a certain number of transformations, into this complex of myths.

At the level of technique, we find ourselves in many respects in a very different situation from that of Lévi-Strauss: instead of the proliferation characteristic of Amerindian myths, we find in our region a strictly limited number of narratives, usually recorded by administrators and missionaries with scant regard for the requirements of scientific ethnography. However, two exceptional pieces of research yield solid material for comparative analysis: those of Jan Vansina on the Kuba, and of Victor Turner on the Ndembu, in the Lunda culture area. Turner deserves particular praise for his perception, rare among field workers, of the semantic organization of ritual. We readily agree with him that, among the Bantu, magico-religious practice commonly prevails over mythical discourse, which seems like a poor relation in the realm of the imaginary. But one must also wonder whether customary secrecy has not combined in many cases with resistance to colonization in concealing sacred traditions, which have moreover been the object of relentless hostility from the Christian churches.

The more important narratives which provide the substance of our analysis appear as founding charters of divine kingship. Their grand themes justify the use of the word "epic" (*geste**). Unfortunately, not one conforms exactly with the oral tradition. Stylistic flaws resulting from the process of translation into French or English have made it necessary to present each text without further alteration, and as concisely as possible while including all significant details.

These dry summaries give us no hint of the poetic qualities which other and more fortunate researchers will one day be able to describe, once a systematic and scrupulous program of myth collection has been set in train. It seems necessary to insist once again on the urgency of this task, given the rapid changes in Africa which threaten to destroy the continent's heritage of oral literature. While an abundance of animal stories has been collected in Central Africa, historic myths and legends have usually not received the same attention. Moreover, being ignorant of the special "tone" of each narrative, we are aware of having done less than justice to the vaguely sensed beauty in them.

Even the heroes' names have been fragmented by the recorders. No attempt has been made to restore the Luba or Lunda words, and the reader should see no more in the choice which it has been necessary to make between the more fanciful spellings than an arbitrary standardization, intended to facilitate reading. To denote the names of peoples, current usage has been followed in employing the root of

*The term refers to the *chansons de geste*, medieval French verse-chronicles of heroic exploits, which have no precise counterpart in English literature. (R.W.)

each term. Specialists will forgive us, to take one example, for speaking of the "Lunda" and not of the "Aruund" to designate the people who founded a veritable empire in the heart of Central Africa.

The chapters devoted to the Luba and Lunda epics were produced during the period when I was privileged to teach in the Religious Sciences section of the École Pratique des Hautes Études [in Paris] from 1966 to 1968.

We are grateful to the staff of the Cultural Anthropology Center of the Institute of Sociology in Brussels for assembling the relevant documents for the book;[4] a grant from the Foundation for Social Research (Fonds de la Recherche Fondamentale Collective) has enabled these documents to be retained at the Center, where they may be consulted by specialists in Bantu religions. In dealing with this material, we have followed the golden rule formulated by Lévi-Strauss, that a myth consists of the sum of its variant versions.* The different versions throw light on one another, so structural analysis can only reveal the meaning of the myth in all its richness where these variant versions are numerous. Such is notably the case with the epic account of the foundation of the Luba state, and for this reason it serves as our point of departure. At the risk of trying the reader's patience at the very outset, we have found it necessary to repeat the same narrative every time a new formulation introduces a significant nuance or change of emphasis. There is a list of the myths and their variants at the end of the book, with appropriate page references.

The Western reader will find one among many *mythèmes*† particularly familiar: the Tower of Babel throws its shadow across our African heroes. It was Frazer who first noticed the universality of this image, and recorded the first known African examples.[5] But his atomistic approach is not ours. Here we avail ourselves, without preconceptions, of the conceptual tools employed by Lévi-Strauss in *Mythologiques*. When the comparison seems appropriate from a structuralist viewpoint, and only then, do we risk promoting a transatlantic dialogue between African and Amerindian thought. Historians will certainly look askance at this confrontation, which the reader is asked to

*"We define the myth as consisting of all its versions" (Lévi-Strauss, 1955: 435). (R.W.)

†*Mythème,* a neologism coined by Lévi-Strauss to denote a constituent element in the structure of a single myth (1968:211). De Heusch here uses the term in a different sense to mean a motif or theme occurring in many myths from different culture areas. (R.W.)

see as no more than a tentative design for a future project calling for the collaboration of many specialists interested in distinguishing the universal from the culturally contingent. For the time being there is too much to be done in Africa that requires resistance to the calls of the sirens inhabiting the world of Frazer, our common master. Divine kingship, which it was his great merit to have identified for the first time, here meets the questioning gaze cast by Engels nearly a century ago over the beginnings of history.[6]

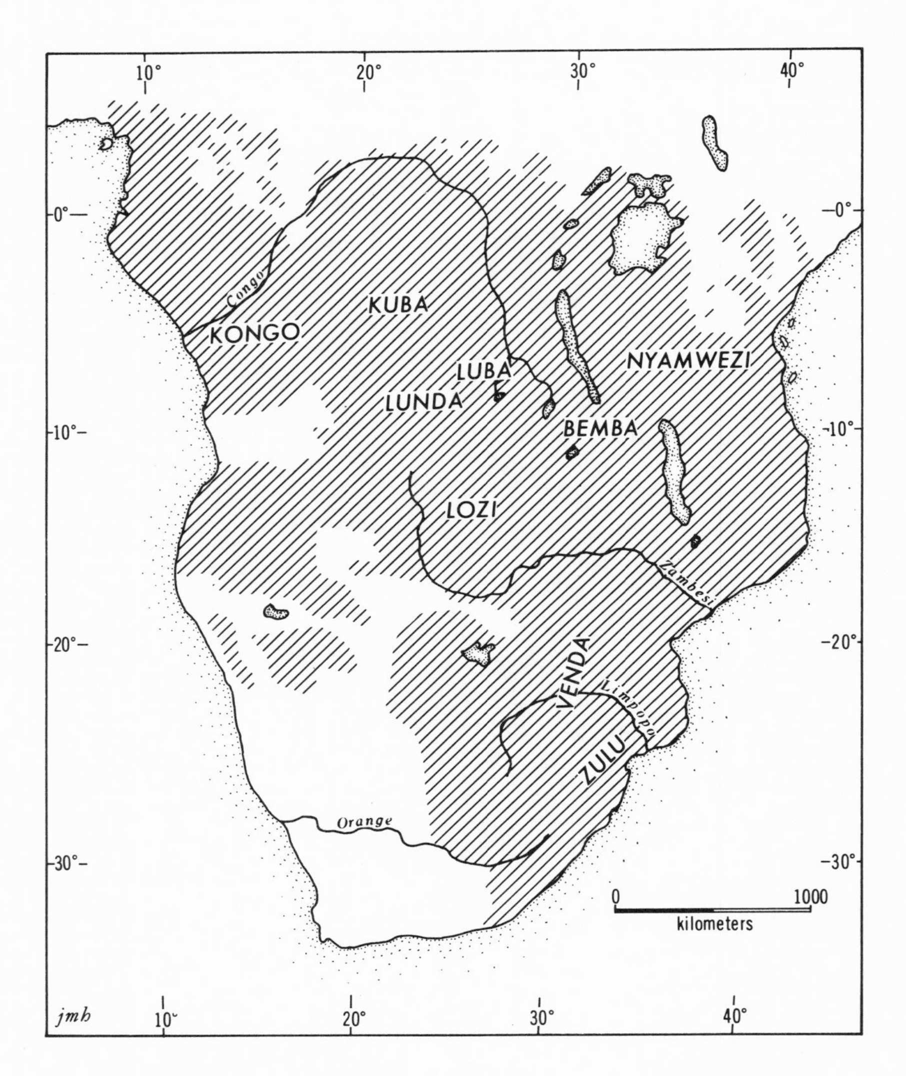

Sub-Saharan Africa. The shaded area indicates the extent of Bantu linguistic predominance. Some of the major Bantu groups are also shown.

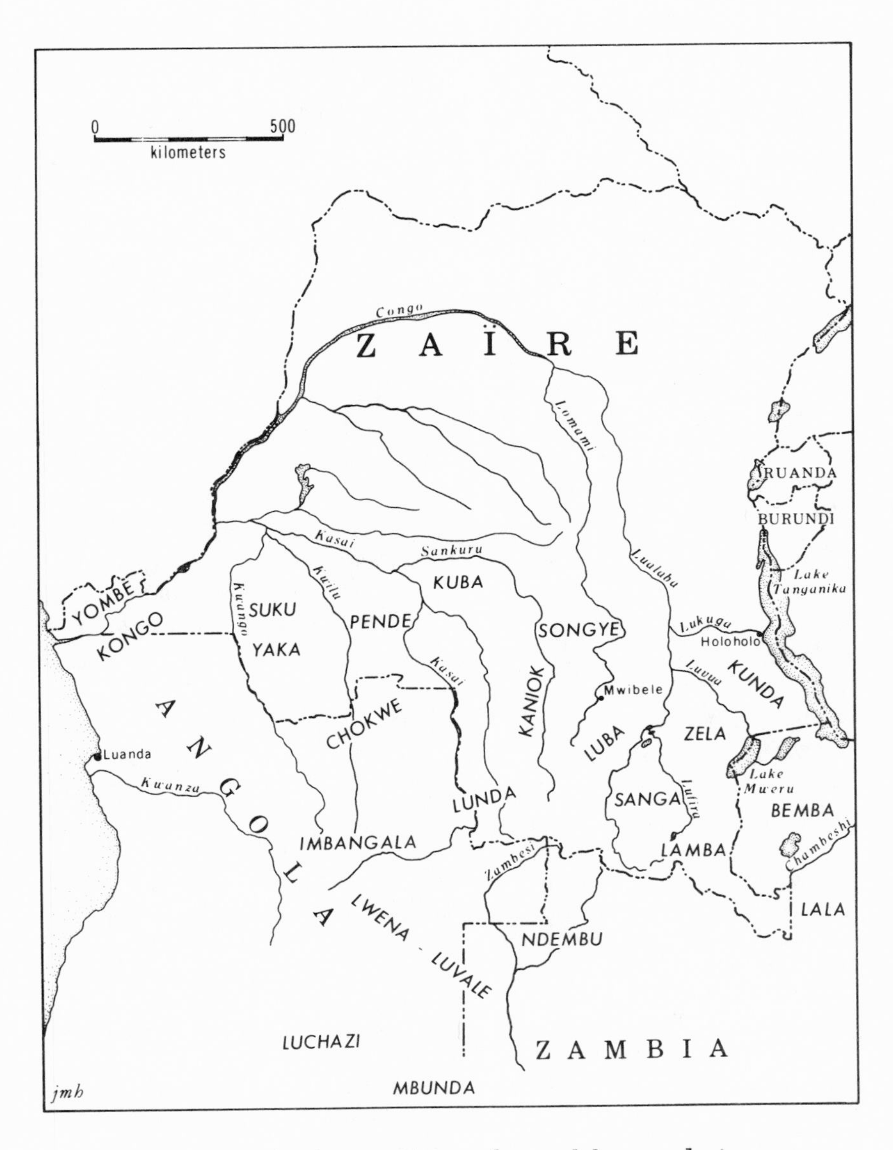

Location of ethnic groups, places, lakes, and rivers mentioned in the text.

[CHAPTER ONE]

Kingly Manners

Myth and History

Do the foundation myths of African kingdoms provide us with the keys to their histories? Or do they firmly lock the doors on such a prospect? Or again, are they likely to lead us on a wild-goose chase ending in the trackless wilderness of the heroic fable or the romantic novel?

The ethnohistorians generally adopt the first position without feeling any need to justify their choice, and briskly ignore what appears to them as merely a mythological excrescence on the body of narrative history. In contrast, instead of brutally eliminating it, we are going to take the marvelous seriously: for we intend to reconstruct the mythological universe within which Bantu historical thought has developed. It will then be seen just how paltry is the residue remaining from the oral traditions after they have been put through the filter of ethnohistory.

Vansina reduces the Luba epic to the following outline:

> Towards 1500, when the region between Lake Tanganyika and upper Kasai contained a multitude of petty chiefdoms, an immigrant called Nkongolo founded the first Luba empire. There are various traditions about his origin. However that may be, he built his capital at Mwibele, near Lake Boya. Soon afterwards, a hunter called Mbidi arrived from the east with some companions. He was welcomed by Nkongolo and married his two half sisters, Bulanda and Mabela. But soon there was a quarrel between the stranger-prince and his brother-in-law, "an uncivilized man who refused to learn from the newcomer the manners and customs appropriate to a chief." Mbidi left the country of Nkongolo. After his departure, Bulanda and Mabela each brought forth a son. Kalala Ilunga, son of the former, helped his uncle to conquer the southern part of his realm. But Nkongolo was offended

> by the renown of Kalala and tried to kill him. Kalala took refuge in his father's country and returned with an army. Nkongolo fled. Betrayed by his sisters, he was captured and killed. Kalala took over the kingdom and built his capital at Munza, some miles from Mwibele. Such were the beginnings of the "second Luba empire."[1]

I accept Vansina's hypothesis that the narratives refer to effective contact between an existing Katangan chiefdom and intruders from a more highly organized polity. After a period of marriage alliances, the newcomers inflicted a military defeat on their hosts. The new dynasty, which reigned over a great part of Katanga [Shaba]* until the end of the nineteenth century, is of Hemba origin.[2] This vague term refers to the eastern Luba, who occupy territory between the Lualaba River and Lake Tanganyika. A tradition from the court of the Luba chief Kasongo Niembo enables us to formulate the historical problem more precisely. According to this tradition, Mbidi Kiluwe, father of the founder of the second dynasty, is sometimes called *Mwenge a Bukunda*, "Mwenge of Kunda country."[3] The Kunda nowadays are associated with a number of broken-down petty chiefdoms, about which little is known; however, their distribution within Hemba territory suggests they were once part of a powerful political entity. The Kunda were closely associated with the Boyo, a people whose sculpture—which I was lucky enough to come across in Manyema in 1949—attests a high level of cultural achievement. Further, the dynasty of the minor kingdom of Kikonja, founded by a close relative of Mbidi Kiluwe, claims to be of Kunda origin.[4] The royal genealogy suggests moreover that the Luba kingdom was founded at the beginning of the sixteenth century; the enmity of two rival princes weakened it at the beginning of the Belgian colonial period.[5] It then split into two chiefdoms (Kasongo Niembo and Kabongo) and a number of outlying and more or less autonomous lesser chiefdoms.

But these conclusions are misleading, even when strengthened with material from the epic of the Lunda, a neighboring kingdom occupying western Katanga and northern Angola. The foundation myth of the Lunda fuses to some extent with the Luba epic after one generation. A Luba prince, Chibinda Ilunga, leaves the royal court during the reign of Ilunga Walefu, son of Kalala Ilunga.[6] A notable hunter, Chi-

*The old province of Katanga in southeast Zaïre was renamed *Shaba* in 1972. (R.W.)

binda Ilunga marries Lueji, daughter of the Lunda chief Konde, whose heir he becomes. The Bemba kingdom of Zambia belongs to the same historical tradition, because its founder, Chitimukulu, was a Luba aristocrat established at the Lunda court. A contemporary of Chibinda Ilunga, he may have belonged to the latter's following.[7] The foundation myth of the Bemba kingdom contains just as many incredible elements as the preceding epic, and describes the departure of Chitimukulu and his followers after a quarrel with the "prince consort" of the Lunda, Mukulumpe.[8]

Assuming, in accordance with at least one of the Lunda versions, that Chibinda Ilunga was a younger brother of the Luba king Ilunga Walefu,[9] each of the personages in this cluster of epics can be situated in the following genealogy:

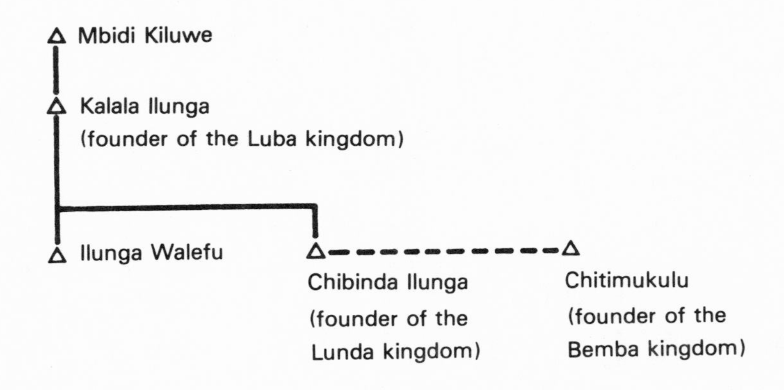

This summary outline contains the essence of our historical knowledge of this region (in the absence of a systematic study of all the relevant traditions). But what we have is probably no more than a symbolic reflection of a much more complex reality which includes military conquests and a variety of marriage alliances linking together the principal states of Central Africa.

Luba civilization, in which metallurgy and wood sculpture reached a remarkable level of development, emerged in a region which had already seen the growth of a highly elaborate culture. The Sanga tombs near Lake Kisale, dated by Nenquin from the second half of the seventh to the ninth century, contained artifacts of iron, copper, and ivory.[10] Vansina describes the present state of our knowledge in the following terms: "The history of the peoples in the savanna in the five centuries preceding 1900 is the story of the development of a Luba-Lunda civilization in the east and of a Kongo and colonial Portuguese civilization in the west."[11] Here it is necessary to understand the term "civilization" in its ethnographic sense, without value judgment, for there is no doubt that the Portuguese colonial "civilization" was continuously destructive of the diverse cultures which had become polarized in opposition to the ancient Kongo state, situated on the Atlantic coast south of the Zaïre estuary.

Ethnohistory also reassures us that the comparative study of the Luba, Lunda, and Bemba epics is not an empty mental exercise, since this study relates to a relatively homogeneous cultural region. We shall soon discover nonetheless that deeper understanding of the myths requires us to venture beyond the limits of this region.

The Principal Sources

We have a dozen versions, variously elaborated, of the story in which Kalala Ilunga is the dominant figure. Unfortunately no vernacular texts have been preserved. Even so, the versions are sufficiently concordant and complementary to inspire confidence in the accuracy of the translations.

The oldest version is due to Colle (1913) and was collected among the Luba-Hemba, in the hero's country of origin.[12] The other versions, collected in Katanga, have been published by Donohugh and Berry (1932), Verhulpen, Van der Noot (1936), Burton (1939; new edition, in the original English text, 1961), Van Malderen (1940), Makonga (1948), Orjo de Marchovelette (1950), Sendwe (1954), and Theeuws (1954, 1962, 1964).[13]

We begin with one of the richest texts, that of Orjo de Marchovelette. This version is also noteworthy in having been recited by one of the established tradition-bearers of the Kabongo chiefdom, Inabanza Kataba.

M1: The Luba Epic (Orjo de Marchovelette's version)

A. *The peopling of Luba territory*

In the country of the east (Buhemba), on the right bank of the Lualaba River, there once were a man and a woman. Their names (Kiubaka-Ubaka and Kibumba-Bumba) mean respectively "he who builds many houses" and "she who makes much pottery."

They lived in ignorance of each other. Guided by the sound of chopping, the man discovered the woman, who was preparing firewood. They lived for a long time under the same roof, sleeping in separate beds. The copulation of a pair of jackals gave them the idea of sleeping together. They brought forth twins of opposite sex, who became inseparable companions. One day the twins found a locality which was exceptionally rich in fish. They took to spending the entire day catching fish, spending the night in the bush in each other's arms. They finally obtained permission from their parents to leave the village and devote themselves entirely to fishing. In their turn, they brought forth twins, who lived in the same incestuous manner, far from their parents. This new generation took up trapping. So pairs of twins, moving in each generation a little further westward, populated the country.

B. *The origin of divine kingship* (bulopwe).

Nkongolo,[14] the first divine king (*mulopwe*) of the Luba, was the offspring of Kiubaka-Ubaka and Kibumba-Bumba. He brought all the lands of the west under his authority. He soon crossed the Lualaba, arriving with a large following at Lake Boya, where he built a great village, Mwibele. About the same time, a hunter called Ilunga Mbidi Kiluwe left his natal village to conquer the peoples living between the Lualaba and Lubilash rivers. On the way home he met his brother-in-law Nkongolo, who gave him a hearty welcome. In the course of the ensuing festivities, Mbidi Kiluwe was shocked to see that Nkongolo ate and drank in the company of his people. Nkongolo, on his side, was astonished to see his guest disappear behind a screen at mealtimes. He was also struck by the fact that Mbidi Kiluwe never laughed. Nkongolo mentioned this to him and Mbidi Kiluwe then burst out laughing. Nkongolo thereupon noticed that the other had his two upper incisors filed to points. He again expressed his surprise, but this time Mbidi Kiluwe flew into a rage, and retorted angrily: "You have conquered the country, but you fail to observe the elementary prohibition which obliges a king to hide himself when he eats or drinks." He thereupon took leave of Nkongolo. When Mbidi Kiluwe arrived at the Lualaba River, he told the local chief: "Nkongolo the Red has grossly insulted me and I have parted from him. I have left behind at Mwibele this man's sisters, my wives Mabela and Bulanda, who are pregnant. I have entrusted them to the care of the diviner Mijibu.[15] I am certain that the sons they will bring into the world will rejoin me. You will recognize them by their black skins. If a red-colored man asks permission to cross the river, refuse him; but if a black man asks, agree immediately."

At the village of Nkongolo, Mabela and Bulanda each gave birth to a boy; the son of the first was called Kisula, and the second was called Kalala Ilunga. They grew up under the vigilant eye of Mijibu. As adults they continued to live with their maternal uncle. One day Nkongolo invited his nephew Kalala Ilunga to a game of *masoko*.[16] Mijibu gave the young man an iron object skillfully fashioned to resemble the fruit employed in the game and Kalala Ilunga had no trouble beating his uncle. Wishing to save her son the disgrace of further defeats, Nkongolo's mother begged him to destroy (fill in?) the small hole into which the players threw their counters.

A short time later, Nkongolo invited his nephew to a game of *bulundu*, which is played with a rubber ball. Mijibu gave his protégé a magic ball which broke all the pots in Nkongolo's kitchen. Nkongolo's mother again asked her son not to take on Kalala Ilunga. Angered by the growing renown of his nephew, Nkongolo decided to get rid of him. He caused a pit to be dug, lined with iron spikes, and hidden under a mat. Then he invited Kalala to dance in his honor. The hero asked Mijibu for advice. Mijibu gave Kalala two spears, and told him to brandish one while using the other to test the ground during his dance. Kalala Ilunga began dancing some distance from the mat. When the drum rhythm speeded up, he leapt and hurled his spear at the mat. The weapon passed right through it, revealing the trap.

Kalala Ilunga fled, determined to join his father. Nkongolo pursued him, but the nephew had already crossed the Lualaba River when his uncle reached its bank. Faithful to Mbidi Kiluwe's orders, the local chief refused to allow the king to cross. Groups of Nkongolo's followers twice attempted to cross the river on craft they found to hand, but both groups were drowned. Nkongolo tried in vain to build a stone causeway across the river: his iron implements were useless against rock. Nkongolo then decided to lure Kalala Ilunga to his side of the river. He compelled the diviner Mijibu and a certain Mungedi to climb to the top of a great tree and call the fugitive back. One shook a rattle while the other struck a gong. Nkongolo had the ladder of vines removed which the two had used to scale the tree. There was no response from Kalala to their calls. Mijibu and Mungedi spent two days without food at the top of the tree. The diviner suggested to his companion that he jump into space with him, holding onto his [Mijibu's] belt. But Mungedi refused to take such a risk. Mijibu escaped, thanks to his magical powers. He crossed the Lualaba with a mighty leap. But poor Mungedi died of hunger.

Mijibu succeeded in joining Mbidi Kiluwe, who raised a great army and entrusted its command to his son. To defend himself, Nkongolo conceived the unlikely scheme of diverting the course of the Lomami River so as to isolate himself on an island in midstream. But his men gave up the project when they heard that Kalala Ilunga's army had seized the capital. Nkongolo then took refuge in the Lwembe gorges. A woman discovered him while he was warming himself in the sun, together with a small band of followers. When he heard of this, Kalala Ilunga reconnoitered the place by moonlight. Nkongolo's hideout was encircled. The next morning he was captured, then beheaded and castrated. The head and genitals of the dead king were packed into a basket (*dikumbo*), which Kalala Ilunga sent to his father. A miracle happened at the village of Lenga. When the man who was carrying the basket placed it on the ground, a termite hill formed over it with extraordinary speed, burying it under a mound of red earth. Lenga village was thereafter called Kimona.[17]

Kalala Ilunga sent messengers to his father, seeking permission to continue his conquests. Mbidi Kiluwe gave his approval. He also reminded his son of the precise ritual observances required of divine kings. A king was obliged to take food and drink alone, and out of sight. A special hut had to be devoted to the preparation of royal meals because it was forbidden for the king to eat in a place where fire had been made. Two wives wearing special raffia dresses (*kibanga*) had to undertake the royal cuisine. The first was responsible for the cooking, the second for serving the various dishes. They had to be replaced by other women whenever indisposed. A cook was forbidden to address the king directly. Instead, she had to let him know silently and in secret when a meal was ready. Without hurrying himself, the king made his way to the dining room by a devious route so as not to attract attention, while the women withdrew. No one was allowed to eat the remains of a royal meal, nor to use utensils served to the king.

After securely establishing his rule over the country, Kalala Ilunga took the name of Ilunga Mwine Munza.[18] He assumed a praise-name which said he was the son of Mbidi Kiluwe, the hunter whose bowstring broke when he was hunting at the source of the Lomami River.

Burton's version adds some further details. The Protestant missionary's account lengthens the chronology, says something about the childhood of Mbidi Kiluwe, and considerably extends the list of prescriptions concerning divine kingship.

M1: The Luba Epic (Burton's version[19])

The author briefly summarizes the traditions concerning the founding ancestor Kiubaka-Ubaka and his wife Kibumba-Bumba, adding the detail that their son was born holding a bow and arrows. He also carried an ax attached to a belt round his waist. This remarkable child taught his father the use of these arms on the very day of his birth.

Later a fisherman called Muleya Monga lived near Lake Boya. He had three children by one of his wives, who was called Mwamba or Ndai. Of the children, one was a boy called Nkongolo ("Rainbow") because of his pale skin. There were also two girls, Mabela and Bulanda. By his second wife, Kaseya, Muleya Monga had another daughter, called Sungu.

One day, Nkongolo was struck by the sight of a column of ants carrying off termites. He had the idea of organizing a merciless army. He gathered some followers about him and soon showed himself to be so tyrannical that he was driven out of the country. Some time later, however, he returned to Lake Boya and, with the help of the diviner Mijibu, reasserted his domination over the Kalanga people. These people were of lighter color than the Luba. Nkongolo was a brutal and ruthless chief. Being suspicious of the power of women, he decided to avoid marrying outside his own family. So he took his half sister Sungu as wife.

At the same time, the hunter Ilunga Kiluwe reigned in Bupemba (presumably Buhemba, a country to the east). He had two sons, Mbidi Kiluwe and Ndala, and a daughter called Mwanana of whom he was very fond. When he became old, Ilunga Kiluwe wanted his daughter to succeed him, while his subjects wanted Mbidi Kiluwe. Mwanana had a pet lion. This animal escaped while Mbidi Kiluwe was playing with it. Enraged, Mwanana threatened to have her brother put to death unless he recaptured the lion. Mbidi Kiluwe was obliged to pursue the animal. He took with him ten of his wives, fifty slaves, and his youngest son,

Mwema Mwimbi. He lost the lion's trail at the Lualaba River. He went on until he came to the river Lovoi, where he found a country rich in game. He began hunting, killing men and animals without discrimination.

When he came to the confluence with the Kiankodi River, his wives and slaves refused to go any further. Mbidi Kiluwe continued on his way with his son Mwema, who carried the bows and arrows.

Meanwhile, at Lake Boya, the diviner Mijibu warned Nkongolo that "power is coming." He advised his master, on pain of losing his life, to give a generous welcome to the chief who was approaching. Mbidi Kiluwe and his son followed the Kiankodi River upstream to its source in the highlands. Then they followed the course of the Luvidyo River downstream to the Munza lake. There they met two beautiful young women, Nkongolo's sisters Mabela and Bulanda, who were trying to drag from the water a net full of fish that was too heavy for them. Mbidi Kiluwe drew it out with ease and took his leave of the two young women, who had fallen in love with the hunter. They were greatly impressed with his beauty, his strength, and his dark color. They begged their brother to spare the life of the handsome stranger, for because of the prophecy of Mijibu, Nkongolo either killed or enslaved all foreigners. Mbidi Kiluwe remained on the alert. When he saw some of Nkongolo's soldiers approaching, he hid in a tree. The two young women tried in vain to find the hunter's trail. While they were resting by a stream, they saw in the water the reflection of Mbidi, who was watching them from his hideout in the branches of a tree above them. They begged him to come down and accompany them to the home of Nkongolo. Mbidi agreed, and instructed his son Mwema to fetch his wives and slaves.

Nkongolo received his guests with ill grace. He was uneasy and consulted his diviner. Why did the stranger not respond to the greetings of his own followers? Why did he refuse to eat in public? Mijibu told him to rejoice because the hunter was introducing the proper customs of divine kingship. He advised Nkongolo to build an enclosure for his guest. Mbidi married Mabela and Bulanda. But things soon became difficult. Nkongolo adopted an insulting attitude toward his brother-in-law. He laughed uproariously whenever he saw the gaps left by the removal of the stranger's two lower incisors.* On his side, Mbidi reproached Nkongolo for

* Luba treat both upper and lower incisors (see p. 22 below). (R.W.)

eating in public and for sitting on the ground with his legs crossed. While in a trance, Mijibu secretly whispered in Mbidi's ear, inviting him to a meeting at dawn the following day. Mbidi duly met Mijibu and was warned that Nkongolo meant to incite Mbidi's own followers against him. Mbidi thereupon decided to leave. He gave each of his wives a curiously fashioned arrow and told them to give it to the child each would bring forth, so that their father would be able to recognize them. He entrusted the care of his future offspring to Mijibu and disappeared.

When Mbidi Kiluwe returned to his native land, his father had died. His sister Mwanana and his brother Ndala were both away, looking for him. After losing Mbidi's trail, Mwanana arrived in Lunda country, where she married the king. At Nkongolo's village, Bulanda brought forth a son, whom she named Ilunga after his paternal grandfather. Mabela brought forth twins: a boy, called Kisula, and a girl, Shimbi.

Ilunga soon became the fastest runner and the best dancer in the whole country. His military exploits led to his being called Kalala, "the conqueror."* Mabela's son, however, was a rather stupid giant of a man. Kalala Ilunga also regularly beat his uncle at the game played with stones of the wild olives.† Nkongolo felt a growing resentment about this. Sneeringly, Nkongolo's mother told him that Kalala would soon take over political power also. Nkongolo became angry and his mother burst out laughing. Nkongolo then dug a ditch with his own hands and buried his mother alive in it. He decided at the same time to do away with his nephew. He tried to lure Kalala into a trap during a dancing competition. Kahia, Kalala's personal drummer, noticed a slight depression in the ground made by a pit hidden under a mat. As his master approached the trap, Kahia warned him of the danger in drum language. Kalala revealed Nkongolo's trick by piercing the mat with his spear. Then he jumped right over the gathered people like a wild animal. He took the arrows his father had left and fled to Kiluba, the only place where there was a boat to cross the Lualaba River. He arrived there before nightfall, pursued by

*According to Van Avermaet's dictionary, the root *-lala* in Luba has the senses of "splitting, breaking, piercing, operating a separation" (Van Avermaet 1954: 380), connotations which agree very well with de Heusch's identification of Kalala Ilunga with the category of "pointed, fabricated objects" (see below, p. 25). (R.W.)

†Burton says: ". . . the game of spinning wild-olive kernels was common. It is similar to European 'marbles' and the winner takes the kernels of the loser" (Burton, 1961:7). (R.W.)

Nkongolo and several soldiers. Jumping into the boat, Kalala ordered the oarsman to deny the crossing to the red-colored man who was pursuing him. After taking Kalala across, the owner of the canoe hid his craft in the reeds. When Nkongolo arrived the next morning, he was told that a stranger had stolen the boat. Nkongolo tried in vain to construct a raft. In a fury, he ordered Kahia to climb a tree and beat his drum until his master returned. But Kalala was already far away. Kahia escaped from the uncomfortable position where Nkongolo had meant him to die.

At his father's, Kalala received a warm welcome. Mbidi gave him an army to beat Nkongolo. Nkongolo was seized with panic when Mijibu prophesied the fatal outcome of the confrontation. With his two sisters, Mabela and Bulanda, Nkongolo took refuge in the caves of Kaii Mountain in the west of his country. But the two women told people where they were going so that Kalala Ilunga could find them.

Nkongolo climbed early in the morning to the top of the hill to enjoy the sun, while his sisters, whose treachery he did not suspect, gathered great quantities of firewood under the pretence of preparing for a siege. Mabela saw the advance guard of the hostile army. She advised the soldiers to surprise Nkongolo the next morning, while he warmed himself in the early sun. She told them of her plan to bar the entrance to the cave with a pile of wood. Nkongolo saw his enemies climbing the hill and fled to his cave, only to find the entrance blocked. Kalala's soldiers fell on him and cut off his head. This was buried the next morning under an enormous red anthill (termite mound?). At this spot the trees, rocks, and earth all became red.

The story ends with an account of the conquests of Kalala Ilunga, ending in hand-to-hand combat with his half brother Kisula. Kalala beat Kisula with the help of his half sister Shimbi, who was in love with him. She seized Kisula "in a very awkward manner" and forced him to let go at the moment when Kalala was about to be brought to the ground.

The version reported by Verhulpen is briefer than the two preceding ones, and we limit ourselves to presenting the new details included in it.

M1: The Luba Epic (Verhulpen's version[20])

A prince from the east, a native of Bukunda called Mbidi Kiluwe, came hunting in the land of the king Nkongolo. Mbidi Kiluwe was in the habit of drinking and eating alone. Nkongolo, who had incestuous relations with his two sisters, Bulanda and Mabela, lent these women to his guest. Bulanda became pregnant and brought forth a son, Ilunga, while Mabela was delivered of a boy and a girl. A quarrel erupted between Mbidi Kiluwe and Nkongolo, each claiming that Ilunga was his son. Mbidi Kiluwe returned to his country of origin. Nkongolo established his rule over all the peoples living between the Lwembe and Lualaba rivers. Ilunga found favor with the inhabitants, who were tired of the excesses of the old king, who was a cruel drunkard. Nkongolo was indeed a great drinker. He was also given to cutting off the noses, ears, hands, and breasts of his subjects. Convinced that Ilunga was plotting against him, Nkongolo decided to kill him by luring him into a trap (see preceding versions).

Ilunga (Kalala) fled to his father. He caused the canoes to be hidden so that Nkongolo could not cross the Lualaba. The king tried without success to build a bridge of straw. Then he tried to make Ilunga return by means of a trick. He had a platform built in a tree and ordered his own brother, Kaniamba, whom he suspected of being in league with Ilunga, to beat a gong, together with a certain Majibu, to call the fugitive. Nkongolo forbade the two men to leave their post. Majibu nonetheless managed to get down while Kaniamba died of hunger without succeeding in making Ilunga return.

Ilunga mustered an army of followers in his father's country. He beat his uncle, who took refuge on the left bank of the Lomami River. Fearing that his mother would fall into enemy hands, Nkongolo buried her alive in a ditch. He fled to the gorges of the river Lwembe, where he was captured and beheaded. The body was buried. Ilunga carried off the head in a basket, which he caused to be placed on a mound. The next day its contents, having been carried off by termites, had disappeared under the ground. It was thus that Kalala Ilunga became the founder of the second Luba empire.

The same story is told, with slight variations, among the eastern Luba: that is to say, according to the epic, in the country of origin of the hunter Mbidi Kiluwe, father of the hero. The following are the particular features of this version, recorded by Colle among the Luba-Hemba.[21]

M1: The Luba Epic (Colle's version)

Kahatwa, coming from a country situated to the west of the Lomami, settled with his two wives on the shore of Lake Kisale. One wife was sterile, while the other, Ndai, brought forth a boy, whom she dedicated to the guardian spirit of the family, the rainbow-serpent; thus he was named Nkongolo-Mwamba. Ndai also brought forth two girls, Bulanda ("Poverty") and Keta ("A Little Meat"). The family also included a little niece called Bubela ("A Lie"). They were all of a reddish color. In those days the earth was soft: a man's foot and the hoof of an antelope left imprints in rocks which today are very hard.

While on her way to the lake to draw water, Bulanda met a hunter who was drinking there. To her surprise, the stranger did not respond to her greeting and ignored her. Bulanda ran to warn her brother, who consulted an oracle on the spot. He learned that the stranger was Mbidi, a hunter from the country of the east (*Kiluwe kya Buhemba*). The oracle advised Nkongolo to build a ritual hut for this distinguished visitor. The hut should be surrounded by a fence and provided with kindling to make a fire. Nkongolo followed this advice and invited the stranger to his home. They passed a few days together. Soon Mbidi Kiluwe married Bulanda. When she was pregnant, the hunter took leave of his affines, saying there was nothing to keep him in that place. He returned to his own country.

Bulanda brought forth a son, whom she called Kalala Ilunga. From the day of his birth the child gave evidence of extraordinary powers. After observing a colony of ants pillaging a termite mound, the child Kalala decided to imitate them. He captured and killed several members of Nkongolo's entourage; he lured other men into the forest and enslaved them. This conduct annoyed Nkongolo, who decided to entice his nephew into a trap. Nkongolo invited Kalala Ilunga to dance over a pit concealed under a carpet. Tapping the earth with his spear, Kalala Ilunga was able to frustrate the criminal plan of his uncle. The ground yielded to the weapon and the young man drew back in fury, saying he would inform his father. "Then," he said, "we will see which of us is the stronger."

Kalala left immediately and crossed the Lualaba River in a canoe. Nkongolo pursued him, but was refused passage over the river. He tried to build rafts, but these overturned, drowning the men who were on them. He then ordered his drummer to climb to the top of a great tree (*muvula*) and to send a conciliatory message to his nephew. But Kalala made no response to this appeal. In his fury, Nkongolo condemned the unfortunate drummer to die of hunger in the tree. Nkongolo then tried to build a barrage of rocks to get across the river. But his followers exhausted themselves in this project without success. At last Nkongolo decided to turn back. Fearing his nephew's vengeance, Nkongolo lived the life of a fugitive in the Mita Mountains, going from one cave to another.

Mbidi Kiluwe refused to give armed help to his son. Nevertheless Kalala went in pursuit of his uncle. Eventually Kalala ran Nkongolo down and cut off his head with a stroke of his knife. He wrapped the head in raffia and placed it in a basket with a conical lid (*kihau*). This basket he deposited in a ritual hut. Since that day political authority (*bufumu*) has remained in the house of the ancestors. Kalala Ilunga succeeded his uncle and united in his person political authority (*bufumu*) and the sacred blood of royalty (*bulopwe*). He fathered several sons, who divided between them the country between the Lomami and Lualaba rivers.

Kalala Ilunga, the Residuary Legatee

The totality of these concordant accounts conveys a single message, of varying degrees of richness, within the same armature.* The less elaborate versions of Colle and Verhulpen cannot be neglected in favor of the more comprehensive ones (Orjo de Marchovelette and Burton), because they contain details which add to the wealth of meanings of an epic which should not be reduced to any one canonical or "authentic" version. Let us begin by examining the overt meaning of the myth: the origin of divine kingship.

All versions contrast the primitive rule of Nkongolo, a cruel, drunken, and incestuous king and a wicked uncle, with the civilized kingship represented by Mbidi. For Sendwe, Nkongolo is a tyrannical chief who imposed immensely burdensome labors on his people. Notably, he altered the course of the Lomami River, a work in which hundreds died of exhaustion.[22] The incestuous relations of this ancient and brutal king express an unwillingness to relate to the external world. Notice

**Armature*, a term used by Lévi-Strauss to mean "a combination (*ensemble*) of properties that remain invariant in two or several myths" (Lévi-Strauss, 1964:205). (R.W.)

Burton's significant commentary: Nkongolo had decided against marrying outside his own family.[23] Theeuws combines the readings of Verhulpen and Burton: Nkongolo, who had sexual relations with his sisters Bulanda and Mabela, married his half sister Sungwe[24] (Sungu).

The picture presented of Mbidi Kiluwe is different in all respects. He marries a complete outsider after being driven from his native country by his own sister. Alone, cut off from his family, abandoned by his former wives (Burton), all that remains to him are certain personal qualities (beauty, and a gift for hunting) on which to build a home. This hero from afar is the bearer of a superior culture. That culture is expressed in fundamental symbolic terms as a revolution in table manners. It is precisely this matter that engenders conflict between the two brothers-in-law. Nkongolo eats and drinks in public and sits on the ground, while the royal stranger takes care to withdraw from the common gaze at such times.

The new prohibitions mainly affect the mouth. Even Mbidi's speech is restrained: he does not reply to Bulanda's greeting at their first encounter. The astonished Bulanda tells her brother that she has just met a stranger who refuses to speak.[25] According to Orjo de Marchovelette, Nkongolo expresses his amazement that his guest never laughs. Caught off guard by this bold but pertinent comment, Mbidi reveals his filed teeth, causing Nkongolo renewed surprise. In Burton's version, Mbidi has two lower incisors missing; this peculiarity provokes Nkongolo to endless mirth. The versions of Burton and Orjo de Marchovelette complement each other to produce a symbolic image in conformity with ethnographic fact: the Luba of Katanga remove the four lower incisors and file away half of two upper incisors.[26] It is notable that Sendwe, a Luba authority who reports this cultural peculiarity of his people, comments on it in a way that echoes the myth: these teeth have been selected as "distinctive signs" because the mutilation becomes evident when a person laughs.

It is clear that the princely stranger differs from his rude host not only by his distinctive manners at mealtimes, but also by the cultural deformation which has been imposed on his mouth. Nkongolo's comment on Mbidi's teeth is offensive, and probably indecent, focusing as it does on a critical point of articulation between the natural and cultural orders. The stranger-prince shows himself to be extremely sensitive on the subject. If Mbidi peremptorily leaves his brother-in-law, plainly convinced that no relationship is possible with such a savage, it is because Nkongolo does not hide himself when eating (Orjo de Marchovelette's version).

Three series of antinomies can already be drawn out:

Nkongolo	*Mbidi Kiluwe*
incest	hyperexogamy
laughter	discreet use of the mouth
primitive (open) eating and drinking habits	refined (closed) eating and drinking habits

The version of Orjo de Marchovelette makes a point of emphasizing the last opposition at the end of the story. When Kalala Ilunga respectfully requests permission from his father to embark on a campaign of conquest, Mbidi solemnly reminds his son of the *culinary duties of royalty*. The royal cuisine requires discretion and silence. Further, the ritual consumption of food and drink takes place elsewhere than at the site of cooking. In other words, the court of Mbidi Kiluwe recognizes the bourgeois separation of kitchen and dining room. It is no surprise that the magic rubber ball given by the diviner Mijibu to Kalala Ilunga affects the *kitchen* of Nkongolo with the (noisy) destruction of utensils.

Let us venture into the logic of forms proposed by Lévi-Strauss[27] and observe that the dialectic of opening and closing (of the mouth) is projected in the theme of the ditch concealed by a mat. Nkongolo tries to deny the new code of royalty by turning it in some way against his adversary. He hides a dangerous hole in the hope of seeing his nephew fall into it. The relation between the yawning pit and the opening of the mouth is established when Nkongolo's mother perishes in a ditch for having laughed mockingly at her son (Burton). These connections are the more striking when one notes that this hilarity has become proverbial: the Luba speak of "bursting out laughing like Nkongolo's mother."[28] Sendwe's version emphasizes the connection between laughter and the mother's murder: "Nkongolo, in an extremity of anger, buried his mother alive to stop her laughing." The saying to which this horrible event has given rise ("thou laughest as unfortunately as Nkongolo's mother") is a warning given to someone who takes a serious matter lightly.[29] The oral orifice, a vital organ which should not be opened immoderately, and the ditch—a pitfall in which one may perish if lacking in prudence or reserve—are thus in a relation of homology. Nkongolo's mother and Nkongolo himself are characterized by intemperate opening of the mouth, whereas the stranger uses his with the utmost discretion. It would seem that excessive opening (forbidden for reasons of good manners or convenience) is a deadly danger.

In this dialectic, opening connotes the abandon of nature and of death, closure connotes the refinement of civilization. "Closed" conduct is the guarantee of the sacred power of *bulopwe*. Further, closure relates directly to fecundity and fertility. In a study which continues my preliminary analysis of the Luba epic at the École Pratique des Hautes Études in 1967–68, one of my students, John Studstill, basing himself on Van Avermaet's excellent dictionary, demonstrates the relation between the ditch where Nkongolo's mother died and sterility.[30] The expression "hole of Nkongolo" is applied to a barren woman.[31] Studstill observes in this context that the word *ki·nà* (hole, excavation) also designates a young woman whose labia minora have not been extended by the appropriate manipulations (these being normally carried out in the bush, at regular intervals, under the supervision of adult women). This custom has the explicit purpose of making young wives sexually desirable to their husbands.[32] The term also seems to have a more general symbolic significance. This idea is supported by the adage *udi enka na ki·nà*, used by women to make fun of prepubescent young girls.[33] Van Avermaet offers, without further comment, a prudish Latin translation of this saying: *habes tantum aperturam, labia interiora non videntur.** We should understand that the manipulations effect a ritual modification of a natural opening which, as such, is not held to excite male desire. Paradoxically, a vagina with an unmodified orifice signifies the lack of an opening into fecundity, in the same semantic zone where "the hole of Nkongolo" connotes the absence of life, and indeed death itself.

Verhulpen's version, lacking the connection between laughter and death, obscures the deep sense of the *mythème* by imputing the mother's murder to filial piety. The narrator thus loses both the metonymic sense (excessive laughter as the cause of death) and the metaphoric sense (immoderate opening of the mouth in the act of uncontrolled laughter suggests by analogy the image of the ditch where one dies of suffocation).

It seems that Luba symbolic thought is wary of every kind of hole, including the vagina if it is not modified, like the mouth, by a cultural

*"Thou hast such a hole that the lips inside are not seen." (R.W.)

operation. This fear of holes appears again in a prohibition applied to pregnant women: they may not eat the flesh of an animal taken in a pit-trap, for fear that the unborn child be dragged into the tomb in its turn.[34] This formal analysis is supported by a pertinent comment by Studstill, who observes that the original world of Nkongolo is "a world of holes." Colle asserts that Nkongolo belongs to the family of *Bwina-mbayo*. The meaning of the second term of this patronym is not clear, but the word *Bwina* is significant because Nkongolo has a special predilection for holes and caves. He learns from insects that dig holes: ants and termites. And *Bw-inà* means "region of holes."[35]

It is appropriate to compare the world of dangerous holes and of pitfalls with the *pointed* signs that characterize Mbidi Kiluwe and Kalala Ilunga. The first gives his wives an arrow signifying his fatherhood, the second brandishes his spear. When Kalala Ilunga seizes power by planting his spear in "the hole of Nkongolo"* he combats death and sterility (symbolized by the gaping ditch) by means of a sharp weapon, thus vigorously setting in opposition two important formal categories: that of *natural openings*, which are dangerous, and that of *pointed, fabricated objects*. Recall that the world of Nkongolo is sometimes described as one of soft earth, marked by the imprints of man and beast (Colle's version). Openness and softness go together. The dialectic of nature and culture is expressed here in terms of a purely formal code, to complete the following table of oppositions:

Nkongolo	*Mbidi Kiluwe*
primitive royalty	refined royalty
incest	hyperexogamy
sterility, death	procreation, life
natural openings	pointed, fabricated objects
softness	hardness

Van Malderen's version, of which we have not so far taken account, makes an absolute cultural distinction between Mbidi Kiluwe and Nkongolo, who is described as chief of the Twa (Pygmies). After parting from his brother-in-law, Mbidi is welcomed on the Kibara Mountains by a yet more savage people, the Tumandwa twa Maseba, who live by fishing and hunting. This dwarfish people, reddish of skin and

*Kalala Ilunga hardly "seizes power" at this moment, but his act sets off the train of tragic events which ends in his final victory over Nkongolo. (R.W.)

covered with russet hair, inhabit vast termite mounds and caves. They appear to have been driven onto the high plateau by a slightly taller, less hairy, darker people, the Twa, under the rule of Nkongolo.[36] Mbidi Kiluwe, a tall black man, is said to have taught the Tumandwa twa Maseba how to cook food, use the bow and arrow, and build huts. This eccentric version doubles the *nature/culture* opposition by situating Mbidi Kiluwe in relation to *two* inferior peoples (in terms of height and degree of civilization). To both peoples he becomes an ancestral figure, giving a son to Nkongolo's sister and marrying the daughter of the Tumandwa chief, begetting four children who grow up to found various chiefdoms.[37]

In this doubling process, the Tumandwa, as the truly autochthonous people, assume the qualities of redness and of living in holes, qualities which in other versions belong to Nkongolo himself. Three peoples are ranged on the ladder of progress in the following hierarchical order:

Tumandwa	*Twa*	*Blacks*
very short	short	tall
red	red-black	black
very hairy	less hairy	(smooth-skinned)

In this perspective, Mbidi Kiluwe appears as the cultural unifier of a human race fragmented into three radically different races which are classified according to their relative distance from the animal world. This original scheme of differentiation has disappeared in Orjo de Marchovelette's version, in which Mbidi Kiluwe and Nkongolo are descended from the same primordial ancestor. But they are no less deeply divided by custom, whether marital or culinary. Mbidi Kiluwe's hyperexogamous union ends the ancient series of incestuous marriages. Here it is necessary to take account of the prologue to the myth, which consists of a desperately monotonous history of the founding ancestors (Orjo de Marchovelette's version). This drab introduction has not been fortuitously tacked on by the narrator to the body of the story. It deals with the beginnings of culture, whereas the substance of the myth is concerned with the introduction of a supposedly superior civilization to a truly primitive and long-enduring social universe.

A Minor History of Technology

The culture heroes of the primordial society are pairs of incestuous twins, all of whom appear to be cast from the same mold. Properly speaking they have no history, each generation repeating the movement of its parents toward the west. The primal couple are set apart from the others. The man (*Kiubaka-Ubaka*) and the woman (*Kibumba-Bumba*) both appear completely devoted to a particular cultural enterprise, and know nothing of sex. He builds houses (for whom?), and she is busy with pottery. At first each lives alone. When they eventually meet, it is because of a signal of cultural origin: Kiubaka-Ubaka is drawn toward Kibumba-Bumba by the sound of her ax. They experience no desire for one another, and live together in chastity. These primordial ancestors discover sexuality through the example of two mating jackals. When at last they make love, a new paradox affects the human condition: the successive generations to which they give rise diversify productive techniques and practice incest, whereas the initial couple, situated as it were at the zero point of the institution of matrimony, obey the law of exogamy without either knowing or willing it. Kibumba-Bumba and her husband emerge from different backgrounds, each with a particular technological talent. The pairs of incestuous twins that make up the two following generations discover, respectively, fishing and hunting with traps. Then, with technology stabilized, the local founding heroes pursue lives of monotonous incest in which the only progression is geographical: each new couple moves westward, gradually populating the whole of Luba country.

Nkongolo is the last heir of this tedious early world. His father, Muleya Monga, is said to have been a fisherman (Burton, Makonga), and the only economic activity credited to his reign in the myth is the netting of fish by Mabela and Bulanda. The relative poverty of this world is symbolized by the names of the two young sisters: according to Colle, Bulanda means *poverty* and Keta (here substituted for Mabela), *a little meat*. The name of the ancestral fisherman, Monga, may be connected to the verb *onga*, which suggests a shriveling.[38] Like his ancestors, Nkongolo lived incestuously with his sisters; he pursued the drive westward, but this time as a conqueror. The great village he built on the shore of Lake Boya (Orjo de Marchovelette) made Nkongolo a magnified example of the primordial ancestor Kiubaka-Ubaka, builder of houses. One sees why ancient pottery fragments found in the present-day village of Kimona, supposedly Nkongolo's residence, are called *Kibumba-Bumba*.[39]

The myth encloses the succession of techniques in a historical spiral: the acquisition of pottery, fishing, and trapping entail no social development because the primordial couples successively separate themselves from their parents in order to live wrapped up in themselves. The only progress is demographic. It is to this world of a people both numerous and clever, but devoid of manners, that Mbidi Kiluwe, Nkongolo's contemporary, offers renewal in two different ways. First, he marries exogamously; second, he introduces an art of eating.

The origin of cooking, shown by Lévi-Strauss to signify the passage from nature to culture in a group of Amerindian myths, barely concerns the Luba. Fire and cultivated plants exist from the beginning of time. A brief Luba-Hemba myth (M2, Colle) says merely that the first man, Kyomba, received from God instruments for making fire and seeds of cultivated plants.[40] Cooking fire is implicitly present in the first part of M1, signified in an acoustic code: the primordial ancestor hears the noise made by the ax of Kibumba-Bumba, who is cutting firewood. This (culinary) call brings together the man and the woman, who are devoted from the first to the work of culture. Fire and agriculture are thus taken for granted by the Luba, who for centuries have lived in the Iron Age. The age of iron is twice celebrated in the person of Kalala Ilunga. A diviner forges for him a magic counter, with which he beats his uncle at a game; and his deftly handled spear discovers the trap in which Nkongolo had hoped to catch the son of the great hunter like any game animal. These moments of mythical wonder also speak of a new and active force: they inaugurate the reign of the charismatic hero, possessor of magic and of the wily science of kingship. Nkongolo, too, uses iron instruments, but they fail him when he tries to build a dam of rocks (Orjo de Marchovelette). The last great work of Nkongolo is an absurdity when faced with the new instruments of power: the arrow of Mbidi and the spear of Kalala Ilunga.

Mbidi's very name (Kiluwe) shows him to be a skillful hunter.[41] He distinguishes himself by a new way of hunting, evidently more effective: he uses a bow and arrow. Technical innovations follow one another in a mythical order which curiously inverts the historical progression from the paleolithic to the neolithic economy:

architecture and pottery,
fishing,

trapping,
hunting with bow and arrow.

Bringer of food and bearer of a refined culture, Mbidi Kiluwe crowns the series of technological achievements evoked in the prologue to the myth. His sudden, enigmatic appearance puts an end to a history which has been going round in circles. Given over completely to labor and reproduction, men were denied the wider horizon of exogamy, just as they were ignorant of the customs of divine kingship. The dreary repetition of incestuous pairing up to the time of Nkongolo has no other function than to highlight this abrupt change in mood. A recital devoid of dramatic tension and literary interest gives way to a helter-skelter succession of complex events leading to the necessary victory of the central personage, now elevated to heroic status. The scene overflows with violent and passionate action, extremes of love and hate. The heroic tale of Kalala Ilunga marks the beginning of true history, which emerges from the ancient mold of mythical thought in the shape of a national *epic*. In it, we see above the clash of arms a people politically united and in full possession of the necessary technology.

Note also that the birth of Kalala Ilunga marks the end of the prestige accorded to the birth of twins, which from then on becomes inauspicious.[42] In this respect an epilogue to the myth, which to our knowledge Burton is the only one to report, echoes the prologue we have been considering. The final and initial sequences throw a reciprocal light on each other. But let us first recall that Mbidi had only one son by Bulanda, whereas her sister Mabela gave him twins: a boy, Kisula, and a girl, Shimbi.

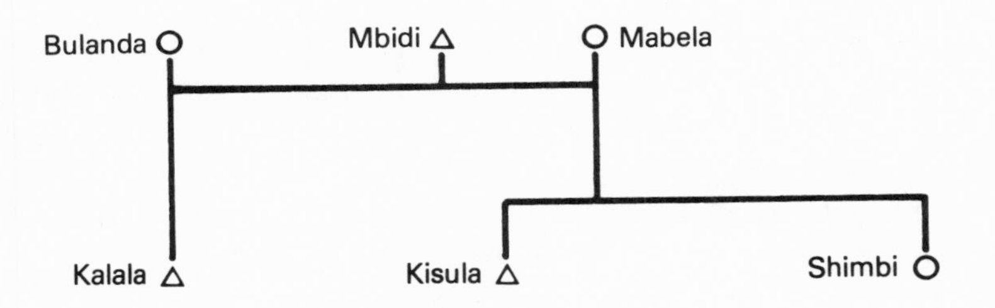

Epilogue to M1 (Burton's version[43])

Nkongolo had two children by his sister Nsungu. When he died, killed by the advance guard of the followers of Kalala Ilunga, the people refused to recognize the authority of Nkongolo's elder son. Power therefore had to go to one of the sons of Mbidi Kiluwe. The people decided to let Kalala and Kisula decide the issue in mortal combat. Shimbi, who was in love with her half brother, betrayed her twin, who was physically stronger than Kalala. When Kalala was on the verge of defeat, Shimbi flung herself screaming on Kisula. By seizing him in an embarrassing fashion ("in a very awkward manner"), Shimbi forced him to release his adversary. Profiting from this diversion, Kalala had no trouble killing his rival. Later, Kisula's son avenged his father by killing Shimbi, after driving her from her home.

This epilogue, which celebrates the end of the supremacy of incestuous twinship, retrospectively illuminates the structure of kinship. It was necessary that Mbidi marry Nkongolo's two sisters so that the myth could oppose the only son of one to the twin offspring of the other. The true heir of Mbidi, the hyperexogamic hero, had to be an only son, devoid of a twin sibling. The incestuous relationship, which until then had harmlessly united the pairs of twins, undergoes a profound change, becoming the tragic passion of a sister who prefers her half brother, an only son, to her own twin brother. This radical alteration in kinship spells the end of endogamy, until then characteristic of human society. It is possible that the name Kisula derives from the verb *-sula* meaning "to be the origin of unhappiness" (*-sula byà malwa*), which is to say, to have incestuous relationships.[44]

Kalala, only son of his mother, and Kisula, the twin, are opposed in other respects. The former is agile and intelligent, the latter a giant of sluggish intellect.[45] These characteristics evidently relate to the general code we are investigating: Kalala, the only child, distinguishes himself from his half brother by specifically cultural qualities, whereas Kisula's endowment is doubly natural, combining physical superiority with the fact that, like the primordial ancestors, he possesses a twin sister.

The crazed love of Shimbi here plays an essential dialectical role. By striking the genitals of her uterine brother, she breaks with the natural tradition followed by the human race,* and she acts thus to save a half brother who shows himself completely ungrateful. Far

*That is, the "tradition" described in the myth of incestuous love between opposite-sex twins. (R.W.)

from being rewarded by the victor, she is compelled to take flight. She pays with her life for her equivocal passion, of which the mythical function is entirely transitional: it merely effects a displacement, in the psychoanalytic sense, of the incestuous attachment, without truly establishing exogamy.

The domestic crimes which tragically embellish the epic of Nkongolo suggest in Shakespearean vein the downfall of the immoderate gods, devoted to violent laughter and passion (Shimbi). The luckless woman is in love, as was her own mother. Her offense derives its significance from the ambiguity of her choice. She causes the death of her twin brother and loves her half brother passionately, while her mother's love for Mbidi Kiluwe, the stranger, prefigures the matrimonial destiny of humanity. Shimbi brings a tragic end to a tradition that she tries desperately to deny, when her mother had already inaugurated the new epoch of exogamic unions. Van Malderen's version highlights this decisive cultural revolution. The two sisters of Nkongolo were also his ritual wives; when they become the mistresses of Mbidi Kiluwe, they incite him to claim the paternity of the child each carries in her womb. Nkongolo then decides to rid himself of his guest, who flees.[46] The abrupt departure of Mbidi is then explained by the contradiction that exists between incest and exogamy; this contradiction is not resolved until the following generation by the desperate act of Shimbi, herself indeterminately either the incestuous child of Nkongolo or the daughter of Mbidi Kiluwe, the stranger. The utter solitude of the heroine, to whom Kalala Ilunga finally owes his victory, is prolonged into the next world: the mediums possessed by her spirit avoid all contact with the mediums of Kalala or of her twin brother.[47]

A surprise awaits us when we compare the myth with the royal installation ceremonies which it legitimizes. For while the myth celebrates the abolition of incest, the ceremony incorporates this shameful legacy of Nkongolo. A new sovereign has ritual relations with his mother and sisters at the time of his investiture; his daughters and his brothers' daughters become his wives.[48] We have discussed elsewhere the general symbolic significance of these sacred marriages.[49] We can now see how Luba royal ritual unites in a particular way the two systems of oppositions we have extracted from the myth, in order to realize a dialectical synthesis. Divine kingship has two faces: as the residuary legatee of all mystical powers, Kalala Ilunga inherits from both the incestuous Nkongolo and the cultured Mbidi Kiluwe. Assuming these two contradictory symbolic orders (*bulopwe* and *bufumu*), the Luba king finds himself projected into a zone of absolute solitude, at once beyond and above the profane cultural order. The king's incestuous relations with his mother and sisters take place in a suffocating environment, without communication with the external world in the sociological sense, and *without any opening* in a formal sense: a hut lacking doors or windows, called "the house of unhappiness."[50] Children born of these unions have no claims to power.[51] The incest that Nkongolo practiced openly is thus ritually hidden. These unusual restrictions remind us of the secrecy and precautions which, since the time of Mbidi Kiluwe, have surrounded the preparation and consumption of food and drink in the royal palace. These ritual measures are probably an indirect reference to exogamy: since the work of Lévi-Strauss, we can no longer doubt the universal equivalence of the sexual act and cooking. But, as we shall see, the symbolism of the cooking fire also introduces the whole universe into the confined space of royalty.

Let us approach this particular code by a macabre detour and compare the royal funeral customs in myth and in rite. An appendix to Burton's version says that the defeated followers of Nkongolo temporarily diverted the course of the Lomami to bury the mutilated body of their chief; afterwards the river covered his grave.[52] And we already know that the head was denied to Kalala Ilunga when it disappeared beneath a magical termite mound. And Burton also tells us that the severed head of a dead Luba chief is kept in a secret basket, the *dikumbo*, while the corpse is often buried near a river or even under the chief's bed.[53] Verbeke's account is notable in conforming exactly to the myth. According to this authority, the chief's skull was preserved as a relic only when the chief died a violent death; otherwise one of his brothers was killed during the funeral ceremonies and his mummified head kept in a sacred basket.[54] It seems justifiable to conclude that the ensemble of these revered skulls symbolizes *bufumu*, the primordial power of Nkongolo, the original ritual victim. The complementary power of *bulopwe* is associated with a figurine called *mboko*, which represents a kneeling woman holding a bowl of white clay.[55]

Other accounts provide implicit confirmation of Verbeke's report. According to Theeuws a succession war erupts at the death of a king between the dead king's youngest brother and the various pretenders. The victor in this struggle, which would seem to have a ritual character, is believed to have been chosen by God.[56] For his part Burton writes that the majority of kings succeeded to office only after putting all their brothers to death.[57] Verhulpen states that the skull of a vanquished prince was accorded ritual significance during the installation ceremony. The tragic sacrifice then offered is evidently a reenactment of the foundation myth of the State. The victim is decapitated, in the manner of Nkongolo, after receiving special treatment. He is invited to become drunk on palm wine in the company of a woman who shares his fate. When the two victims have drunk themselves insensible, they are placed face down and asphyxiated with red powder (*kula*). The dead prince's head is then separated from his body, which is buried in a trench dug in a riverbed. The head is kept in a basket; every four days it is taken out, exposed to the sun, and anointed with oil.[58]

This death by suffocation calls for explanation since it does not form part of the mythical plot, which simply described the decapitation of Nkongolo. To begin with, it can hardly be doubted that the *kula* powder relates to Nkongolo the Red. The death by suffocation inflicted on the beaten prince goes back to the dialectic of opening and closing that we have already outlined. Mouth and nose stuffed with red powder, the victim is delivered to the closed universe of the victorious king.

In this ritual the defeated prince assumes the tragic role of Nkongolo facing the heir of Kalala Ilunga. But the dead king himself appears as Nkongolo when he is ritually slain: in this case his own skull is preserved in the *dikumbo*, together with those of previous ritual victims. The court dignitaries of Kasongo Niembo could recall only one case of a *mulopwe* who died a natural death,[59] suggesting that decapitation of royal corpses was the rule.[60] It is obviously because the dead king is symbolically assimilated to Nkongolo that his decapitated corpse is buried in the bed of a diverted river.[61]

It is time to explore the cosmogonic dialectic underlying this partition of the royal corpse; the new light thrown on Nkongolo will also illuminate the hidden face of Mbidi Kiluwe, the Prince of Night.

[CHAPTER TWO]

The Rainbow and the Lightning

Bantu cosmogonic thought has rarely been the object of scientific inquiry, either because it has appeared impoverished to hasty observers, or because it has been concealed in initiatory teachings barred to ethnography. The authorities seem resigned to considering particular religious systems as heterogeneous collections of practices devoid of any coherent ideological basis. In this area, the work of Turner on Ndembu ritual constitutes a remarkable exception. It is all the more striking therefore that this explorer of the Bantu "forest of symbols" contents himself with two brief references to mythical narratives: texts concerning respectively the origin of circumcision and the ritual curing of menstrual disorder.[1] There can be no questioning the wisdom and competence of an investigator of Turner's exceptional merit. This singular absence of mythical development, together with a proliferation of ritual, would seem rather to be the rule in Central Africa.

But although the overt traditions are disappointing, may there not exist a body of esoteric myths which remains hidden from outsiders? In the whole area of Lunda expansion, which includes the Ndembu, we possess only fragments of the initiatory ritual of the religious society called *mungonge*. As to the society's anthropo-cosmogonic teachings, we have only faint echoes in several mythical narratives which pose almost insurmountable problems of interpretation. We would not have dared interpret Kuba cosmogony in the existing state of the written evidence had Vansina not had the good fortune to undergo initiation with the young men. But no such privileged experience has opened the doors of Luba religion, despite an abundant literature. The facts are always described from the outside and from such disparate perspectives that it seems impossible to determine a common symbolic basis. Tempels's misguided attempt at interpretation, based on an appeal to the outdated theory of *mana*, has hardly served to advance our understanding. The "logical system" presented by Tempels under the fallacious title *La Philosophie bantoue* is a metaphysic of "being-forces" that blocks all true comprehension. In the view of Tempels and his disciples it seems that as the prey of a driving ontological obsession the Luba (and the whole of the Bantu peoples) are unable to understand or act on the world other than in terms of magical appropriation: "The whole energy of the Bantu is directed toward the vital force."[2]

The relative absence of cosmogonic speculation in popular beliefs, the lack of consistency between several mythical narratives recorded by Theeuws,[3] and the apparent incoherence of ritual have been taken to exclude any possibility of a true Luba natural philosophy. No authority seems to have asked whether such might not be found elsewhere, and notably in this prime pseudohistorical text which constitutes the foundation myth of the State. This hypothesis becomes more plausible when one realizes that one of the heroes of this myth bears the very name of the rainbow, Nkongolo. In following this lead, and drawing out all the consequences, we hope to reveal a large part of the Luba cosmogonic* system.

For Colle, the historical Nkongolo was dedicated to the rainbow spirit cult from the day of his birth; for Verhulpen, he was an incarnation of the spirit.[4] The rainbow makes visible the celestial union of two serpents, respectively male and female, who live in two different rivers. These two multicolored creatures prevent rain or stop its falling.[5] On this last point, decisive for the decoding of our myth, Van Avermaet contradicts Verhulpen, who asserts that Nkongolo causes the rain to fall.[6] There is good reason for accepting Van Avermaet's interpretation. For one thing it conforms with that of Theeuws, who says that the Luba believe the rainbow prevents rain;[7] it is also compatible with the Songye belief according to which the rainbow-serpent

*De Heusch's use of the term "cosmogonic" (*cosmogonique*) here and elsewhere in this book is somewhat puzzling, because the dominant ideas at issue typically concern the continuing structure of the universe rather than its creation and would seem to be more appropriately rendered by *cosmologique* (cosmological), as in the mythological studies of Lévi-Strauss. However, in this case I have not felt justified in departing from a literal rendering of de Heusch's term. (R.W.)

Nkongolo "binds" the rain and the spring from upstream.[8] Again according to Theeuws, when the two aquatic serpents join together in the sky the fire they emit burns the earth.[9] That this fire adversely affects rain is evident from a saying reported by Van Avermaet, according to which the rainbow "burns" (drives away) the rain.[10] By a strange reversal, the burning power of the rainbow explains Nkongolo's praise name as "master of the clans, peaceful lord of the sky."[11]

It can easily be shown that the popular beliefs about the rainbow-serpent, enemy of rain, and the personal characteristics of Nkongolo in M1 are in detailed correspondence. The one and the other are associated both with terrestrial waters and celestial fire. Let us begin by examining the first aspect through the mythical topography.

Nkongolo follows a trajectory which varies from author to author, but which is invariably punctuated with lakes and rivers. He comes moreover from a family of fisherfolk; his sisters occupy themselves with the nets. In Colle's version, Nkongolo establishes himself on the shore of Lake Kisale, on damp (soft) ground; when he sets off in pursuit of his rival, he is unexpectedly stopped short by the Lualaba River; deciding to return to his ancestral home, he wanders from cave to cave. Orjo de Marchovelette's version identifies Nkongolo's residence as on the shore of Lake Boya. It is from there that he pursues his nephew until prevented from crossing the Lualaba River. Theeuws situates Nkongolo's village at the confluence of the Lomami and Lubishi rivers. Verhulpen's version describes an even more symptomatic itinerary. Nkongolo founds an empire between two rivers, the Lwembe in the west and the Lualaba in the east. He is really imprisoned within these boundaries, because he is unable to follow his nephew across the Lualaba; pursued by his nephew in turn, Nkongolo retreats as far as the Lwembe gorges, where he is captured and beheaded.

Nkongolo's journey from one river to another (or from a lake to a river) immediately evokes the image of the rainbow uniting two watercourses. It will also be remembered that Colle's version describes the reign of Nkongolo as characterized by an excess of humidity: the earth was so soft that the feet of antelope and man left imprints in places which in our time are rock-hard. This soft, water-swollen earth is opposed to the hard, dry earth of the termite mound which suddenly appears at the end of the narrative and buries the hero's head. The opposition between wet and dry recurs later: while the upper part of Nkongolo's body is raised up by the termite mound, which grows with miraculous speed, the lower part of the decapitated corpse is buried in a remarkable manner beneath a river. Nkongolo's men diverted the course of the Lomami and dug a pit in the dried-out bed large enough to contain the bodies of twelve sacrificed concubines. The remains of Nkongolo were laid on their knees. This work completed, the dams were destroyed so as to submerge the tomb.[12]

The decapitation of the divine Nkongolo marks a separation of the dry (or burning) aspect of the rainbow (represented in popular belief as a celestial fire) from the humid aspect, associated with terrestrial waters. The rainbow effectively embodies a contradiction: at once male and female, it unites fire and water, high and low. Nkongolo's death connotes a failure; he dies on a high place, midway between sky and earth (on the Mita Mountains according to Colle, on the summit of a hill in Burton's version); and he is cut in two. The rainbow hero of the Luba epic fails in his attempt to unite the terrestrial waters (from whence he came) and the burning sky, of which he aspires to be the master. In the final episode of the myth, Nkongolo associates himself with the sun through some rather odd behavior. A fugitive from his nephew, he climbs each day to the summit of a hill to receive the gentle rays of the early morning sun (Burton). Nkongolo thus divides his time between the fresh dampness of the cave where he has taken refuge and the moderate warmth of the rising sun. This daily to-and-fro-ing prefigures the definitive spatial dismemberment of Nkongolo after his capture, the head going to a dry place, the trunk to a wet one. But what is most interesting here is the discreet affinity suggested between the rainbow spirit and the sun. At the metaphorical level, the sun is equated with Nkongolo's head, the burning superior part detached from the humid body of the rainbow. If, as we have suggested, the ritual funeral of the rival prince who dies in the succession war is inspired by Nkongolo's death, it should be no surprise to find the victim's desiccated head taken out every four days from the hut where it is carefully preserved and exposed to the sun.[13]

The affinity between Nkongolo and the sun is further strengthened by the belief of the Luba-Hemba that every night the sun traverses the country of the Tumandwa twa Maseba, little people covered with reddish hair who live in termite mounds near a mythical lake called Endelende.[14] The name of these autochthonous "red" people ("the little conquered people of the bare uplands") reminds us even more of the tragic end of Nkongolo, if we take into account Van Malderen's statement that the Tumandwa twa Maseba lived in *caves*.[15] In a word, these little beings are associated with the world of holes of Nkongolo. But there is a difficulty here: Nkongolo did not reign over other savages (who were even ignorant of cooking) but over the Pygmies, darker and less hairy people, who had supposedly driven the red people into the highlands (see p. 26). The symbolic correspondences we have just mentioned are nevertheless so striking that we are prepared to risk repairing the gaps in the picture with a hypothesis. In taking refuge near the end of his life in high country, in caves, Nkongolo may have rediscovered, like the setting sun, these little red-colored aborigines. The bloodstained head of the hero would then correspond with the beautiful image of the nocturnal sun, as invented by the Luba-Hemba.

The mythical termite mound which swallowed up the solar head of the rainbow hero also occurs in the belief system. For the Zela, a Luba-ized people of Katanga, the rainbow python lives in a termite mound, from which it emerges only in rainy weather; to escape its deadly breath, one must make a noise.[16] A similar tradition is found among the Luba-Hemba: "the rainbow is really the vapor or smoke which comes out of the mouth of a great red serpent called Kongolo." The same black smoke sometimes comes out of termite mounds, takes the form of a cloud, and kills anyone in its path.[17] Later we suggest an explanation of this mysterious smoke, which is analogous to the rainbow. For the moment it is enough to observe that popular belief, faithful to the serpentine model of the rainbow, substitutes a snake for the mythical head of Nkongolo buried in its termite mound. From its lofty vantage point in the cosmos, which M1 portrays as the sky, the rainbow serpent launches fearsome attacks on men during the wet season. He makes his presence particularly felt, as we shall see, during the transition from the dry season (which he incarnates) to the wet season (which he opposes). The cosmogonic portrait of Nkongolo can already be sketched in broad strokes:

Head of Nkongolo:	celestial fire (sun)	dry earth (termite mound)
Body of Nkongolo:	terrestrial water (rivers, lakes)	wet earth (riverbeds)

Nature and culture collaborate in this surgical separation of contradictory categories. A natural prodigy robs men of the head (sheltering it in a high, dry place) while Nkongolo's family buries the mutilated remains under the water. Nkongolo's head thus belongs entirely to the dry season and the sun, while the body is culturally integrated in the aquatic natural order. The decapitation of the rainbow separates fire and water, sky and earth. We shall see how it also inaugurates the dialectic of the seasons.

Mbidi Kiluwe and Kalala Ilunga, the Rain Heroes

Master of terrestrial waters, burning enemy of rain in the sky—thus does Nkongolo now appear to us. One may easily deduce that his adversaries, Mbidi Kiluwe and Kalala Ilunga, are the masters of the wet season. This hypothesis is confirmed by popular belief: rain signifies fecundity and life.[18]

The kingdom of Mbidi lies to the east, that of Nkongolo to the west. This topography also connotes the opposition of high (sky) and low (earth), because the east is mountainous country, while the west is not. The Lualaba River separates the two domains. In spite of all his efforts, Nkongolo is unable to cross it, for the canoe master is a servant of Mbidi and of his son. The tumultuous waters which engulf the rafts of Nkongolo powerfully evoke the image of a river in spate at the height of the wet season, a river which has ceased to belong to the master of drought and terrestrial waters. This spatial barrier thus also marks along the temporal axis the transition of the seasons, according to the following code:

west	Lualaba River	east
low		high
earth		sky
dry season		wet season

It is significant that Nkongolo places a magician (Mijibu) and a musician in an elevated position (at the top of a tree) to call back the vanished hero when the river prevents Nkongolo's further advance eastward. This elevation becomes ascent in Orjo de Marchovelette's version, when Mijibu leaps without difficulty through the air and finds himself on the further bank where the country of the east begins. The same symbolic notation occurs in Makonga's version: Mijibu literally flies while shaking his bells, his companion in misfortune hanging on to his clothing.[19] Mbidi is found up a tree when Nkongolo's sisters see his reflection in the water (Burton's version). The son of this celestial hero is characterized by an airy lightness. Given to dancing and jumping, he makes a wonderful leap over the crowd to escape the trap laid for him by Nkongolo (Burton's version). He has no trouble in finding the canoe so he can cross the river, which separates the western kingdom from the eastern, the earth from the sky.

Two versions introduce an initial separation between the two domains, before the river. According to Theeuws, Mbidi has to cross burning mountains on his way west.[20] According to Van Malderen, Mbidi's way is barred by "two insurmountable walls of rock" between which flows a tributary. Mbidi follows its course westward until he reaches the main river, which he crosses on a raft of bark.[21] The first obstacle evokes the fire which the rainbow serpent causes to appear in the sky. The second seems to prefigure, on the vertical axis, the river barrier which Nkongolo will be unable to overcome.

Mbidi, the prince from on high, in no way assumed the airs of a conqueror in Nkongolo's realm. On the contrary, he appeared shy and reserved, avoiding all contact and ignoring the young women who greeted him (Burton and Colle). But note that Orjo de Marchovelette's version qualifies this picture: here Mbidi hunts with a large following and brings the native peoples under his sway before meeting Nkongolo. In this account, Kalala Ilunga's distinctive martial quality has already emerged. Nonetheless, Mbidi has no intention of fighting Nkongolo and, in Colle's version, even denies his son military assistance. Kalala, in contrast, is from the earliest age a fearless warrior. His prowess displeases his uncle, who decides to get rid of him (Burton, Colle, Makonga). Kalala belongs totally to the terrestrial world of Nkongolo in which he was born and reared. He plays, dances, makes war, and earns public acclaim, whereas his father is mannered, taciturn, and withdrawn. Before meeting Mbidi, who teaches him culinary ritual (Orjo de Marchovelette's version), Kalala seems not to have known the aristocratic code of royalty. He competes with Nkongolo on his own ground (games, war). The colorful picture of Kalala contrasts with that of his father: a purely celestial being who is temporarily exiled on earth, Mbidi would seem to strive to maintain a distinction between the lowly kingship of Nkongolo and the royalty above. He restricts himself to leaving a trace of his presence by impregnating his host's two sisters. His opposition to Nkongolo is peaceful, whereas Kalala opposes his maternal uncle with violence.

Let us try to correlate the successive operations of our two heroes and the peculiarities of the rainy season. The abrupt departure of Mbidi, his return to his native land, provides an excellent starting point: the reference here is undoubtedly to the short intercalary dry season which separates the wet season into two unequal parts. Here our argument is essentially in agreement with the work of Studstill, who has independently attempted to draw parallels between the Luba calendar and mythical events.[22] Following this observer, one can note that the long journey and diverse hunting expeditions of Mbidi, before his entry into Nkongolo's country, can be situated at the height of the dry season, during the month *mpulu*, when hunting activity is most intense. The beginning of the wet season is marked by the benign appearance of Mbidi Kiluwe, just at the moment when Nkongolo's sisters are busy fishing. This incident strongly suggests the time of spawning and regeneration that, according to Sendwe, characterizes the end of the dry season and the appearance of the first rains.[23] Similarly, the pregnancy of Mbidi's two wives seems homologous with the second month of the wet season (called *Kyongwe*, "maturity"), when the first harvest takes place. The unceremonious departure of Mbidi would correspond to the interruption of the rains in the month of *lwishi* (fog).

The birth and exploits of Kalala and his conflict with Nkongolo belong to the latter part of the wet season, when rain is at its heaviest. The return of the rains, after the brief intercalary dry season, is marked, according to Sendwe, by the appearance of the red ants who give their name to the month (*mpaji*). In this context Colle's account tells how Kalala Ilunga, soon after his birth, observed a column of ants returning from a successful raid on a termite mound; the sight fascinated him and gave him the idea of enslaving the followers of Nkongolo. The deadly conflict which, in all the versions, ensued between uncle and nephew is evidently that between the rainbow and the storm. At this level Kalala the Violent, the Black, could well be the anthropomorphic transformation of the black goat with the fiery tail (*nzadji*) which personifies the lightning (*nkuba*).[24] It may be objected that this hypothesis is unsupported, whereas the very name Nkongolo means "rainbow." However, we should remember that in Luba as in French the word *foudre* (lightning) has both a real and a figurative sense: the term *nzadji* designates both the lightning animal and a ferocious warrior,[25] and the latter expression fits Kalala Ilunga exactly.

At the cosmogonic level, Mbidi and his son Kalala would seem to represent respectively the first rains and violent storms. The final victory of Kalala Ilunga is understandable only in the perspective of a truly dialectical logic. The tragic death of Nkongolo takes on a spatio-temporal function; his decapitation not only separates sky and earth, it also establishes the cycle of the seasons. The amputated head is made safe from harm in the dry earth of a termite mound. The death of the master of drought is followed by a partial resurrection. The preservation of Nkongolo's head puts drought in its proper place in time and space, denied the privilege of unlimited duration. We know that termites are adept at defending their home against atmospheric water.[26]

These conclusions would remain hypothetical unless we knew that at least one Zaïrean culture explicitly employed the cosmogonic code which we have just outlined. A Mayombe myth is from this point of view the exact structural equivalent of M1: it describes the conflict of the rain and the lightning animal. This narrative makes manifest the latent cosmic drama that the Luba disguise as history.

M3, Yombe: Rainbow and Lightning Quarrel[27]

One day Mbumba the Rainbow left his hole beside the water and went up to the sky where he found Nzazi, the Lightning. Together they built a village. Nzazi, who is the master of the sky, wanted to make Mbumba the guard of the village. But Mbumba refused and returned to earth. He threw himself in the water. Some women came fishing and caused the hole where he was hidden to dry up. They took him for a great red catfish. When they tried to kill him, Mbumba bit a finger off one of them. Like a snake, Mbumba rose out of the water, which had turned red. The sister of the woman he had bitten tried to strike him but fainted before she could do so. Mbumba assumed a menacing appearance and ordered the remaining women to retreat. He went up to the sky, where he learned that Nzazi had descended to the earth to kill six men. But Nzazi soon returned to the sky and greeted Mbumba with a mocking expression. Mbumba recognized that Nzazi was the lord of the sky and offered him a slave. At the same time he warned Nzazi not to strike this man on pain of being drenched by a great downfall of rain. Nzazi refused to believe this; to show his independence, he slapped the slave, who began to cry. Mbumba returned to earth and visited his friend Phulu Bunzi, master of the waters. Mbumba asked him to kill Nzazi. Phulu Bunzi came out of the water dressed as a great chief and summoned Nzazi by magical means. No sooner had Nzazi reached the earth than he was engulfed by floodwaters. Phulu Bunzi settled Nzazi's quarrel with Rainbow and concluded a pact of friendship with Nzazi, who returned to the sky.

Phulu Bunzi stayed long at Mbumba's village. He left on a day when it was raining. He plunged into a river. Back home, he learned that his son had died. Mbumba came to visit him and was severely reproached by Phulu Bunzi. His child would not have died, he said, had he, Phulu Bunzi, not been absent at Mbumba's. He demanded compensation. But Mbumba was unable to meet this demand. So he was killed and his head was cut off with a knife. Phulu Bunzi ordered Mbumba's head to be hung high up on the fence surrounding the royal enclosure near the chief's house, and he ordered the trunk to be buried.

Popular beliefs about Mbumba the Rainbow help us to understand this myth. A water serpent, he reaches toward the sky by climbing trees. Once in the sky he stops the rain falling.[28] Whereas Nzazi the Lightning rules the sky, Rainbow rules the earth.[29]

There are numerous points of convergence with Luba symbolism. The rainbow is associated with terrestrial waters and the color red. He dies on being beheaded on the orders of Phulu Bunzi, master of rain, who has power to cause floods. Phulu Bunzi is the ally of Lightning against Mbumba the Rainbow. He is a water spirit and a prominent member of the Yombe pantheon. At times of storms and heavy rains he appears in the swollen rivers where, with his following, he makes a great commotion to the sound of drumming.[30] In the myth, Rainbow, a water spirit of earth who is dangerous to approach, makes several journeys between earth and sky. Between Lightning and himself there is a profound incompatibility of temperament. Let us analyze this antagonism and these cosmic journeys in relation to seasonal change.

1. Celestial conjunction of Lightning and Rainbow. The latter stops the rain falling (*dry season*).

2. Return to earth of Rainbow, who lodges in a hole beneath the waters. The opposition between high and low, celestial fire (lightning) and terrestrial water is maximized. Rainbow threatens the women who fish (*dry season well established*).

3. Lightning begins to cause harm on earth. Rainbow goes up to the sky. He tries to make a bargain with Lightning by which the latter will not return to earth. But Lightning has no intention of abandoning his attacks on men (*beginning of the wet season*).

4. Return to earth of Rainbow, who seeks an alliance with the water spirit to finish off Lightning. Phulu Bunzi is master of rain and flood: he emerges from the riverbed and soaks Lightning. But he makes peace with him soon afterwards. Lightning then returns to the sky while the water spirit lingers in Rainbow's village (*establishment then interruption of the wet season*).

5. It rains. The water spirit leaves Rainbow's village and returns to his aquatic domain. He causes Rainbow to be beheaded (*resumption of rains after the short dry season*).

These data can be related to the characteristic pattern of rainfall in the Lower Congo, as reported for Luozi.[31]

June–September: height of dry season
October–December: wet season
January–February: attenuation of wet season (little dry season)
March–May: wet season

In decisively separating Rainbow's head from his body, Phulu Bunzi, the master of rain, acts exactly like Kulala Ilunga in the Luba epic. Yet there is a noticeable rigidity about Yombe mythical thought. Although the red rainbow serpent is presented as an aggressive being, M3 minimizes the dangers of his appearance: Rainbow does no more than bite a finger off one woman and cause another to faint. On the other hand, the angry nature of Lightning is accentuated. All in all, Rainbow appears as an unsuccessful mediator between sky and earth. He tries vainly to protect men from the onslaughts of Lightning (and he has compassion for the slave he gives to Lightning). The Yombe present an unflattering portrait of this formidable ally of the benign spirit of rain. For the Luba, Lightning is a martial hero, son of the master of rain (Mbidi). The same hierarchical relationship between the two personages is expressed by the Yombe in another mode: Phulu Bunzi is a great chief who is able to summon Nzazi by magic and impose on him a pact with Rainbow. In this context, Phulu Bunzi is certainly equivalent to Mbidi: Lightning depends on him like a son on his father. There is nevertheless a permutation of function: the master of rain orders the execution of Rainbow in the Yombe myth, whereas it is the lightning (Kalala) who performs this act in the Luba myth. The common armature of the two myths is now apparent: the fire of lightning (Nzazi, Kalala Ilunga) and celestial water (Phulu Bunzi, Mbidi) are united in the great struggle which opposes the wet season to the season of drought. With more clarity than the Luba epic, the Yombe myth expresses this cosmogonic drama in aquatic terms: the low terrestrial waters are the domain of Rainbow; the appearance of Phulu Bunzi marks rivers in spate. It is clear that the wild waters of the river which carried off the frail rafts of Nkongolo in M1 belong to this semantic complex. In both cases the rising of the earthly waters, in unison with rain and storm, announces the death of the rainbow serpent.

Evidently, this cosmogonic myth belongs to the most ancient common heritage of the Bantu peoples, for the Venda of southeast Africa possess it in an inverted form.

M4 (1), Venda: Python and His Two Wives (Roumeguère-Eberhardt version[32])

Python married a second wife who knew nothing of his animal nature. At night she was surprised to feel a cold presence at her side. When she questioned him, Python told her to be quiet. During the day she worked in the fields with the first wife. She was very curious about her husband, but her co-wife forbade her to go to the village in the daytime. Pretending one day to be looking for a spade, the second wife saw her husband peacefully smoking in the men's courtyard. Python was furious at being discovered, and disappeared into a lake. From then on the rain ceased to fall. The crops perished, a great famine arose, and the springs dried up. Divination showed that all this had happened because Python wanted his young wife with him. So the young women prepared the ritual beer and all the people gathered by the lake. While the women brought beer, the men danced, played the flute, and invoked the ancestors. Holding a calabash of beer, the guilty young wife disappeared under the water. Immediately the rain began to fall again.

Roumeguère-Eberhardt, to whom we owe this text, compares it to the version published by Stayt in 1931.[33]

M4 (2), Venda: Python and His Two Wives (Stayt's version)

The first wife of Python knew he was a serpent, but the second wife did not know. All her questions to the first wife were turned aside with the order to be silent. For several nights running, the second wife woke up soaked with water. Through the intermediary of the first wife, Python offered the second wife a necklace, at the same time begging her not to ask questions. The first wife served the morning meal, the second the evening meal. When the two wives were working in the fields, the second tried to slip away on the pretense of looking for her box of tobacco. But the other forbade her to go to the village and herself went and procured the box. The same thing happened on the following days until the young wife escaped from the other and surprised her husband catching flies. Then Python threw himself into a pond and disappeared. The rivers dried up, and only the lake where Python had taken refuge still contained water. The first wife revealed the cause of the trouble and the chiefs ordered preparation of an offering of beer. The guilty young wife entered the water holding the calabash of sacrificial beer, while the men played the flute. As the music became increasingly loud, the young wife disappeared. Thereupon the water returned to the rivers and the people rejoiced.

The Yombe and Luba myths here undergo a double transformation.

The aquatic serpent ceases to be associated with the rainbow and to signify the dry season: instead it goes over to the side of rain. And now it is the disappearance rather than the presence of the serpent that causes a general drought and famine. The rain no longer falls and the terrestrial waters dry up, with the exception of the lake which hides the hero. The beneficent presence of the aquatic serpent among men therefore signifies the wet season, his absence the dry season. During the wet season, killing of pythons is prohibited.[34]

Yombe and Luba: rainbow serpent = terrestrial water (or celestial water)
Venda: serpent (but not rainbow) = terrestrial water + celestial water

For the Venda the aquatic serpent is cold, whereas the rainbow serpent is burning for the Luba. The Venda water spirit smokes a pipe, whereas Nkongolo avoids it because for the Luba he is classified among the spirits of the west and only the spirits of the east consume tobacco.[35] Lack of information prevents an interpretation of this point, but at least it is clear that the terms of the Luba myth are inverted by the Venda. The Venda seek to gain favor with the python spirit by offering a noisy sacrifice, whereas the Luba put the rainbow serpent to flight by making a din (this acoustic code will be examined later). As for the Yombe, they fear and venerate Mbumba, who is the reigning spirit during *khimba* religious initiations.[36]

The domain of water assumes a double form in the Yombe myth, where Phulu Bunzi, spirit of floods and rain, opposes Mbumba (spirit of the low terrestrial waters) and ends by putting him to death. The dialectic of the seasons is more simply coded by the Venda in the disappearance of the aquatic serpent. But a complementary dialectic opposes masculine water to feminine fire.[37] Roumeguère-Eberhardt, one of the few authors to have taken Bantu symbolism seriously, has shown very well how these two cosmogonic principles are joined in complementary opposition. The wet season is introduced by a feminine rite associated with the sign of fire and which consists of cooking a representative array of the plants to be cultivated. Conversely, the dry season, the appearance of which coincides with the harvest, is greeted with a masculine rite associated with the water sign. In this rite, all the men, grouped by age class, wander through the country and assemble in the east by following the course of rivers. They then sacrifice a bull and throw the ritual parts in the water. The rite celebrates an origin myth according to which the world was created in a whirlpool.[38]

The following summarizes the semantic data we have been considering.

Luba: rainbow serpent = terrestrial water and celestial fire (dry season)

Yombe: rainbow serpent = terrestrial water (dry season)

Venda: serpent = terrestrial water and celestial water (wet season)

The "burning" of the rainbow is absent from the Yombe myth, which is otherwise close to the Luba version, as it is also to the Venda. In M4, the drought is the result of a feminine fault (the indiscretion of Python's young wife); correlatively, fire becomes feminine in contrast with the single source of water, which is masculine. Luba symbolic thought doubles up masculine water (Nkongolo is to Mbidi as terrestrial water is to celestial water) and masculine fire: in face of the celestial fire of Nkongolo (the sun) it is necessary to take account, since Mbidi's descent to earth, of a new terrestrial fire.

A New Cooking Fire

Mbidi, the heroic bringer of rain in M1, is also the hero of cooking fire. The converse of the rainbow, which emerges from earthly waters to inflict a savage burning on the sky, Mbidi brings a new cultural fire to the earth, a novel art of cooking calling for many precautions. In this respect, the tiny but highly refined court, replete with culinary prohibitions, which Mbidi establishes at the center of Nkongolo's realm appears like a fragment of heaven on earth. Foreseeing the arrival of the celestial hero, the diviner Mijibu recommends that Nkongolo prepare a special hut for his guest, equipped with fire-producing tools. Van Malderen's version even alleges that Mbidi taught cooking to an archaic people ignorant of the art. However that may be, Mbidi manages domestic fire with aristocratic polish, while Nkongolo eats and cooks like a rustic. Mbidi particularly reproaches his brother-in-law for sitting on the ground during meals, emphasizing the rude manners of his terrestrial host. Cooking fire is mentioned only once in connection with Nkongolo, and in a negative form: while he warms himself in the sun, his treacherous sisters collect firewood, not to prepare a meal but to facilitate their brother's capture by blocking the entrance to the cave. It is as if Nkongolo, by approaching the sun, was distancing himself from the terrestrial fire associated with Mbidi. Remember that the head of the prince (similar to Nkongolo) who is put to death after the succession war is periodically exposed to the sun.[39] But Nkongolo is fundamentally an earthling who tries to approach the sky, whereas Mbidi is a celestial prince by nature. Without being able to adduce decisive evidence, we shall argue that the supercultural fire he brings from above is related to the planet Venus (see p. 51).

In this perspective, Mbidi's marriage with the sisters of Nkongolo is a true hierogamy, a careful union of sky and earth that brings all the categories of the universe into play. Mbidi keeps his terrestrial brother-in-law at a distance. He is particularly careful about using terrestrial water (which, as we have seen, belongs to Nkongolo): Makonga's version says that the stranger-prince's water is drawn by night, as if in secret. If the operation took place in daylight, a man preceded the calabash bearers, advising passersby to hide; a ringing of bells warned Nkongolo's men of the party's approach.[40] Even in our time, women are supposed to avert their gaze from watercarriers going to the house of a *mulopwe*.

Nkongolo and Mbidi perform a strange dance together. Nkongolo is a terrestrial and aquatic being, who tries unsuccessfully to impose the burning regime of drought on the watery heavens; Mbidi, a celestial being, easily crosses the flaming barrier on high (Makonga's version) to bring to earth rain and ritual fire. Both are particularly associated with water and fire, but in complementary fashion. Nkongolo's fire rages on high, while Mbidi's burns below; Nkongolo's water belongs to earth, that of Mbidi to the sky. The two heroes avoid rather than support each other. The prudent marriage of sky and earth, the uneasy alliance of the prince of the east (sky) and the prince of the west (earth), bears fruit after an interval: Mbidi returns home (the sky), but he leaves an unborn son on earth.

It is obvious that Kalala Ilunga fills the role of cosmic mediator as a son of the sky through his father and of the earth through his mother. By right of descent from his celestial father, Kalala takes possession of the world below, where he was born. Mbidi, initiator of ritual fire, and Kalala, hero of storm and lightning, follow converse and complementary courses between sky and earth. Mbidi leaves the heavenly kingdom for a relatively brief period, and returns with family ambitions thwarted (see p. 17). Kalala flees Nkongolo's kingdom for a time, visits his father in the sky, and returns to earth gloriously successful. Rainbow, for his part, is unable to reach the sky despite two attempts: Nkongolo fails to cross the frontier between sky and earth (the Lualaba River) and dies between the two realms at the top of a mountain, abandoned by his followers. The victorious adventure of Kalala is thus situated between the utter failure of his uncle and the relative failure of his father.

Cosmogonic journeys of the heroes

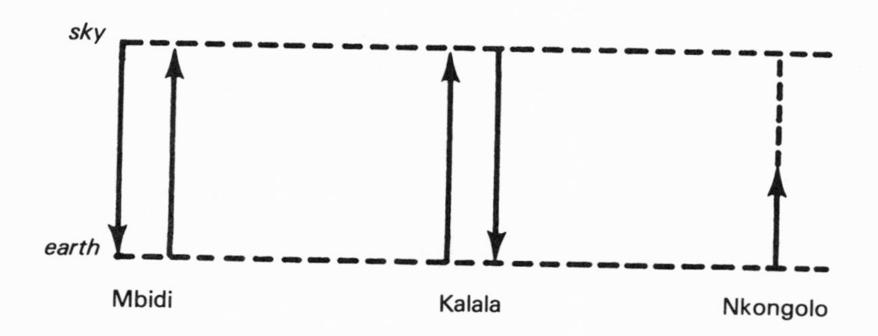

The images of cooking fire, rain, and lightning vividly express the double mediation of Mbidi and Kalala, against which Nkongolo makes his unsuccessful attempt at a burning conjunction of earth and sky. Had he succeeded, drought would have reigned for all time and men would have known nothing of divine kingship. This is why Kalala the Founder at first assumes a disjunctive function: in beheading his uncle, he definitively separates sky and earth. Between them there is thenceforth interposed ritual fire, rain, and lightning.

Lunar Fantasies

Luba thought associates rain and the moon and opposes the latter to the sun. A fragment of cosmogonic narrative tells how the moon keeps the world fresh and alive whereas the sun dries it up.[41] M5 describes the quarrel between the two heavenly bodies.

M5, Luba: Conflict of the Sun and the Moon (Theeuws)

The sun and the moon each claimed to be greater than the other. They brought their dispute to God, who decided in favor of the moon, because it gave life to men: on one of its thirteen annual journeys, the moon brought back the rain, so causing the plants to grow. Incensed at this verdict, the sun threw mud in the moon's face. Since that time the moon has produced less light than the sun.

The cosmogonic code is transparent:

sun	moon
dry season	wet season
maleficent	beneficent

The Luba foundation myth reproduces this opposition in a somewhat disguised form. We have seen that Nkongolo is associated with the sun. We would have hesitated to make the corresponding equation between Mbidi and the moon if Studstill had not compared the second encounter between the hero and Nkongolo's sisters with a story in which a woman sees her lover as a crescent moon which she draws from a well with the aid of a jar.[42] Our hero does indeed find himself in an elevated position, being lodged in the branches of a tree when the amorous young women notice his reflection in the water (Burton's version). Other parallels exist. The moon, like Mbidi, has two wives.[43] Theeuws identifies them respectively with the morning and evening stars, that is, with the two complementary aspects of Venus.[44] Further, the term which designates this brilliant planet (*lu-bangà* or *ki-bangà* according to Van Avermaet's dictionary[45]) is also applied to the ritual headdress of raffia worn by the two women in charge of the royal cuisine, in conformity with the instructions given by Mbidi to his son (M1, Orjo de Marchovelette's version). The word *kibanga*, given without tonal marks in this second context, should almost certainly be related to the preceding semantic complex rather than to the term *ki-bàngà* (jaw). The hypothesis that Mbidi is a moon-king, the husband of Venus, becomes highly probable.

The irreconcilable opposition between Nkongolo and Mbidi in M1 reproduces the conflict between the sun and the moon (M5). By separating the two personages after a brief conjunction, M1 demonstrates more precisely the impossibility of coexistence between the two heavenly bodies, between the day and the night. This is doubtless the major reason why Mbidi keeps his distance from Nkongolo.

Note once more that Nkongolo died decapitated at the western extremity of his kingdom, like the sun, which a popular image describes as "bleeding," whereas Mbidi disappeared conversely in the east, like the moon at the end of its monthly cycle. In this respect, the first pacific episode in the myth, contained between the sudden arrival and abrupt departure of the Prince of the East, is analogous to a lunar cycle. It evokes the short cyclical rhythm, whereas the long rhythm of the seasons is expressed more precisely through the second episode, full of noise and anger, which opposes Nkongolo the Rainbow to Kalala Ilunga the Lightning. But the death of the rainbow hero, master of the dry season, is also the death of the sun and the promise of solar resurrection—in brief, the establishment of the shortest cycle, the alternation of day and night. The three cosmic rhythms thus appear in two temporal modes in the progression of the mythical narrative:

1. lunar cycles
2. { seasons / day and night }

The masculine moon is, in fact, the middle term in the Luba cosmogonic system: on the one hand, he is held to bring the rain (M5); on the other hand his wives, the evening star and the morning star, are also, in M1 (if we accept the identification of Mbidi with the moon), the incestuous sisters of the sun: they announce his disappearance at dusk, and his reappearance just before dawn. Did not Mabela, one of the two sisters, inform the followers of Kalala that Nkongolo exposed himself in early morning to the first rays of the sun (Burton's version)? We therefore propose the following attributions:

Mabela	*Bulanda*
morning star	evening star

According to this hypothesis, it is now evident why it is Kalala Ilunga, son of the evening star, and not Kisula, son of the morning star, who is called to succeed their moon-father. Kisula, as son of Mabela, is indirectly associated with the rising sun and with heat. That is why, with a sure sense of the cosmogonic code, Orjo de Marchovelette's version shows us Bulanda's son exploring by the light of the *full moon* the places where Nkongolo has taken refuge in hope of escaping death.

By the mediation of Venus, the monthly lunar cycle is related to the short cycle of days and nights. It is also related to the long cycle of the seasons by another aspect of the symbolic system which we will now consider. The Luba of Katanga hold that the moon presents two contradictory aspects. When its crescent points east, toward the place of origin of divine kingship, the moon is "good" and men rejoice. Conversely, when the crescent is pointed to the west the moon is "bad" and people are sad because deaths and misfortunes abound.[46] Observations show that the first position (related to Mbidi, hero of the east) characterizes the waxing phase of the moon, and the second (related to Nkongolo, master of the west) the waning phase. Every lunar cycle therefore reproduces on a reduced scale the spatiotemporal oppositions we have discovered in M1, as if the seasonal cycle were projected into lunar cyclical time; in the process the moon takes on a certain coefficient of ambivalence that has been well described by Theeuws. The two cyclical systems, of long and short periodicity, are articulated with each other because one of the lunar cycles brings rain. This time is also the critical moment in the calendar, for it is then, as we shall see, that the Luba expect to suffer from violent gales.

The duality of the moon, which is sometimes "good" and sometimes "bad," is related to the moon's two wives in the following belief: when the moon reappears in the west, Kilonda, the second wife, accompanies him in the firmament; but she feeds her husband badly and he recovers his strength only with the cooking of the principal wife, who awaits him in the east.[47] Probably one should use a mirror to read this image, which Tempels has inverted: it seems most probable that the Luba associate the waxing phase of the moon with good nourishment, and vice versa. Only in this form could the belief reported by Tempels be reconciled with the preceding material. As the moon in the course of each cycle effects an apparent movement from west to east, the waxing, beneficent moon grows in size *thanks to the wife in the east*, for the tips of the crescent are turned in this direction during this first phase. Conversely, when the moon is waning and the crescent is turned to the west, the maleficent direction, the second wife, Kilonda, allows him to waste away to extinction. In other terms, and in conformity with the general spatial code, the moon gets fat through the east and thin through the west.[48]

The beginning of each lunar cycle is associated with intense ritual activity.[49] The day following the moon's reappearance is sacred to the dead. Armed with staves, the spirits of the departed bar access to the fields, and no one dares go there. All magical charms are regenerated. No one except the diviner can have a lighted fire in his house. The diviner, or the local chief, purifies every villager with magic water. Women who have borne twins exchange obscene jokes with anyone they see. Pregnant women anoint their bellies with oil. In the evening, dances and songs greet the new moon.

The Rainbow, the Termite Mound, and the Tower

Nkongolo appears in a double epiphany: as rainbow, arising from the terrestrial waters to burn the rain, and as serpent, emerging from the termite mounds to threaten men. It is time to look at the connection between these two images. For the Zela, the serpent Nkongolo only shows himself, like the rainbow, during the rains.[50] The deadly breath he produces directly affects the rain, according to a belief of the Luba of Kasai, who make a precise equation between the rainbow and the breath of the serpent *nkongolo*.[51] This colored breath becomes black smoke among the Luba-Hemba, who say that when the Nkongolo spirit is abroad people see a dense and somber vapor moving about, ravaging everything it touches. One might take this belief to refer to whirlwinds, except that Colle, to whom we owe this information, reports that the same smoke is sometimes exhaled by termite mounds.[52] This "dangerous vapor" rising from the ground toward the sky can hardly be other than the nuptial swarm leaving the termite mound at the beginning of the wet season. An eminent entomologist, Jean Feytaud, describes this "single, short-lived flight" in the same terms as the myth: the larger termites mass in such numbers that "the observer has the impression of black smoke rising above the nest."[53]

In mythical terms, this dark vertical cloud that moves and then dissolves is nothing other than an abortive attempt by the chthonic serpent to emerge from its hiding place in the termite mound and to burn the rain: the termite swarm, in the visual code, is a transformation of the rainbow concept. The Zela make it clear that the python Nkongolo emerges from the termite mound *at the beginning of the rains.* The termite mound has a pivotal significance in the Luba calendar. According to Sendwe, the last month of the dry season is called *kansense kaswamitunda* (little termites of the great termite mounds): it marks the appearance of winged termites and the first rains. The first month of the wet season is called *kuswamukata* (great termites) because it is the time when these insects are gathered for eating. It will be remembered that the martial ardor of Nkongolo (Burton's version) or of Kalala Ilunga (Colle's version) was inflamed by the spectacle of a column of ants attacking a termite colony. The fragile kingdom of Nkongolo is comparable to a vast termite mound, well protected against the rain, where men are engaged in gigantic construction projects (Verhulpen's version). The invasion of Kalala's army resembles a column of ants breaking into a human termite mound, inside which shelters a society with but a rudimentary form of organization.

This world of holes reminds us of Nkongolo's patronym, of which the first term, *bw-ina*, signifies "a region filled with dangerous excavations" (see p. 25). The perilous fire of the rainbow bursts out of the cosmic termite mound in two *burning* forms which are transformationally related: a serpent with lethal breath, or a black smoke (the natural origin of which we have just noted). Once a year, the termite people rise up toward the sky, rehearsing for a brief moment the original cosmic drama. This epiphany is always perilous for men: the black cloud of termites rising skyward at the time of seasonal change has to be magically controlled by noise among the Luba-Hemba, while similar measures are taken by the Zela against the deadly breath of the rainbow python. When men see the "smoke" of Nkongolo, they bring out cooking pots, iron rings, and everything that makes a noise.[54] Theeuws, for his part, says that the Luba of Katanga magically avert the catastrophes threatened by the rainbow by banging together iron hoes and beating drums.[55] This acoustic code should be noted because it occurs in the foundation myth, in connection with an ascent effected on the orders of Nkongolo (M1).

The general structure of the narrative projects the opposition of earth and sky along a horizontal axis (west-east), but a vertical cosmogonic axis takes form at the moment when Nkongolo reaches the river which marks the uncrossable boundary of his kingdom. Abandoning his attempt to cross, he orders the magician Mijibu and an assistant to climb to the top of a tree; the two men are obliged to beat a gong and shake a rattle to summon their master (Orjo de Marchovelette). It is at first sight surprising that Rainbow orders the making of noise to attract the rain spirit. But what is occurring is a ruse, an inversion of the ritual by which men stave off the evil designs of Nkongolo. Mijibu, who had earlier helped Kalala avoid the trap laid by his uncle, finds himself in a false position. By the intermediary of the diviner, Nkongolo tries to draw his enemy into an ambush by utilizing the magical techniques used by men to defeat himself. In this context noise constitutes a means of long-distance communication, founded on normal speech. Another version (Burton) condemns Kahia, Kalala's personal drummer, to transmit signals. But, by using drum language, Kahia had earlier been able to warn his master of the danger threatening him during the dance arranged by Nkongolo. Condemned to die of hunger, Kahia nevertheless escapes. For Colle, it is also a drummer who is perched in the tree and dies of hunger after the ladder he used to climb up is removed. In Verhulpen's version, the magician, Mijibu, finds himself on a platform in the branches together with Kaniamba, Nkongolo's own brother; Mijibu manages to escape while Kaniamba, who beats a gong, dies before Kalala's arrival. According to Makonga, the magician Mijibu is accompanied by the drummer Mungedi. The magician hurls himself through the air, bearing with him his companion, who holds on to his clothing.

One or two friends of the fugitive hero thus find themselves in an elevated position on the orders of Rainbow, who thereby tries to realize through them his double cosmogonic purpose: to reunite sky and earth, and to burn the rain. These mediators, the captives of Nkongolo, are Kalala's men, and hostages: the magician accompanies the musician, who, in several versions, dies without having recalled the vanished lord. This episode is no more than a truncated variant of a cosmogonic myth, widely distributed throughout Central Africa, in which men build an enormous tower to reach the sky and regain immortality. The parallel is the more impressive in that Verhulpen's version cites among the great works undertaken by Nkongolo the building of just such an edifice that would join the sky to the earth.

M6, Luba-Kasai: The Tower and the Musicians (Denolf[56])

> At the beginning of time, men lived in the same village as God. Tired of the noise of their quarrels, the Creator despatched humankind to earth. There they suffered from hunger and cold, and came to know sickness and death. A diviner advised them to return to the sky to find immortality. So they began to build an enormous tower of wood, with its foundations in a *lusanga* tree. After many months of labor the builders arrived at the sky. They entered the celestial domain, beating a drum and playing a flute to make the news known to those who remained on earth. But these were too far away to hear. When He heard the noise God became angry and destroyed the tower, killing the musicians.

In this narrative, the earth is separated from the sky and the earthlings are afflicted with hunger and sickness. God has broken the original spatial conjunction which guaranteed immortality. Men try in vain to reestablish both the one and the other. The musicians' call was intended to summon men on high and overcome the disjunction between sky and earth. But the message is not heard; instead, the din harms its makers because it arouses the anger of God, who hates noise. Let us compare this situation with the ritual exorcism of Nkongolo:

M6:

1. Ephemeral conjunction of sky and earth realized by a cultural means (the tower).
2. Noise causes a return to the initial disjunction.

Ritual of the Rainbow:

1. An ephemeral, natural conjunction of sky and earth is brought about by a terrestrial demiurge (the rainbow-serpent).
2. A disjunction of sky and earth is effected in a noisy manner to avert a catastrophe.

In the first case, the men who seek a conjunction of sky and earth make much noise in vain in the sky; in the other, men on earth use noise successfully in their struggle to avert a dangerous conjunction (for them and for the cosmos). It thus seems that the themes of the tower and the rainbow are joined by an inverse homology. But the two projects are also different. In M6 men seek vainly to regain a lost immortality; in the rite, they are implicitly struggling against a perpetuation of the dry season, the enemy of rain. The very difference defines a new semantic field, the product of sad reflection on continuity and discontinuity. The tower in the cultural domain, and the rainbow in the natural domain, are equivalent signs of spatiotemporal *continuity*. It is no doubt in this perspective that we should interpret the very name of the rainbow: Van Avermaet derives the term *Nkongolo* from the verb *ku-konga*, "to assemble, bring together, amass."[57] In M6, men create an artificial link between sky and earth to annihilate time, which is destroying their own lives; in the rainbow ritual, however, men conjure a natural element uniting sky and earth and threatening to substitute an unchanging cosmic time for the succession of the seasons. The mythical enterprise fails, the rite succeeds. Noise is the cause of failure as it is of success, because in both cases it serves the same cosmic function: the separation of sky and earth.

In the interior of this semantic field, M1 occupies an intermediary position. It does so first of all because Nkongolo uses a tree (a natural element) as well as a tower (he causes a platform to be built in the tree in Verhulpen's version). There he puts musicians, as in M6. He who, in the ritual, is attributed with a horror of noise compels the musicians to play so as to summon their master. These actors begin against their will the ascent to the sky achieved voluntarily by the musicians of M6. The rhythmic message sent out halfway between sky and earth is deceitful. Nkongolo uses the language which, in M6, calls men to immortality, to entice his adversary to certain death. The musicians or noisemakers are condemned to die of hunger; they are no more successful in reaching the sky than in causing the return of the celestial hero.

The theme of the disjunction of sky and earth, brought about by noisy means, is philosophically ambiguous. It carries a negative value for the man permanently separated from his Creator and condemned to mortality (M6), whereas it possesses a positive value on the cosmogonic level (ritual). In M6 men attempt to reestablish for their benefit the conjunction of sky and earth. The noise with which they displease God makes definitive the separation of the world above from the world below, and perpetuates death. To the contrary, when noise resounds in the ears of the rainbow-serpent, the spirit is forced to abandon his attempt at a malign conjunction opposed to the mediating action of the life-giving rain. In the end, noise has the same result, that of maintaining for better or worse the principle of separation, of discontinuity. The death of Nkongolo is also the death of man himself, the price paid for the life of the cosmos.

	time	*space*
	A. *The search for continuity*	
M6	human immortality	cosmic tower
M1	permanent drought	rainbow, tree-tower
	B. *Introduction of discontinuity*	
M6	human finitude* (death)	destruction of the tower
M1	dialectic of the seasons	beheading of the rainbow

A Chokwe variant of M6 serves as a bridge leading toward the Kuba cycle of Woot, which we shall examine in chapter four. It is a restatement of the Babel myth; it explains, through the destruction of the tower, another form of discontinuity: the dispersion of peoples. The overt quest for immortality disappears; instead, men build the tower to hear the secret words of God.[58] This variant is entirely deployed along a spatial axis: the diversity of peoples is homologous with the separation of sky and earth. God casts from him men who seek to know the ultimate secrets of life, including, in all probability, that of immortality.

Let us examine the whole set of situations considered in order to reconstitute the acoustic code in relation to this metaphysical picture.

M6: *Noise in the sky (musicians at the top of the tower)*

purpose: a search for immortality
modality: message inaudible to earthlings, who are too far away
result: disjunction of sky and earth, sickness, short life

Ritual: *Noise on earth*

purpose: magical control of dangers emanating from rainbow-serpent

*I have preferred the archaic word "finitude" to translate the French *finitude* because of its superior philosophical and poetic resonance in comparison with "limitation," its prosaic modern equivalent. (R.W.)

modality: message understood by the terrestrial demiurge
result: in accordance with the purpose: disjunction of sky and earth

Only the ritual noise produced on earth is effective, for it puts the rainbow-serpent to flight and therefore staves off the danger of death; but as it is also disjunctive at the cosmogonic level, it can do nothing against death itself since immortality implies the conjunction of sky and earth. Immortality would have been possible if the call of the musicians who reached the sky could have been heard by men. But, unluckily, it is inaudible to them, whereas for the master of heaven it is an insufferable din. The hope of immortality is therefore completely vain. A third possibility is explored in the myth: the noise produced halfway between earth and sky, up a tree, condemns the musicians of M1 to an absurd situation, intermediate between life and death.

The acoustic code may be summarized thus:

noise in the sky (call too distant to be heard)	failure of quest for immortality
terrestrial noise	prolongation of a brief life
noise between sky and earth	death from hunger

The first part of M1 succeeds in evoking a situation comparable to ritual. Kalala's drummer (whom several versions later condemn to perish up a tree) successfully uses drum language to warn his master of the danger represented by the concealed pit. The hero understands the message at once and makes a prodigious leap, afterward fleeing to the east as if returning to the sky. With this first intervention the drummer as it were causes a disjunction of earth and sky to save the hero's life. The message means nothing to Nkongolo, who is ignorant of drum language; it represents, in relation to speech, the analogue of the ritual noise by which men demolish the attempted malign and burning conjunction of sky and earth. In the myth, the drum message (full of meaning) is addressed to the rain hero, who takes flight, while the ritual noise (incomprehensible) drives away the evil spirit of drought. Whatever the significance of this difference, we should note the presence of drums in the battery of weapons deployed by men against the rainbow.[59] Whether sounded on earth or in the sky, drumming has the same disjunctive function on the cosmogonic level. The high or low position of the musician-messenger is only significant on the human level. Celestial noise, too feeble to be heard by men, too loud for the ears of God, ratifies the mortal condition; terrestrial noise avoids immediate death without restoring an impossible immortality, which would imply a continuous, unaltering space-time, the conjunction of man and God, earth and heaven. The dialectical time and discontinuous space introduced by the hero of rain and lightning is therefore also that of human finitude.

Silence occurs in a quite different ritual content among the Luba, that of culinary operations. These may now be integrated into the foregoing cosmogonic code, especially since M1 makes Mbidi the bearer of novel customs in this domain where the Luba multiply ritual precautions. Men and women are rigorously separated before and during meals.[60] Food for men must be prepared on a different fire from that used for women's food. This rule applies to young boys as soon as they begin to use the bow and arrow (like Mbidi the hunter). The male dining room includes a compartment containing accessories (pestle, mortar, pots) used exclusively in preparing the husband's food. The female cook has to work in silence. At such times women can communicate among themselves only in a special language of whistles. When the food is ready, the wife calls her husband by snapping her fingers; during the whole meal she remains silently outside. At the end of the meal she breaks a piece of wood into two pieces and touches her mouth with each piece to break the period of silence. These prohibitions cannot be reduced, as Burton thinks, to magical precautions intended to protect the husband against poisoning by his spouse. They mark the separation of the sexes by referring implicitly to the foundation myth where even stricter precautions, which are always observed in chiefly families, recall the cosmogonic function of Mbidi, the reserved and taciturn hero, the mediator between sky and earth.

Silence	*Noise*
ensures the moderate conjunction of sky and earth under the sign of cooking fire	prevents the excessive conjunction of sky and earth under the burning sign of the rainbow and unleashes the rain

The third possibility entertained by Luba cosmology is the tempest, which transforms welcome mediation of the rain into an excessive, wet conjunction (the converse of that caused by the rainbow). The Luba are particularly afraid of this evil the day after the appearance of the new moon because of the close association between the moon and celestial waters. On that day women avoid going into the fields, for fear the angry spirits will send a tempest to destroy the crops.[61] Sexual relations are prohibited during the preceding night. Those most devoted to this "moon cult" fast and avoid lighting fires. The diviner alone is supposed to keep his fire going.[62] Fasting and extinction of fires are impossible to interpret unless they are seen as relating to the restrictions on use of domestic fire for fear of provoking a cosmic disaster. By extinguishing fire or reducing it to a minimum one symbolically separates sky from earth to remove the danger of tempests. Rain and ritual fire are complementary mediating terms, relating equally to the jurisdiction of Mbidi and of Kalala: by acting on the one, the Luba hope to act on the other.

One would expect to find a specific element in the acoustic code, peculiar to the rites of the moon, insofar as these rites imply the danger of a tempest. *Song* and *dance* are found to greet the lunar rebirth.[63] The complete Luba acoustic code is therefore:

Silence	*Noise*	*Dancing and Singing*
ensures the moderate conjunction of sky and earth (cooking fire)	removes the danger of an excessive conjunction of sky and earth as caused by the burning rainbow	remove the danger of an excessive conjunction of sky and earth under the sign of the tempest

In the musical domain, finally, the drum signal of M1, which introduces the disjunction of sky and earth by rendering ineffective the trap laid by Nkongolo for Kalala, was specially apt as a symbol of discontinuity. Modelled on a spoken language which opposes high and low tones, the drum code introduces significant separations in the midst of a sound continuum; merely a senseless noise for Nkongolo, it is a subtle language for Kalala, the hero of discontinuity, the initiator of the rhythm of the seasons. Nkongolo thus finds himself once more on the side of nature: his insensitivity to music is merely the acoustic expression of the principle of continuity (symbolized by the rainbow) which abolishes distance and duration. The presumed etymology of his name, deriving it from a verb meaning to assemble, to bring together, here finds a new validation.

A brief comparison with Amerindian mythology shows up a dramatic reversal of the relations between the acoustic code and the cosmogonic code. We encounter again among the Luba the same double significance of the rainbow that Lévi-Strauss has discovered in South America: it heralds the end of rain, and effects an abnormal and malign conjunction of sky and earth, thus being responsible for sickness and disasters of various kinds.[64] However, in America resort is not made to ritual noise in connection with the rainbow (the significance of which seems relatively minor), but on the occasion of a solar eclipse, interpreted as a conjunction of sky and earth which threatens the world with going rotten.[65] Conversely, among the Luba, noise averts a conjunction which threatens the world with drying up (the burning rainbow, the enemy of rain). The "world gone rotten" results from another kind of conjunction, the danger of which is averted by the same techniques which the Sherente Indians of Brazil reserve for the magical control of drought (a burnt world): dancing, singing, and fasting. But it is also the case that cooking fire, as mediator between sky and earth, requires the same careful attention among the Luba as among the Amerindians.

This particular Bantu cosmogonic code is founded on the positive valuation of the wet season, as opposed to the malign dry season. Kuba mythology, which we shall examine from the same cosmogonic perspective, has some surprises in store. It is based on the contrary idea of an original excessive wetness to which is opposed a benign dry season. But before leaving the Luba world, we shall consider a myth emanating from its eastern reaches. We shall seek to establish it as a transformation of M1, of which it verifies the cosmogonic code. The myth in question is the epic of the Holoholo, a heterogeneous people inhabiting the Lake Tanganyika shore in the Albertville region. The Holoholo speakers live at the boundary of the Lega and Luba communities.[66] In an old monograph, Schmitz reports the origin myth (M7), in which, by a curious inversion, Kalala plays in certain respects the role assumed by his adversary Nkongolo in M1. But this Kalala is no more than the first actor to appear in a long story whose true hero is a young brother, master of water and friend of the birds.

M7, Holoholo: The Epic of the People of Mwamba (Schmitz[67])

In the old days, people knew nothing of war, sickness, and death. Then a woman called Mwamba arrived from the southwest with her fifteen children. Kalala, the eldest, brought spears. On the way he noticed a column of black ants and announced that he would devote himself to war. Hearing this, his mother burst out laughing. Then Kalala, grown evil, buried her alive. Soon afterward he came upon a gigantic tree which joined heaven and earth; at its feet sat five men. Kalala killed three of them and the other two ran away. Kalala caught them and they offered to renounce war and to organize a great dance. The festivities brought together many people in the village of the chief Ilunga Nsungu, who lived on the other side of the Lualaba River.[68]

While Kalala was asleep, the followers of Ilunga Nsungu dug a great ditch, which they covered with a mat. When Kalala woke up, the dancing began anew. The hosts of the pacified warrior deceitfully invited him to rest on the mat. But Kalala stretched out beside the [concealed] trap. Then one of the two men he had spared climbed up the great tree to the sky. Five months later, as that man had not returned, his companion decided to join him. The second man met the first man coming back to earth. The first man told his companion that, in the sky, he had met a great black goat with a fiery tail (*nkuba,* the lightning), which had ordered him to make war. The two companions seized Kalala and threw him into the ditch, which they filled in.

Kalala's fourteen brothers went searching for him. With consternation, they discovered the grave of their mother. Arriving in the country of Ilunga Nsungu, they killed women working in the fields. Ilunga Nsungu defended himself by hurling at his enemies three pots which contained the skin disease called *musa* (smallpox) and some bees. Many slaves were killed, but the fourteen brothers continued the war. Ilunga Nsungu eventually asked for peace, offering drink to his enemies. The next day he asked them to cut his hair, as friends do. But his great mop was unusually tough and only the youngest brother managed to succeed, by licking it. Furious at finding the youngster so clever, the others killed him and cut up his body. During the night, Ilunga Nsungu collected the pieces and put the body together again by magic. The youngster came back to life. Ilunga Nsungu kept him hidden in a hut, lest his brothers find him.

Excessive drink revived the wickedness of Kalala's brothers and war began again. The youngest brother, saved by Ilunga Nsungu, gave his benefactor a great magical calabash. Ilunga poured out the water it contained from the top of a high mountain and the sons of Mwamba were drowned.

The youngest brother remained with his protector. The latter sent him one day to collect bird traps along the river. The captured birds asked him one after the other to save their lives in return for magical aid in case of sickness. The youngster let them go and returned empty-handed. Ilunga Nsungu decided to watch him. He discovered that his protégé talked to the birds and set them free. He attacked the boy and cut him into pieces. But the birds came in great numbers and put him together again. They carried him through the air and left him before the house of his maternal aunt. The people of Mwamba took up arms and a terrible war ensued with Ilunga Nsungu. The latter blew in vain on the magic calabash: no water appeared. He was obliged to sue for peace and pay tribute to the people of Mwamba.

This myth has the dual function of explaining the origin of war and sickness and justifying the political hegemony of a conquering people. Two heroes, the eldest and the youngest, are clearly set apart from the compact and anonymous mass of the thirteen other brothers. The eldest, Kalala, is evil. He kills his mother in circumstances recalling the crime of Nkongolo in M1. He invents war and brings death to men. Kalala combines the characteristics of Nkongolo and Kalala Ilunga. Although he at first avoids the trap laid for him by his enemies, he ends by being hurled into it by the messengers of Lightning, who have received a mandate from the sky. The ambiguity of Kalala is reinforced: far from being the lightning, as in M1, he is its first victim. Who then is this being who fails where his homonym in M1 succeeds?

This question cannot be answered without situating this negative hero in relation to his youngest brother, with whom he forms a couple. The youngster is the friend of Ilunga Nsungu, who resuscitates him after his brothers have killed him. He is the master of magical water; he succeeds in cutting Ilunga's hair after licking it; and he then gives Ilunga victory. The image of water rushing down a mountain and causing a flood symbolizes beyond any doubt the beginning of the wet season in a mountainous country. It is therefore the youngest son and not the eldest who plays the role given in M1 to the adversary of Nkongolo: he it is who "unbinds" the mountain stream, to speak in the clear language of the Songye.*

The eldest and the youngest are thus opposed in the following ways:

eldest	*youngest*
passive victim of lightning	agent of the wet season

The wet season appears twice in the myth. The *messengers of lightning* seize Kalala in a time of peace. Later, after a new armistice, the youngest son pours his *magic water* on his own brothers. How to explain that the wet season is marked by two signifiers (lightning and flood water) which are separated in time? Note that the appearance of lightning shatters the renewed peace, while the eruption of torrential flooding puts an end to the second war. The following is the position of these *mythèmes* in diachrony:

first sequence:

first appearance of death (invasion of Kalala);
peace of five months (Kalala goes to sleep and disappears from the mythical scene);
death of Kalala (invasion of the messengers of Lightning).

second sequence:
first war, epidemics (invasion of Kalala's brothers);
peace (death and secret resurrection of the youngest brother);
second war (appearance of torrential floods).

This alternation of violence and peace which structures the narrative is based on the repetition of two identical schemes, of which one could say that the first is played *piano*, the second *forte*. The departure from the scene of Kalala, whom the myth abandons beside the lethal ditch, is analogous to the concealed presence of the youngest brother, dismembered and secretly resuscitated. This absent presence of the eldest, like the absent presence of the youngest, marks the dry season at the cosmic level because the first situation precedes the appearance of lightning, the second that of torrential floods. The only difference

*As reported by Wauters (1949:237). (R.W.)

is that the eldest is the victim of seasonal periodicity, while the youngest is its hero.

War corresponds to the wet season, peace to the dry season. The cosmic tree, arising in a country of peace which is ignorant of death and sickness, is the natural homologue of the tower which the people of M6 construct to reunite sky and earth and become immortal. The guardians of the cosmic tree belong to the people of Ilunga Nsungu; they succeed in dissuading Kalala from his fearful project and invite him to dance with them, at the same time seeking by trickery to rid themselves of this dangerous intruder who has brought death to the country of immortality. Kalala then gives up his bellicose scheme and seems to sink into sleep. But his project bears the mark of failure from the beginning: he kills only three of the five guardians of the cosmic tree, symbol of immortality and spatiotemporal continuity. He has cause to regret his mercy, because it is precisely those he has spared who kill him. That Lightning in person recommends relighting the torch of war suggests peculiar secret affinities between Kalala and the celestial animal with the fiery tail. It all seems as if Kalala, whose murderous activity ensures seasonal periodicity, is in a state of torpor through the whole dry season. He appears to sleep for five months next to a dangerous ditch; this inactivity provokes from on high, from the top of the cosmic tree, the first intervention of Lightning, of whom men are apparently ignorant. Lightning, in his turn, then tries to introduce seasonal discontinuity through third parties, thus reviving Kalala's murderous project. By striking Kalala, Lightning simply carries out on the cosmic level the task that the hero should himself have carried through instead of sinking into peace and inactivity. The disruptive and feebly murderous arrival of Kalala is therefore the tragic herald of death and seasonal periodicity in accordance with the following code:

peace and immortality	war and death
absence of seasons (union of sky and earth)	alternation of the seasons
continuity	discontinuity

The prudent intervention of Lightning suddenly gives an epic dimension to the narrative: the victim's brothers take up arms. Death claims many victims; but the fourteen brothers survive. They impose peace. All this sound and fury achieves nothing more than reconstituting the period of immobility and sleep espoused by Kalala the first warrior, a soldier little inclined to martial glory whose bragging made his own mother burst out laughing. No more than their elder do the fourteen attain their objective.

The rising tide of war, which appears immediately after the evocation of the lightning, is evidently, like Kalala Ilunga's military intervention against Nkongolo in M1, a metaphor for storm. The alliance which follows peace is clearly placed under the sign of the dry season: Ilunga Nsungu invites his new friends to cut his hair, but this is difficult because it is extraordinarily *dry*. If the youngster succeeds where his elders fail it is because he is the true master of rain, the owner of the magic vessel. It is understandable that he is cut into pieces in this time of peace, which corresponds to the dry season on the cosmogonic level: the hero, whose action as rain master is at that time unseasonable, is withdrawn from the scene and hidden in a hut; resuscitated *secretly*, he remains invisible, like the rain.

Let us compare these speculations with the climatology of the equatorial zone. The Holoholo occupy a territory situated about the 6th parallel south. This location gives them a climate similar to that of the Luba of Katanga in which the wet season is interrupted by a minor dry season. One of the *mythèmes* of M7 provides an objective chronological link: Kalala's five months of sleep before the arrival of the messengers of Lightning evidently connotes the major dry season.

Major dry season: Kalala's five months' absence
Beginning of the wet season: appearance of messengers of Lightning
Major wet season: arrival of Kalala's brothers
Minor dry season: armistice between Kalala's brothers and Ilunga Nsungu of the dry hair, who hides the youngster, master of water
Heavy rains: resumption of war; the youngster pours torrential water on his brothers

Twice over, and with violence (the second time, suffered in his own body) the young master of rain assumes the undoubtedly dramatic principle of discontinuity. By cutting the hair of Ilunga Nsungu, master of the pacific realm of the tree of immortality which unites sky and earth, the youngster puts an end to the principle of continuity, symbolized here by unceasing growth of hair. The fury of the brothers is understandable, since they belong to the opposite party of peace and continual drought. But in fragmenting the body of the cutter of dry hair, they work, in spite of themselves, for the victory of the principle they are struggling against.

Ilunga Nsungu, the man with the tough dry hair, appears here in two contradictory roles. In turn friend and enemy of the master of the rain, he at first puts him together, then dismembers him anew. Showing a helpful attitude, Ilunga Nsungu evidently intends to gain possession of the water remaining after the end of the rains—that is, terrestrial water. The myth indeed takes care to point out that the master of drought keeps the young man hidden in his hut. The action of the youngster is subsequently manifest in a sudden flood, evoking swollen rivers. This temporary association of the two heroes calls to mind the momentary friendship of Phulu Bunzi, master of flood waters, and the rainbow-serpent in the Yombe cosmogonic myth (M3). The final conflict, opposing Ilunga Nsungu and his protégé, transmits the same cosmogonic message as the conclusion of M3: it affirms the triumph of the rain spirit over the master of the dry season and terrestrial waters. But why does this unresolvable antagonism manifest itself when Ilunga Nsungu discovers that Kalala is freeing the birds? Birds are, with Lightning, the only creatures of the above evoked by the myth. By capturing them Ilunga Nsungu, master of the cosmic tree, realizes by another means that conjunction of sky and earth without which, M6 has taught us, there can be no immortality. By liberating these powerful magicians of the sky, the rain hero clearly separates the above from the below; in exchange for this disjunction he receives remedies for the ills which have recently been introduced into the world. Thus does the art of healing appear in the myth in the role of mediator between the newly disjunctive sky and earth, even as death is the price paid for the succession of the seasons. The young hero is effective on the spatial axis as he is on the temporal axis. He partly regains on the first what men have lost on the second: immortality, of which the birds, restored to the sky and liberty, retain the secret.

Enraged, Ilunga Nsungu takes revenge by cutting up his old protégé. But, like the thirteen brothers, Ilunga Nsungu merely ensures his own defeat: by fragmenting the hero's body, marking it with internal discontinuity, he dialectically summons the violent return of the rain master, who will now have the magical help of the birds. The latter are themselves placed beneath the sign of terrestrial waters, for they live near a river.

But what is the cosmogonic role of the other sons of Mwamba, who are initially enemies, then allies, and finally enemies again of Ilunga Nsungu? What is the exact position of these thirteen enigmatic personages who separate themselves from their youngest brother because of his association with water magic? Consider the whole family of Mwamba, which consists of the following elements:

elder	subgroup of thirteen	youngest

The elder sets off alone with his mother, whom he soon gets rid of because she makes fun of his boasting. The youngster, at first one with the subgroup of thirteen, detaches himself from them to form a pair with the vanished elder. One and the other occupy symmetric and inverse positions in the articulation of the narrative. The subgroup of thirteen opposes its amorphous mass to these two clearly defined individuals, and is distinguished only by minute gradations of age. The number thirteen evokes the thirteen months of the Luba year. But note that not one of the subgroup of thirteen bears a name, whereas each Luba month is named.[69] The compact mass of the thirteen brothers thus evokes an undivided, opaque time and signifies, once more, the absence of periodicity.

Furthermore, the group of thirteen, which renounces its mission to make a pact with the master of the dry season, must be homologous with the rainbow, a figure which is singularly absent from this myth. By getting angry when the youngster dampens the resistant hair of Ilunga Nsungu, the brothers manifestly take the side of dry against wet. Appearing in the narrative in a form suggestive of a continuous band of age without definite intervals, these thirteen brothers realize on the temporal axis an image which is rigorously analogous to the rainbow on the spatial axis. We have seen, moreover, that mythical thought easily switches from one axis to the other. The familial code of M1 itself authorizes this transformation of the rainbow into a homogeneous collectivity of thirteen brothers. The family of Nkongolo, like that of the warrior brothers of M7, is matrilineal in type. In the versions of Colle and Sendwe, Nkongolo bears the name of Mwamba, which designates the mother of the fifteen brothers in M7. A positive hero emerges from both families. In M1, Kalala Ilunga, distinguished by the black color he has inherited from his father, holds himself apart from birth from the family of Mwamba Nkongolo, to which he belongs as uterine nephew. The young hero of M7 finds himself in an analogously eccentric position, this time as youngest son in a matrilineal family which he manages to destroy by causing the deaths of his thirteen uterine brothers. There is one striking difference, however: where Kalala Ilunga destroys his maternal family to restore an original patrilineal order, the youthful hero of M7 ends by taking an opposite attitude and joins a maternal aunt. This inversion is congruent with the matrilineal system of the eastern Luba.

	Rainbow	Storm
M1	maternal uncle	uterine nephew
M7	chain of thirteen uterine brothers	youngest brother

The transformation of the rainbow maternal uncle into a continuous chain of thirteen brothers is again accompanied by a doubling of the rival heroes: for Kalala Ilunga there are substituted an elder and a younger brother, whose cosmogonic roles are complementary. The first brings discontinuity in the form of war, the second in the form of rain. By immediately attacking the guardians of the cosmic tree, the elder reveals the profound philosophic meaning of the myth. But the position of this archetypal figure is ambiguous: he does not complete the mission he has taken on, giving himself over to peace and alliance with the master of continuity. If Lightning becomes angry, it is because the warrior has become a dancer.[70] As for the youngster, he struggles unrelentingly against the principle of continuity. This principle is no longer represented in the second part of the myth by the cosmic tree but by the compact group of thirteen brothers and then by the trapper of birds. But this last figure [Ilunga Nsungu] is none other than the master of the land of immortality, where the cosmic tree unites earth and sky. By liberating the birds, the master of rain introduces discontinuity in space: for the sky has to be definitively separated from earth in order to establish the rhythmic alternation of the seasons. From then on birds are mediators between the two separated spaces. If human life is condemned to finitude at the end of this anthropo-cosmogonic drama, these creatures of the above fend off man's inescapable destiny with their magical remedies.

In this respect, the youngster is the antithesis of the elder: the death introduced by the latter is combated by the former. The dismemberment of the younger, and the intervention of the birds who carry him through the air, make him seem curiously like an authentic shaman.[71]

Further concordances between the family of Mwamba and Nkongolo emerge from the transformational perspective just outlined. The dismemberment of the family of Mwamba in M7 corresponds term for term with the dismemberment of Rainbow's body in M1.

M7	M1
elder brother (buried in dry ground)	head of Nkongolo
group of thirteen brothers (covered by waters)	body of Nkongolo

The youngster who destroys the familial body of the decapitated Rainbow is himself twice transformed (when he is dismembered) in the ensemble of his bodily parts. Thus is negated in him, in the most radical fashion, the rainbow image metaphorically created by his brothers. From this utter denial of the principle of continuity, the youngster is reborn as master of the waters, mediator between sky and earth.

In fact, the rainbow theme is divided between two distinct figures in the Holoholo myth: the group of thirteen brothers on the one hand, and Ilunga Nsungu, master of drought, on the other. It is most especially the hair of this autochthonous king which signifies the absence of water, like the head of Nkongolo in M1. The dry hair of Ilunga Nsungu is a metonymic reduction of the latter; it therefore seems likely that this hair can be identified with the sun.

To complete this analysis, it is appropriate to consider the symbolic significance of the Milky Way, which Lévi-Strauss has shown to represent a nocturnal rainbow for the Amerindians.[72] It is surely surprising that the Luba term for the Milky Way suggests an undifferentiated space-time: *kishipo nè kiyô* (literally: the dry season and the wet season).[73] But the other expression designating this continuous group of constellations refers to a myth (of which we know nothing) purporting to explain why the Milky Way is at the origin of seasonal alternation: *mukalangano wà diyo nè bushipo* (literally: the separation of the two seasons).

The Holoholo myth is remarkable in its striking confirmation of one of the most daring theses of *Mythologiques*: that continuity, the domain of small intervals, is opposed to the diachronic discontinuity of the seasons.[74] M7 also verifies our own argument that death is the price paid for seasonal periodicity. In this connection one may note, with Lévi-Strauss, that epidemics (introduced into the cosmic drama by M7) create large gaps in a population, as does war; epidemics therefore belong to the category of the discontinuous, the necessary condition for the establishment of cultural and cosmogonic order. The Sanga myth of the cosmic tower (M6, ii) emphasizes the demographic damage wrought by the disjunction of sky and earth: a chief causes a tower to be built on the bank of the Lualaba River to get hold of the moon. The tower collapses, eroded by water and insects, killing vast numbers of people. The many groups acquainted with this myth call themselves "people of the tower" (Bena Kaposhi).[75] These facts suggest a new avenue of research which can hardly be embarked on at the present stage of our investigations: a systematic comparison of African and Amerindian mythical codes. The singular convergencies we have just noted should not make us overlook the existence of original semantic fields. Nothing could be more foreign to the structuralist enterprise than the construction of a new archetypology which would restore from a different perspective the metaphysical system of Jung and Eliade. However, we already know enough to conclude that these symbolic spaces are haunted by the same type of language and the same mode of philosophic reflection.

Despite these resemblances there is a remarkable difference between this first group of Bantu myths and Ameridian mythology: the former contains a veritable political ideology which is absent from the latter. These Bantu myths develop a dual concept of power. This is evident in M1 where the *bulopwe* of Mbidi, the sacred magic from the sky which is the source of fecundity, rain, ritual fire, and the rules of right conduct, is opposed to the *bufumu* of Nkongolo, who is at once terrestrial authority, gross violence, and incestuous sexuality. The same duality is found, though less strongly emphasized, in M7, in the antagonistic and complementary elements of the pair constituted by the eldest and youngest brothers. Hero of the rain on whom the birds confer magical powers, the youngster returns to his native land through the sky. In contrast, the eldest dies in a ditch on the orders of Lightning, a celestial being, after attacking the guardians of the cosmic tree which joins earth and sky. This ideological function dominates the narrative of M1, masking the cosmogonic symbolism. The converse applies to M7. M1 is a true myth of sovereignty, articulating the time of origins with historical time.

This special thematic strikingly recalls the primary function of protohistoric Indo-European mythology, of which Dumézil has demonstrated the structural coherence in so masterly a fashion. The comparison is the more impressive in that Indo-European sovereignty also presents two faces: the terrifying and violent king, the possessor of magic (Varuna, Romulus), is opposed to the benign king who is the founder of juridical order (Mitra, Numa[76]).*

Bantu dual sovereignty obviously has a different content. Its two poles, sky and earth, belong to cosmogony; they establish a relation between royal power and the universe it controls. Pierre Smith has shown that Ruanda royalty conforms to this axial schema: the myth of Kigwa, celestial ancestor of the kings and source of sacred magic, is complemented by the myth of Gihanga, the earth-born, who legitimizes the dynasty from political, technical, and economic perspectives.[77] The Ruanda ideology of power, emerging from a pastoral civilization which differs profoundly from the agrarian cultures of the Congolese savanna, cannot be equated in all respects with that of the Luba. Nevertheless, it is in part its mirror image: the celestial Kigwa practices incest and Gihanga founds the State, whereas the celestial Mbidi practices hyperexogamy and introduces a refined and truly royal cultural order, about which the incestuous earthling Nkongolo knows nothing. There are notable parallels between the Ruanda and Luba royal rituals. For instance, a sacred fire is lit at the beginning of each reign in both kingdoms.[78] Even so, it would be a misleading simplification to identify the two ideologies of royalty. That would mean neglecting the extremely important political and ritual role of the queen mother in Ruanda. But the common fact of duality is still impressive. Its terms may be liable to change, incest being attributed to the heavenly ancestors in Ruanda, to terrestrial ancestors among the Luba, but there is no doubt that the concept of divine kingship has a common source in Central Africa and that it invariably conforms to the laws of mythical thought.

*Dumézil (1948) identifies the mythical Roman kings Numa and Romulus respectively with the pacific (*Mitra*) and the violent (*Varuna*) aspects of the composite Vedic deity *Mitra-Varuna*. (R.W.)

The Bantu myths of the foundation of the State invite us to continue construction of the theoretical bridge which Pierre Smith and Dan Sperber have begun to build between the problematics of Dumézil and Lévi-Strauss.[79] Although our first group (M1 to M7) accords a privileged status to sociopolitical problems, these are not divorced from cosmic rhythms. These problems are all bound up with the problem of death, which constitutes, finally, the most powerful gage in this dialectical game of logical categories, a game which, as we have begun to see, is by no means always tranquil.

[CHAPTER THREE]

The Outraged Father

Unruly Sons

Myth pictures the universe so as to speculate about society. Where the adventures of the three heroes of M1 faithfully reflect the rhythms of the cosmos, albeit in a cryptic fashion, the familial doctrine that defines these adventures is a creation of the unfettered imagination, which in the end legitimizes the real order of things. The network of kin relations is remarkably constant from one version to another. All these narratives tell of a double familial crisis affecting marriage alliance (dispute between brothers-in-law) and the kin group (death struggle between a maternal uncle and a uterine nephew). The foreign marriage of the wandering hunter is abnormal in all respects. Not only is it matrilocal, contrary to the custom which would have a man take his wife to his own home, but also the children are abandoned by their father during their mother's pregnancy. The hero (Kalala Ilunga) is brought up with his maternal uncle, whereas the Luba of Katanga are patrilineal and patrilocal. Nevertheless, Kalala Ilunga shows great loyalty to his father, with whom he takes refuge. When he discovers the trap laid for him by Nkongolo, he exclaims: "I can do nothing against you here. But I am going to inform my father Kakenda Mbidi,[1] and then we shall see which of us is the stronger." Although Colle's version, which recounts these words, comes from the Luba-Hemba, who have a matrilineal system, it is evident that the invariable familial armature of the myth is dominated by the patrilineal ideology of the Luba-Katanga.

But it is necessary to realize that mythical thought, even when it claims to be historical, is deployed in a universe of the imagination in which the situations described never truly correspond to sociological fact. In the case we are examining, Nkongolo lives in a confused kinship system wherein incest and marriage alliance cancel each other out with the eruption of a violent conflict between Nkongolo and his brother-in-law. This conflict is provisionally resolved by the departure of the real father (Mbidi), making possible the constitution of a curious incestuous family of pseudomatrilineal type, consisting of a maternal uncle, his sisters, and his nephews. The narrative takes pains to show that this situation is untenable. Nkongolo's mother dies by the hand of her own son, whom she has held up to ridicule. Nkongolo in his turn falls victim to the uterine nephew who has aroused his jealousy. All the relations peculiar to this pseudomatrilineal configuration are therefore negated.

In contrast, the father-son relation is given a high value. Mbidi Kiluwe never doubts that his son will join him one day; even though Mbidi abandons his pregnant wives, he gives them arrows which represent an acknowledgement of paternity (Burton's version). He is careful to teach Kalala Ilunga the duties of divine kingship, which is unambiguously shown to be transmitted from father to son. On this point, the myth conforms to the custom of patrilineal inheritance of the Luba-Katanga. There can be no doubt that M1 belongs to this ethnic group, because the matrilineal Luba of the east have a mirror-image version of the familial armature just described, contained in a myth which is an African version of *Totem and Tabu.** The relation between this myth and M1 is the more patent in that the theme of the lethal trap recurs in this converse situation where the father is his son's victim while a positive association develops between maternal uncle and nephew.

M8, Luba-Hemba: The First Patricide (Colle[2])

When Kyomba, the first man, became old, his sons decided to get rid of him. They dug a ditch into which they set spears, then they hid the trap with a mat covered with sand and grass. They invited the old man to drink beer. When he was drunk they led him into the trap, where he was fatally injured. He had just

*The reference is to the *Totem und Tabu* of Sigmund Freud, published in 1940. In this book Freud posits a "primal patricide" when the junior members (the "sons") of a primordial horde banded together to kill the leader of the horde, their oppressive "father." (R.W.)

> enough strength to summon his uterine nephews, who carefully lifted him out of the trap. To reward his nephews, he invested them with his authority and disinherited his sons.

The explicit function of this brief narrative is to explain and justify the matrilineal descent system of the eastern Luba. The theme of murder by a trap here undergoes a double transformation affecting both kinship and intergenerational relations. In M1 a maternal uncle tries to kill a uterine nephew, while in M8 the sons kill their father. This about-turn makes it impossible to conclude that the latent function of the familial code of M1 is to explain a historical transition from a matrilineal system (symbolized by the reign of Nkongolo, the wicked uncle) to the patrilineal system proper to the Luba of Katanga. In fact, Burton's version describes Mbidi Kiluwe's chiefdom of origin as an already constituted patrilineal society; but paradoxically the myth situates this chiefdom in Kunda country, among the matrilineal eastern Luba.

The true function of the familial code is not historical but ideological. The coexistence of patrilineal and matrilineal regimes within the same culture leads Luba thought to treat them as a system of oppositions in which one can be validated at the expense of the other. All the societies considered here think dialectically in myth about their kinship systems. It is a remarkable fact that the matrilineal societies appear to themselves as degraded forms of an earlier patrilineality. As for the patrilineal societies, they develop a more complex theory, which is admirably illustrated by M1. We shall examine it in Burton's version, which displays the greatest genealogical depth and goes back to Mbidi's country of origin. The first part of the narrative contains other interesting familial conflicts and offers an unexpected link with M8. It begins by positing the existence of a patrilineal system. Ilunga Kiluwe, paternal grandfather of Kalala Ilunga, had two sons, Mbidi Kiluwe and Ndala. He also had a daughter, Mwanana, whom he loved to the point of considering bequeathing his authority to her, even though the people's choice was Mbidi Kiluwe.

The patrilineal system is in crisis: Ilunga Kiluwe has turned away from his son and come close to his daughter (Mwanana). By the same token Mwanana is separated from her brother (Mbidi Kiluwe). She ridicules the future hero, who is obliged to pursue the pet lion he has allowed to escape. This Hercules of the hunt unprotestingly allows

Mbidi Kiluwe's family
(Burton's version)

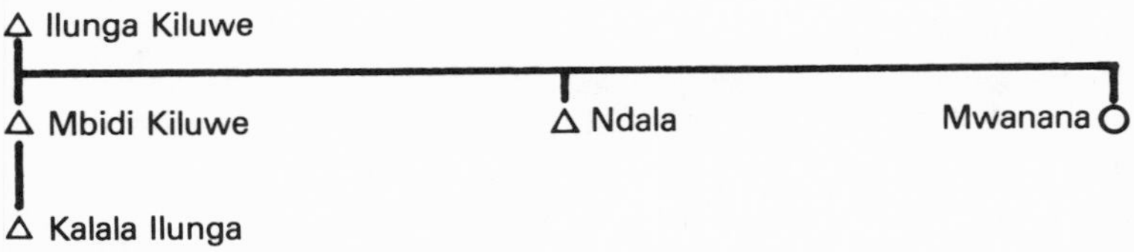

Δ Ilunga Kiluwe
Δ Mbidi Kiluwe
Δ Ndala
Mwanana O
Δ Kalala Ilunga

himself to be humiliated by his Omphale of a sister.* He is soon abandoned by the wives he has taken with him. One son accompanies him thenceforth; although this secondary personage, who does not figure in most versions, makes no further appearance in the story, his discreet presence indicates that the familial drama experienced by Mbidi Kiluwe has not abolished the father-son relationship, the only one to count in the end. In fact, the only result of the uncertain quest of Mbidi Kiluwe is the birth of a marvelous son (Kalala Ilunga) with the promise of a most glorious destiny. But Mbidi Kiluwe is finally condemned to solitude. His adventure ends in failure: when he returns home, having left his pregnant wife with his brother-in-law, his father is dead and his sister and brother have gone away forever. Only the filial love of Kalala Ilunga is saved from this emotional shipwreck. His son joins him briefly before undertaking the conquest of the empire of Nkongolo. This final meeting is important because it reconstitutes the initial patrilineal family which had been imperiled by the excessive love of a father for his daughter. But a generation had to pass before the initial peril, the motive of the whole adventure, had been overcome. The drama appears to unfold in an illusory historical time. The hero, driven out by his sister, goes on a fruitless journey: the weakness of the father, the hatred of the sister can do nothing against the filial love, foundation of the patrilineal order, which is restored in the end. In other words, the story says it is vain to deny the obligatory solidarity of father and son (which M8, on the contrary, vigorously demolishes), since, even when separated from the begetter

*In the mythology of ancient Greece Omphale was a beautiful queen of Lydia who temporarily came to dominate the great hero Hercules. (R.W.)

he has never known, Kalala Ilunga rushes to him to accomplish his own destiny.

Here one may note a curious detail in Sendwe's version. The author describes, among the oddities of Nkongolo's behavior, the following incident. One day he had the cruel notion of separating all the children from their mothers. Having made a certain distance between them, he released the children to see what would happen. He observed with interest that each child ran unhesitatingly into the arms of its own mother.[3] Sendwe draws a dubious moral from this fable, to the effect that Nkongolo is asserting the judgment of the child to be as good as the adult's. But what this episode really does is reconstitute inversely, and at a single stroke, the complicated saga of Mbidi Kiluwe, who, after being separated from his father by the quirks of Mwanana, sees his own unknown son fly to him. Let us look more deeply into the connection between the two situations. Nkongolo, as we have said, seems to be free, after his brother-in-law's departure, to construct a type of matrilineal family, a project which the rest of the narrative shows to be doomed to failure. Nonetheless, the foundations of the system would appear to be solid: children artificially separated from their mothers by the tyrant's whim find their way back unfailingly. One can now better understand Nkongolo's satisfaction, thinking himself to have proved the necessity of a *natural* familial order. The incestuous Nkongolo takes as proven that children are necessarily united with their mothers, whereas the cultural order, the logic of which the myth follows, requires that the son be united with the father, whatever the difficulties of this enterprise. Nkongolo himself invalidates the proof he has proposed: he murders his mother in a ditch, taking up the theme of M8, in which he vainly tries to do likewise to his uterine nephew. Nkongolo's mother is not without significance in this drama. She is for Nkongolo what Mbidi Kiluwe is for Kalala Ilunga. There is a dialectical relation between M8, in which sons in a matrilineal society kill their father, and M1, in which a maternal uncle tries to kill his nephew and succeeds only in murdering his own mother. M1 begins by describing a gross culture in which the incest prohibition has not yet emerged from the reign of the primordial twins; it next draws a caricature of the familial code of matrilineal society before firmly establishing, on the death of the maternal uncle (so that civilization becomes possible), the principle of patrilineality.

The Luba epic (M1) begins by positing a patrilineal situation which is assumed to be normal: a man, Ilunga Kiluwe, has three children by a woman whose name has been forgotten. A crisis ensues, marked by the abnormal closeness of father and daughter, which is an aberrant situation from both patrilineal and matrilineal perspectives. The family structure is overturned: driven out by his sister Mwanana, Mbidi Kiluwe goes on a long search which we may interpret as one for a lost patrilineality. This quest entails an enormous detour; the narrative describes a matrilocal hyperexogamic union, which fails, and a lop-sided familial order based on relations of a matrilineal type (Nkongolo, his mother, his sister, his uterine nephew). Kalala Ilunga is to be the triumphant restorer of the old patrilineal order which had been compromised by an initial excessive conjunction of a father and a daughter.

M1 (diachronic schema):

patrilineality
  patrilineal crisis
    matrilocality and matrilineality
      end of matrilocality and crisis of matrilineality
        patrilineality

The myth has therefore posed a series of absurd, self-contradictory hypotheses, in order to return to the point of departure. This dialectical movement is also present in the matrimonial adventure of Mbidi Kiluwe, for filiation and marriage go together. Let us look at the narrative in this new perspective.

Mbidi marries far away after being driven from home by his own sister. Mbidi's abnormal marriage is obviously opposed to Nkongolo's incestuous sexual life as hyperexogamy to radical endogamy. The first relation destroys the second, since Bulanda and Mabela betray their brother Nkongolo through loyalty to their husband (Burton's version). Nkongolo's sisters are accomplices in their brother's murder at the end of the narrative; symmetrically, Mbidi Kiluwe's sister Mwanana tries to get rid of him at the beginning of the story. From this point of view, the distant marriage of Mbidi Kiluwe and the passionate love Bulanda and Mabela bear for him appear as mediators between two equally untenable situations: the (hateful) disjunction and the (incestuous) conjunction of a brother and sister. There is no restoration of harmony between Mbidi and Mwanana: the sister responsible for his exile goes off and marries among the Lunda, thus repeating on her own account her brother's hyperexogamic adventure.

One may note that in Burton's version, which gives us the most complete picture of familial relations, the disjunction of the brother and sister provides the initial impetus (Mwanana drives out Mbidi) and the final conclusion of the drama (Mabela and Bulanda betray Nkongolo). The myth clearly intends no normalization of this relation. On the contrary, it strives to negate it in favor of the conjugal bond to strengthen patrilineality. Mbidi does not need to give Nkongolo a sister in exchange: the double passion of Bulanda and Mabela reigns over the narrative.

Burton's version extends the familial crisis over three generations, from the grandfather, Ilunga Kiluwe, to the grandson, Kalala, named Ilunga in memory of the first. Mbidi is condemned to remain alone until the end. Doomed to failure as it is, his personal adventure is but a half-measure along the way to patrilineality. It is for the heroes of the third generation to recapture the time that has been lost. At least one version (Colle) says that Kalala Ilunga gives evidence of extraordinary strength from the day of his birth; others describe his precocious exploits in war and games. Colle and Theeuws adopt the most radical position, telling of a child whose feats make him acclaimed on the evening of the day he was born.[4]

This quest for a father by an abandoned child reproduces in every detail the Ruanda epic of Ryangombe, which will be compared with our mythical cycle.[5] But for the moment other narratives from neighboring peoples demand our attention, for these are comparable to M8 or to the first part of M1 (Burton's version). This comparison is necessary if we are to understand in its entirety the familial code proper to the myths.

A tradition of the matrilineal Lamba leaves no doubt that the antagonism between Nkongolo and Mbidi belongs to a triple—political, familial, and cosmogonic—code.

M8 (ii), Lamba: The Origin of Matrilineality (Grévisse[6])

At a time when they cultivated only millet and were still ignorant of fire, the men of the Goat clan found a woman who had become lost, Kinelungu or Konde, who belonged to the Hair clan.

Lwabasununu, chief of the Goat clan, married her. She brought the seeds of various cereals and agreed to reveal the secret of fire to her husband on condition that his people abandon patrilineal filiation. She also demanded that on Lwabasununu's death his power be split between two principles: authority (*bufumu*) would continue to be exercised by men, but sacred power (*bulopwe*) would be transmitted through women. The son who sprung from their union, Kabunda, killed the elder son of Lwabasununu, his half brother. Then all the members of the Goat clan drowned themselves in the Zambezi River with the exception of a woman, Kabilo, from whom all existing members of the clan are descended.

Kabunda became chief of the Lamba. He had incestuous relations with his sister, who gave him a son. The latter combined in his person the two principles of power (*bulopwe* and *bufumu*). He joined himself in his turn to his sister, by whom he had a son. By the matrilineal rule which prevailed thenceforth, the son was considered as the uterine nephew of his father.

This is a total reversal of M1: sacred power (*bulopwe*) goes with the matrilineal system, whereas it accompanies the patrilineal system in the Luba epic; the establishment of matrilineality implies the incestuous conjunction of brother and sister for at least two generations. This transformation is congruent with the emergence of cultural fire, whereas the hero's hyperexogamic marriage and the affirmation of patrilineality are linked with aristocratic customs of cooking and eating in M1.

M1	M8 (ii)
coming of patrilineality	coming of matrilineality
introduction of aristocratic customs of the cooking fire	introduction of cooking fire

In M1, as in M8 (ii), the passage from one familial order to another is accompanied by a cultural acquisition. Renunciation of patrilineal filiation is even, in M8 (ii), the price paid for knowledge of fire. But this transformation also entails incest and the demographic impoverishment of the initial clan, which is reduced to a single member. Transition from patrilineality to matrilineality is therefore treated in mythical thought as a progressive-regressive movement defining a primary cultural advance (the acquisition of fire), whereas the converse transition from matrilineality (or its like) to patrilineality (M1) is mythically associated with the establishment of a superior culture.

But cooking fire and agriculture also go back to the cosmogonic code, since their appearance condemns the people of Lwabasununu to die by drowning in a river. A long variant, published by Marchal, portrays it as a collective suicide; but a third version (Bourgeois-Doke) will soon furnish us with the key to these tragic events. Lwabasununu, alias Chipimpi or Kipimpi, really personifies the rainy season.

M8 (ii), Lamba (Marchal's version[7])

Kipimpi, the first chief, was given fire and cultivated plants by his wife Liulu; a quarrel broke out between Kipimpi's men (the Goat clan) on one side, and his son Kabunda and daughter Lumpuma (both of the Hair clan) on the other. Kipimpi decided to separate these two matrilineal clans. Kipimpi's people suffered a serious famine. This was because they insisted on sowing seeds which had already been exposed to fire; the rain could make nothing grow in the fields. In contrast, Lumpuma and Kabunda enjoyed prosperity. Kipimpi's nephew went to visit his cross-cousins,* who fed him. He spent the night with Lumpuma, who was already pregnant with an incestuous infant by her brother, Kabunda. Then Kipimpi sent all the people of his clan to eat with his children. Lumpuma married her cross-cousin. But the child she brought forth was called "son of an unknown father," although in reality he had been conceived incestuously.

When Lumpuma's husband lost some valuable immortal dogs belonging to his mother-in-law (Liulu), this woman was furious. She obliged her son-in-law to compensate her by killing Kipimpi, who was at once his father-in-law and his maternal uncle. Kabunda, Kipimpi's own son, confirmed this order. So the nephew brought the people of his clan together to associate them with his act. The women refused to do it, but the men agreed. After spearing Kipimpi twice, they cut off his head.

But soon a new dispute erupted between the Goat clan and the Hair clan. The people of the Goat clan then decided to commit collective suicide. Joined together, they threw themselves into a

Cross-cousins is an anthropological term referring to the children of opposite-sex siblings (genealogical or classificatory). (R.W.)

river. One woman only was dragged out in time by her husband, who belonged to the Leopard clan. It was thus that the Goat clan was enabled to survive, thenceforth dominated by the Hair clan.

This strange story serves to explain how the Hair clan seized power from the Goat clan. Evidently it is no longer a question of transition from patrilineal to matrilineal filiation, but of a political crisis that opposes two matrilineal clans. This political struggle is also a family drama in which a mother (Liulu) causes the murder of her husband (Kipimpi) with the complicity of their son: through the intermediary brother-in-law, Kabunda is certainly guilty of patricide. The Doke-Bourgeois version, the structural significance of which appears later, confirms this interpretation. Liulu's sudden hatred of her husband has a cosmogonic dimension: the heroine of agriculture has just lost the mark of immortality, two dogs without offspring that a man of her husband's clan has stupidly allowed to escape. There is reason to believe that the husband's murder ritually introduces the dialectic of the seasons in place of the lost immortality.

M8 (ii), Lamba (Doke-Bourgeois variant[8])

The first chief of the Lamba, Chipimpi, had a son, Kabunda, who quarreled with his father and killed him. After the burial, the villagers were surprised to find the dead man sitting on his front doorstep. They killed him a second time and took the precaution of burning his body. But on returning to the village, they found his head. This still exists. It rolls angrily around whenever one hears thunder.

This variant is, even more clearly than the first version (Grévisse), an inversion of the Luba foundation myth (M1). The victim, Chipimpi, is in all respects the opposite of Nkongolo:

Chipimpi	*Nkongolo*
father killed by son	maternal uncle killed by uterine nephew
head associated with fire of lightning (wet season)	head associated with fire of rainbow (dry season)
body burnt	body buried under water

This comparison shows that patricide means the end of patrilineality in M8 (ii) as in M8, in opposition to the murder of the maternal uncle in M1. Such was indeed the explicit meaning of the Grévisse version, where this *mythème* appeared in a distorted form (murder of the elder brother by the younger).

But in Marchal's version the murder of Kipimpi, chief of the Goat clan, on the orders of his wife and son, who belong to the Hair clan, also expresses the opposition between a dominant, food-providing clan which is secretly incestuous and a dominated, starving clan which is driven to collective suicide. The second group seeks food and wives from the first, to which it is allied by preferential marriage. The opposition between the two clans is expressed in totemic language: the goat connotes pastoralism, while hair is an agricultural metaphor, its growth and periodic cutting being an image of cultivation. This is made clear in the Bourgeois-Doke version, where the female founder of agriculture and her son hide in their hair the seeds they have stolen from the Luba.[9] The third clan to appear in the Marchal version, that of the Leopard, is opposed to the Goat clan in the totemic code as the predator to its prey; but in the narrative the relation of devourer and devoured is reversed, since a man of the Leopard clan snatches a woman of the Goat clan from death, thus preserving the clan from complete extinction. This episode is a timely reminder that matrimonial exchange based on marriage with the matrilateral cross-cousin implies at least three partners. The Hair clan has itself to receive wives from a third clan if it is to give its daughters to the Goat clan and escape from the incest to which Kabunda is provisionally condemned. The original matrimonial structure outlined by the myth can be formalized as follows:

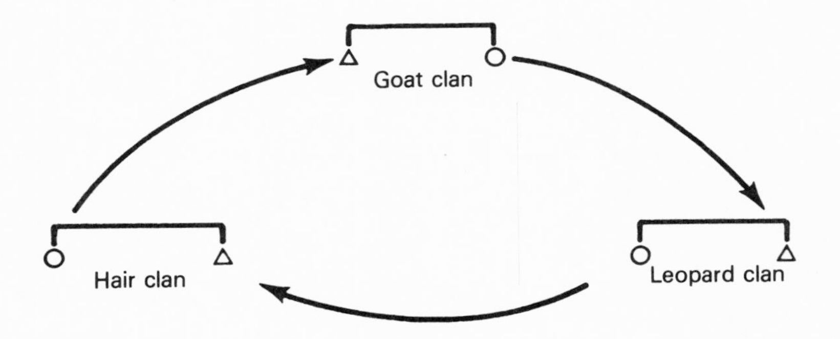

The conflict between the Hair people and the Goat people is thus overcome with the help of a third partner. Moreover, only this structure can justify the superiority of the first group over the second. As giver of wives and food to the Goat clan, Kabunda, the chief of the Hair clan, is able to impose his authority to the extent of requiring suicide, *because he receives nothing in return.*

The conflict between father and son is therefore duplicated in a conflict between brothers-in-law. It expresses a more general problem in terms of alliance: the Goat people are in league with the lightning, and in this way they collaborate, but in a position of inferiority, with the Hair clan, which has charge of agriculture. The death of Chipimpi resembles an agrarian fertility sacrifice acting on the rain. This opposition is also that between fire (brought by the ancestor of the Hair clan) and water (into which the Goat people jump). One can now understand why fire cannot destroy the head of Chipimpi, the external source of rain. More precisely, Chipimpi's death, like the suicide by water of his companions, restores dampness to the seeds sterilized by the untimely action of the flames to which they have been submitted: the Goat people of those days misused the fire given them by the Hair people, so much so that famine reigned instead of the expected abundance. The hero's death ended this unfortunate persistence of dryness.

The myth therefore superimposes on a binary schema (two clans disputing the chiefship) an implicit ternary schema which is the minimum requirement for generalized exchange of women. In so doing, it makes a reasonably accurate translation of the social structure of Lamba society in which numerous exogamic totemic clans (more than thirty in Zambia alone) are associated in pairs by joking relationships based on antithetical complementarity.[10] The ideology behind this twinning considers one partner superior to the other, even though they render one another the same ritual funeral services. This is borne out by Bourgeois's examples and explanations. The Fire clan is associated with the Rain clan because the latter puts out the former, the Goat clan with the Grass clan because the first eats the second, and so on.[11] The clans are effectively allied through matrilateral cross-cousin marriage, even though there is a low percentage of actual unions of this kind.[12] One clan dominates all the others politically; by a curious linguistic displacement it is not the hair of the head (as in the myth) but pubic hair which gives the Lamba myth its totemic title.

M8 makes use of the historic conflict between the new dominant clan and the aborigines (the Goat clan) to describe the permanent dialectical structure of the universe. Comparison of the Lamba myth with the Luba epic shows that the cosmogonic code it uses is one with the politico-familial code. In the patrilineal epic the decapitated victim (Nkongolo in M1) signifies the dry season; in M8 (ii) this relation is transformed in a matrilineal epic in which the decapitated victim (Chipimpi), a member of the originally dominant clan, personifies the wet season. In the present case, this thematic inversion can be at least partially explained by history: the Lamba, who live in the border zone of Zaïre and Zambia, seem to have become detached from the Luba group to their northwest.[13]

The general code remains unchanged from the patrilineal Luba to the matrilineal Lamba. The father's murder in M8 and M8 (ii) cannot be interpreted apart from the murder of the maternal uncle in M1. This code is not peculiar to Luba symbolism alone, for it is found in equivalent forms in neighboring cultures, as we shall shortly see. In particular, the disjunction of father and sons is the basic *mythème* of matrilineality in Kuba symbolic thought. The parallel with M8 and M8 (ii) is the more striking in that the hero of this story is an incestuous brother like Kabunda, the putative founder of the matrilineal system among the Lamba.

M9, Kuba: Origin of Matrilineality and Young Men's Initiation Rites (Vansina[14])

> One day the culture hero Woot, founder of royalty, having got drunk on palm wine, lay naked on the ground. His sons mocked him, but his daughter covered his nakedness after approaching him modestly with her back turned. When Woot awoke, he rewarded his daughter by declaring that only her children would inherit from him. Such is the origin of the matrilineal system. Woot punished his sons by making them undergo rituals of initiation.

M8 and M9 belong to two different matrilineal cultures with only the most distant historical connections. Nevertheless, they transmit the same message (the origin of matrilineality) by means of a nearly identical armature:

—disjunction of father and son (aggression or insult to father)
—conjunction of maternal uncle and nephew (Luba-Hemba) or conjunction of father and daughter (Kuba).

M8 and M9 make it seem that the conjunction of father and daughter is equivalent to the conjunction of maternal uncle and nephew, which is the normal basis of matrilineal filiation. This mytho-logic, which does not conform rigorously to social logic, brings us back again to the first part of M1 (Burton's version). The second element of the armature of the Kuba myth occurs there in an embryonic state at the moment when the patrilineal family of the hero is undergoing a grave crisis. The reader will recall that Ilunga Mbidi wanted to transmit his power to his daughter, Mwanana, whereas the elder brother, Mbidi Kiluwe, enjoyed the favor of the people. The dispute ended with the departure of Mbidi Kiluwe, who thus found himself separated from his father and his people. Formally, the first part of M1 differs from M9 only in the order of events: the conjunction of father and daughter which ends the Kuba narrative begins the Luba one. This difference is justified by the familial message of M1: the patrilineal crisis is not to be resolved as in the Kuba myth (M9) by the establishment of matrilineality. On the contrary, M1 is concerned to show that the project of a matrilineal order is monstrous, and engineers the triumphant return of patrilineality in the person of the grandson, Kalala Ilunga. In M9, however, the grandsons will inaugurate, in conformity with Woot's desire, the matrilineal system of the Kuba, which has since endured for centuries. This myth says unequivocally that the affectionate conjunction of father and daughter marks the beginning of the matrilineal order in opposition to patrilineality. We shall find this feature again in the Lunda myths of the hunter-king, in episodes very similar to those found in the Kuba myth (see chapter five).

Restored to this general mythological content, M1 uses the code of M9 to let it be understood that a royal father (Ilunga Kiluwe) attempts to institute a matrilineal system through the intervention of his daughter who is preferred to the son. The second part (the meeting of Mbidi Kiluwe and Nkongolo) provisionally establishes this matrilineal (and even matrilocal) order; the disjunction of father and sons, the primary source of matrilineality according to M8 and M9, is maintained in M1 to the second generation (Mbidi Kiluwe abandons his son even before his birth at his brother-in-law's). But the hero of the third part, Kalala Ilunga, gets rid of his maternal uncle and restores the patrilineal order, which is thenceforth to regulate dynastic succession.

It is interesting to note that M1 associates the ill-fated attempt at matrilineality with a crude state of culture; the kings of this "first dynasty" (Verhulpen) cut sorry figures in all respects. Moreover, although Woot appears as the unique culture hero of the Kuba, the myths make no bones about his defects. Not only is he a shameless drunkard who abandons all modesty in front of his children, but a mythical tradition of the dominant Bushong group unites him incestuously with his sister Mweel. He goes into exile and disappears in the direction of the Sankuru headwaters; his nine children were the outcome of this disgraceful union.[15] We possess at least three versions of this exoteric narrative (Torday, 1911; Denolf, 1933 and 1954; Vansina, 1963). In contrast, M9, according to Vansina, is a secret myth told to young people during their initiation. Paradoxically, Kuba mythology presents the existing state of society as the result of a double regression. The drunkenness and involuntary immodesty of Woot cause the impious reaction of his sons, from which flows the matrilineal system. Exile, the consequence of incest, explains the loss of an original cultural and linguistic unity. Kuba origin myths are thus apparently situated at the opposite pole to the Luba epic, which associates the foundation of a powerful and conquering state with the coming of an aristocratic patrilineal culture, superior to that of the incestuous Nkongolo. However, as we shall see, these Kuba myths belong to the same ensemble as M1.

M10, Kuba: The Incest of Woot, the Cry of Animals, and the Going of the Sun (Denolf's version[16])

After committing incest with his sister Mweel (Muele), Woot (Woto) fled to the east and set himself up beside the Sankuru River. Mweel tried to make her brother return, for the village had been plunged into perpetual night since his departure. First, she sent human messengers to him. But these found the imprint of royal feet on a rock and turned back. Mweel then sent the tempest (*mvula*) to her brother. But Woot refused to receive him. Next Mweel sent the dog Bondo, to whom Woot gave a bundle of meat wrapped in the mottled skin of the wild cat, *nshimba*. He explained that day would come if the skin became white; but if it

> became completely black, night would continue to reign over the village. Woot expressly forbade the messenger to eat the meat. But on the way back the dog could not resist temptation. Thus he lost the power of speech. A richer variant of the myth gives the dog two traveling companions, the fly and the tortoise. Woot offered his guests a house for the night, at the same time telling them not to touch anything. But the fly drank the palm wine, the tortoise smoked the pipe, and the dog ate the meat and cassava. To punish them, Woot deprived them of speech. He sent them back and blocked the road with a great stone. Then Mweel sent the woodworm Bombo, which bored a way through the rock. The insect found Woot asleep. The cry of the leopard awoke him. The new messenger begged the fugitive to return to his sister so that daylight might reappear. Woot did not accede to this plea, but he called his daughter Bibolo and told her to collect presents for Mweel; these were a monkey (*mfunga*), a cock, a sparrow (*chapodia*), the *mukuku* and *junje* birds, and a cricket. He gave these animals to Bombo, who returned with them to Mweel. The next day the animals presented by Woot began to make their cries and the sun came up again.

According to one version, Woot put these animals in a chicken basket and gave them to his *son*, Bibole. Bibole was sent to Mweel. In this version Woot had taken a son and a daughter with him into exile; the daughter was called Ibengu. The Dutch text, which is unfortunately ambiguous, makes it seem that Bibole and Ibengu return together with the basket to the village.[17]

The cosmogonic wealth of this myth is obvious. The animals named are the heralds of the sun, which rises in seeming obedience to their cries. Torday reduces the list to three birds: the Natal cuckoo (*mokuku*), the cock, and the *japodya* ("a little black bird that builds nests in great abundance in trees near villages"). The cries of these three species are said to succeed one another and to connote respectively the night, the dawn, and the rising of the sun.[18] We shall explore the implications of this *mythème* in the following chapter. Here we restrict ourselves to consideration of the familial code.

Since the Kuba themselves invite us to compare the esoteric and exoteric versions, one cannot fail to notice that the extreme modesty characterizing the father-daughter relationship (M9) contrasts with the immodesty of the brother-sister relationship (M10). Moreover, the first version recurs in the epilogue of the second, where one learns that a daughter accompanied Woot into exile. The solar hero entrusts this daughter with collecting the animals of light. She thus appears as a mediating figure between a brother (Woot) and a sister (Mweel) who, from having been too close, are now too far from each other. One variant even suggests that this daughter goes with her brother to the village. The reestablishment of the solar motion, the alternation of day and night, is analogous to the symbolic reunion of brother and sister who have been separated by the shame of incest. Mweel wants Woot to come back not only because the village is plunged into darkness, but also because a matrilineal society is inconceivable without the close socioeconomic association of brother and sister. M9 and M10 evidently go together. It is not enough for Woot to separate himself socially from his sons and approach his daughter for the matrilineal system to work. The same decision leads to an impasse in the Luba epic, which shows us a stunted caricature of a matrilineal family. It is necessary that Woot return in some way to his sister after separation from her. M10 describes this situation metaphorically by comparing the distant brother to the vanished daylight. The morning cries of the animals at once salute the coming of the dawn and a new form of relationship between brother and sister that lies halfway between incest and complete separation. While the incestuous conjunction threatens the social order, the disjunction of the incestuous lovers overturns the cosmic order. M10 describes the search for a compromise solution between incest (which continues to characterize divine kingship) and its excessive negation. This compromise solution is realized precisely in the moderate conjunction of brother and sister which is peculiar to matrilineal society: the motion of the masculine sun around the earth is comparable to the exogamic initiative of men who give their sisters in marriage without truly separating from them.

Only the cosmogonic aspect remains in the variant recorded by Torday, in which Mweel (Moelo) has become the brother of Woot (Woto[19]). The first sends three male messengers to the second. For their mission to succeed, they must not loiter or fish in the rivers. One man violates these prohibitions, while the others turn back. But Mweel sends them away again to look for Woot, accompanied by a dog. Woot is moved by the messengers' appeal and gives them the three birds whose cries signal the end of night and the rising of the sun: the

Natal cuckoo, the cock, and the *japodya*. This variant is notable in that it contains a new seasonal notation: the story unfolds in a time when fishing is forbidden. Vansina tells us that fishing, hunting, and gathering prevail over cultivation between May and August, that is, during the dry season.[20] There is therefore reason to believe that the myth refers to the abolition of this period. We shall indeed see in the course of the next chapter that the eternal night into which Woot's exile plunges the world is homologous with the wet season.

A brief story (M11) provides articulation between M9 and M10. This tale, which is something of a moralizing fable, requires attention because the incest theme appears in it in a weakened form; otherwise its explicit purpose (explaining the origin of young men's initiation) suggests it is no more than a replica of M9.

M11, Kuba: Origin of the Initiation Ceremony (Torday[21])

> A certain lad who had reached manhood was in the habit of drinking palm wine with his mother and not offering any to his father. When the father protested at this conduct, the son rebuffed him. The father decided to punish his impertinent son. After dark he hid by the path that led to the palm grove. When he saw his son coming back along the path with two large calabashes of wine, he began to try out a musical instrument he had just made. By rotating a palm tree frond at the end of a string he produced a mournful sound which greatly alarmed the young man. The latter dropped his calabashes and fled back to the village. The same thing happened several times. One day the father called his son and slyly asked him why he no longer drank wine. The son replied that a ghost near the palm grove had threatened him. The father then suggested that he make fun of the ghost as he had already made fun of his begetter. The son repented and the ghost no longer appeared. The son became obedient and thenceforth shared his wine with his father. Heartened by this result, the father called the old men together at night and they decided to inaugurate initiation rituals so that sons might no longer cow their fathers because of their superior physical strength.

One sees here the excessive closeness of a man and his mother substituted for the incestuous conjunction of a brother and sister that lies at the heart of the Woot cycle (M10). Otherwise, as in M9, the narrative is dominated by the eruption of a dispute between a father and his son over palm wine. The chaste association of the father and his daughter in M9 is the inverse homologue of the near-incestuous conjunction of mother and son in M11; this association is in its turn equivalent to Woot's incest with Mweel, who, in the symbolism of initiation, is proclaimed as the primordial mother (see pp. 109–117). M8, M9, and M11 establish matrilineality on the same problematic. The Oedipal drama—hostility of sons toward the father, the temptation of incest—is fully evoked in this group of myths explaining the foundation of matrilineal society and the initiation of young men. A primary dichotomy sets up the familial order: the modest daughter is joined socially with the father while the impious sons are sent away. But this operation makes sense only on the removal of the threat of incest after dealing with the danger of drunkenness; the relations of mother and son (M11), brother and sister (M10), and father and daughter (M9) have to be covered with the same mantle of prudery.

M11 pivots between M9 and M10 and is constructed out of the same primordial conflict between the father and his sons.

M9	M11	M10
chaste conjunction of father and daughter	immodest conjunction of mother and son	immodest conjunction of brother and sister
drunkenness	drunkenness and incest	incest

The incestuous temptation of Woot (M10) is the transformation of the near-incestuous temptation of the protagonist of M11, who gets drunk in secret with his mother. But the incestuous Woot of M10 is also the drunken Woot of M9. M11 offers the richest message under the most anodyne appearance, since in it drunkenness and incest are found together and condemned. The existing matrilineal society is presented as the product of a double regression toward natural disorder, under the sign of the original, derided father, at once a victim (of his sons' impertinence) and guilty (of intemperance and incest). It is in this structural sense, far removed from the preoccupations of Malinowski, that the ensemble of M9, M10, and M11 could pass as a founding "charter" of Kuba matrilineality. Matrilineality is thought of as an alternative to (and a degradation of) the initial patrilineal order. It is defined mythically, as in M1, by the affectionate conjunction of a father and daughter. This *mythème* makes no sociological sense. From the point of view of social praxis this aberrant choice can be understood only in the light of a certain propositional logic: this relation is the symmetrical and inverse replica of another and more primary relation, the conflict of a father and his sons.

the code of matrilineality

disjunction of father and sons	conjunction of father and daughter: Woot approaches his daughter in the same movement that separates him from his sons

This affectionate bond is the only positive relationship in this group of myths. Woot's daughter restores the respect which has been compromised by drunkenness. It is she who makes up for the unfortunate consequences of the father's lapse, when she collects the animal heralds of the suspended dawn. This detail must remain inexplicable unless one takes account of the variant of M10 in which Woot's daughter and son return together to the village. For the chaste conjunction of father and daughter of M9, M10 substitutes a moderate conjunction of brother and sister that guarantees matrilineality and the harmonious alternation of day and night. This code also applies to the Luba epic as a constitutive charter of the patrilineal order. But here the initial *mythème* (affectionate conjunction of father and daughter) is accompanied by a definitive and hateful disjunction of the brother (Mbidi) and the sister (Mwanana), thus paralyzing all development in the direction of matrilineality. In the language of myth, the movement toward patrilineality implies the rejection of the brother by the sister (or the converse) and distant marriage.

Luba	*Kuba*
aggressive sister driving her brother far away	incestuous sister
hatred of sister for brother, then hyperexogamic marriage	sister striving to communicate with exiled brother
patrilineality	matrilineality

This code curiously verifies the existence of an unconscious property of matrilineality that we have posited in a preceding work. As a prudent cultural decision, the matrilineal option defines itself, in relation to patrilineality, as halfway between incest and exogamy.[22] M9 asserts that this choice is the indirect consequence of intemperance and unchastity.

The postincest exile of Woot leads not only to the disappearance of the sun, but to the disintegration of primordial society. In leaving his own people, Woot systematically creates linguistic diversity. The setting up of the cultural universe and its extension in space never cease to be thought of as a curse, as the revenge of the incestuous father whose absence the sons regret to this day.

M12, Kuba: The Succession of Woot, the Migrations, and the Diversity of Peoples (Vansina[23])

Before going into exile, Woot regulated his succession in the following fashion. He summoned Ishweem, his elder son (he who founded the Ngeende tribe), and told him to come the next morning, just before dawn. He would call him by whistling softly. To make himself recognized, Ishweem would ask for the chicken basket. But a Pygmy, who had overheard this conversation, told another of Woot's sons, Nyimilong, saying: "Thou, his sister's child, wilt thou let power escape thee?"[24] Nyimilong was the first to present himself [next morning] to Woot. Annoyed at this mischance, Woot at first offered him a box of clothes. But Nyimilong refused it, demanding the chicken basket. In it Nyimilong found the insignia of royalty: the eagle's feather, the leopardskin, the skin of the genet (*mbiidy*), the pangolin's scale; another informant adds cowrie shells and the national costume to this list. Nyimilong put on this costume and danced the coronation dance in the village for the first time ever.

Woot was furious and uttered a curse on his people. The millet began to rot, the poultry died, the sun stopped rising, the animals became wild. Woot burned the original village, the name of which says even today that is was destroyed by fire, and the rivers burst their banks. A niece of Woot was delivered of a sheep. In the hurried departure, Woot's wife injured herself on a tree stump. She applied plants to the wound and felt a burning—she had discovered salt, which is got from the ashes of a certain plant.

The rest of the story, in conformity with M10, tells how Mweel sent messengers—a dog, a fly, a tortoise—to Woot in order that the sun might rise again. Mweel left the Kuba in her turn, while the different tribes, led by Nyimilong, went searching for Woot. Some informants say that Woot became head of the Kete, of the Luba, or of certain Kuba tribes; on his way he gave certain groups the names they now bear. Using a magical technique, he changed the language of each group on leaving it. Thus journeying, Woot created the diversity of countries, plants, and animals. To prevent his sons' joining him, he hurled rocks into the river. Then, according to some informants, he left behind two corpses, of an idle person and a sorcerer, to discourage his pursuers. Finally, Woot disappeared toward the east, carried off by a whirlwind. One informant claims he fell into the Lake Itaangwa dika, a name said by Vansina to mean "the sun at its zenith."

Here Woot's succession is inconsistent with the decision taken in M9: devolving on to an incestuous son, it is truly neither matrilineal nor patrilineal. The myth is situated at a critical moment when incest has confounded alliance and kinship. It is a stranger, an indiscreet Pygmy, who holds the future of divine kingship in his hands. Above all, the conflict between father and son which began in M9 is intensified and takes a dramatic new turn. The fury of the frustrated Woot is now extended to his whole people, who undertake a long and fruitless quest for the vanished father; but the search merely multiplies the physical and cultural obstacles between the father and his children.

Paradoxically, however, the exiled Woot pursued the work of linguistic creation begun when he gave a proper name to the Kuba, before the peoples' dispersion.[25] Here he is depriving the animals of speech (M10) while giving each people a separate language. Woot the linguist is thus in all respects the creator of differences within the human species, which he separates from the animal species, driven from the primordial village where they apparently lived on good terms with men (M12). But these cultural innovations are made in a spirit of anger, contempt, and revenge. Woot's attitude is ambiguous: in burning the primordial village he does not put an end to culture but instead destroys his original home, causing migration and the diversity of peoples.

This new stage of cultural development is felt as a dramatic loss of original unity. The discovery of the technique of making salt by

Woot's wife, in consequence of a painful accident, is symptomatic of this singularly pessimistic historical philosophy. A natural catastrophe, which could well have been some kind of flood corresponding with the disappearance of the sun, is a prelude to this leap forward in human culture: the rivers overflow and millet rots. This eclipse and flood are signs that the distinction between the seasons and the alternation of day and night are abolished, and that rain has taken over.

We shall develop this cosmogonic code in the next chapter. Here it is merely necessary to emphasize that this catastrophic suspension of cosmic rhythms is provisional, and that Woot will liberate the sun. He will also introduce discontinuity in natural domains hitherto unmarked by any system of differences; on his way he creates geographical, zoological, and botanical diversity, even as he sets up the diversity of peoples and languages in the cultural order. It also seems, as we shall see, that he introduces death and the necessity of labor.

M9 and M12 express the father-son disjunction by different means, which convey complementary messages.

M9	M12
Drunken and immodest Woot	Incestuous Woot
Woot punishes his sons	Woot abandons his sons
Origin of matrilineal society and initiation	Origin of cultural and linguistic diversity

In M9 the sons of Woot, condemned to undergo the ordeals of initiation, are symbolically and provisionally excluded from society. Conversely, in M12 Woot really and definitively abandons his sons. M9 preserves tribal unity although the initial patrilineality is lost. M12 engenders the dissolution of cultural and linguistic unity.

Considered together, M9 and M12 explain the existing cultural order by the progressive degradation of an ideal society in which only one language was spoken, and where harmony reigned between father and son. Woot's drunkenness explains the beginning of matrilineality and the initiation of young men; a consequence of Woot's incest, the loss of linguistic homogeneity is also the creation of new cultures. Cultural diversity emerges dialectically from incest: Woot's onward flight, entailing loss of his sister forever, seems like a journey to the limit of the incest prohibition. This aspect is particularly prominent in a brief variant of M12 from the Byeng tribe which makes a maximum separation between Woot and Mweel after their excessive conjunction in solitude.

M12 (ii): Woot's Incest and the Dispersal of the Peoples (Vansina[26])

> Woot, being stricken with leprosy, went to live in the forest with his sister Mweel and his successor Yoncolo. It was during this isolation that he discovered the symbols of power. Mweel gave him many children, destined to be the founders of diverse tribes. When he was healed, Woot returned to the village. But he was driven away because of his incest. He fled upstream, while Mweel disappeared downstream. Yoncolo stayed with the Kete and the Twa (Pygmies).

The radical separation of the incestuous lovers is defined by the opposition downstream/upstream. In the space created by this stark division, tribal discontinuity arises. From being positive, Woot's linguistic function becomes negative. He no longer invents languages to impede communication as in M12: here it is the sons who, peopling the void created by the disjunction of the incestuous mother and father, institute cultural differences. But the linguistic diversity which results in both cases from the breakup of the primal intimacy and the petulant affirmation of the incest prohibition simultaneously nullifies the function of that rule, which is returned to zero point. Effectively, tribal differentiation means a fragmented cultural universe. In creating different languages (M12), Woot compromises the matrimonial exchanges between the peoples which have issued from him. He isolates the groups one from another, enclosing each in endogamy on its own account.

The incestuous Woot's flight toward the unknown therefore recreates incest at a higher level. The original defect is projected as in a mirror image. Even within the Kuba tribe, matrimonial customs reflect this internal contradiction of clan exogamy approaching its limit: geographical endogamy. Any woman with whom kinship can be traced is forbidden; this prohibition concerns eight or sixteen clans, for the Kuba recall their genealogical links bilaterally for three or four generations. But this sizable enlargement of the exogamic field is balanced by a converse tendency toward alliance between groups which are nearest in space.[27] The clan hyperexogamy of generalized exchange goes together with local endogamy. The breaking of linguistic communications, a direct or indirect consequence of Woot's incest, implies the breaking of relations of alliance between tribal groups, which thenceforward have their own speech and customs, their own women.

That in no way means that language and kinship obey the same laws. Matrimonial communication, which is necessarily exogamic, requires a homogeneous linguistic universe (the primordial village that Woot destroyed by fire) where words are accessible to all and circulate freely, without restriction. One could say that exogamic exchange requires a community in which speech is incestuous, available to all. By the same logic, the myth presents us with an incestuous cultural hero who devotes himself to the creation of linguistic diversity, abolishing the primal unity of tongues. Reality, like its reflection in the mirror of myth, tends to support a thesis we have argued elsewhere: that language and kinship are inversely homologous.[28]

As at Babel, the diversity of peoples is the consequence of a sin, but this time it is the demiurge himself who is guilty. In the biblical account the confusion of tongues halts the building of a tower which would have joined heaven and earth.[29] We find an analogous cosmogonic representation in the Woot cycle, when the hero's departure causes the sun to disappear. In both cases there is the same kind of correlation between the cultural code and the astronomic code of the myth: the loss of an original linguistic unity is associated with the breaking of a means of communication established naturally (the rays of the sun) or culturally (the tower) between the sky and the earth.

A common Kuba tradition (which we have found in M12 (ii)) projects the opposition of high and low on a horizontal axis: Woot and Mweel turn their backs on each other after their incest, the one going upstream (high) and the other downstream (low).[30] The spatial separation of the incestuous lovers is analogous to the separation of sky and earth, as is clearly conveyed in a proverbial saying (the complex meaning of which we shall consider later): "Mboom in the sky, Ngaan in the water, Mweel downstream, Woot upstream."[31]

This formula makes an explicit relation between the definitive separation of Woot and Mweel (the origin of cultural and linguistic discontinuity) and the conflict that opposes the creator gods Mboom and Ngaan, formerly united. Now the sky, the domain of Mboom, is opposed to terrestrial water, the domain of Ngaan. The dispersion of the peoples (the subject of M12) returns implicitly to the abolition of this vertical axis.

In other words, the Babel story makes a fleeting appearance in our myth. The Babel story and the myth make a correlation between the collapse, real or metaphoric, of a cultural work created in linguistic unity, and the end of this same unity. Although the psychological motives credited to the actors in the mythical drama are obviously different, it is nonetheless remarkable that in the one case an outraged Creator, in the other a guilty and outraged culture hero, realize the same project with incalculable consequences for the history of civilization.

In effect, the nostalgic quest for the vanished father inaugurates historical time for the Kuba. The Kuba oppose the time of creation (the subject of numerous stories, none of which is generally accepted) to two preceding periods, the epoch of migrations and that of the founding of the kingdom.[32] This pluralistic vision emphasizes the contrast between Kuba thought and that of the Luba, for whom the epic foundation myth, which is remarkably consistent in all its versions, marks the very beginning of history. The Luba heroes are only weakly cultural. Nkongolo is the heir of a long line of technological innovators; Mbidi contents himself with bringing the aristocratic use of fire and a new hunting technique; and Kalala Ilunga is but a conqueror. For the Kuba, in contrast, the first sovereign, Woot, is the initiator of basic social institutions and the inventor of ironworking.[33] This mythical culture-history, which is distinct from the history of migrations, is in essence the work of a drunken, lustful, and incestuous king whose magical powers are still the ultimate guarantee of fecundity. It is a history that unfolds according to a singular process, which we have called progressive-regressive. Each new institution is felt as a loss in relation to a preceding state of harmony and unity.

The second founder of Kuba culture, the king Shyaam a Mbul, is by contrast associated unequivocally with progressive historical time. The advances in civilization achieved during his reign no longer present the ambiguity associated with comparable developments in the time of Woot. Following a dynastic crisis this adventurer seized power and reorganized the Kuba state, probably about the beginning of the seventeenth century. He introduced sweet corn, which became the staple diet of the population. He diffused the arts of weaving and woodworking throughout his realm, and developed commerce.[34] The Kuba attribute to this authentically historical sovereign the transition from a primary cultural order to a refined civilization, which was in fact one of the most brilliant in Central Africa. This precise break between myth and history is completely foreign to Luba thought, which otherwise adopts a resolutely evolutionist diachronic schema.

The Kuba royal epic, which the reigning sovereign recited in 1953 in the presence of Vansina and Jacobs, contains only a passing reference to the Woot cycle,[35] as if the myth were but a prologue to the history; the latter is a description of migrations and the late reunion of the wandering tribes under the rule of a divine king, the more or less spurious heir of Woot. This epic, which is singularly lacking in magical elements, contrasts in both tone and form with the Luba epic, the founding charter of a unitary state. The Kuba epic, as Vansina and Jacobs remark, exalts the unity and indivisibility of the nation; the property of the governing institutions, it tells of glory and triumph. In contrast, the myth says that the primal unity did not survive the burning of Byengl, the primordial village; that original unity can never be restored. The epic ranges in outline over the whole historical field, from Woot's departure to the present time (1953). It ends by recalling the motto of the present capital ("the hunt for money") and proclaims the benefits of wealth, which makes man proud and powerful whereas "poverty is the occasion of flattery"—with such remarkable and cynical ease are the industrious Kuba people relegated to colonial degradation.

Despite all these differences, we shall show that the Luba epic and the Kuba cycle use the same sets of ideas and the same codes. For this reason we have to disagree with Vansina when he includes myths and origin stories among those oral traditions the purpose of which is to instruct.[36] The present investigation will show that the Kuba myths cannot be reduced to their ideological function. Even if the myths occasionally validate one institution or another, their symbolic significance cannot be reduced to this contingent framework; for it forms, with the symbolism of neighboring populations, a vast ensemble of familial, political, and cosmogonic relations. This ensemble is shaped by a general code that is subject to strictly defined transformations, and the present work is devoted to the elucidation of that code.

Let us now consider the other variants of M12, beginning with Torday's version, the closest to the first variant (M12 (ii)).

M12 (iii), Kuba: The Incest and Exile of Woot (Torday[37])

Woot fell in love with his sister, the daughter of his own mother, and by her had a son, Nyimi Lele, who was forced to emigrate because of the general indignation. Nyimi Lele went on to found the neighboring people (the Lele tribe). But popular anger was not appeased. Some said: "How can a man who has shown himself to be worse than a beast go on ruling us?" Woot lost patience and decided to leave the country, but not without first taking his revenge. He decided to call his people together very early on the day of his departure and to hand over his insignia of office to whoever first answered his call, whatever his rank. He confided this project to his Pygmy (Twa) advisers. One of these was a friend of Woot's brother Nyimi Longa (Nyimilong), and he betrayed his master's secret to him. Nyimi Longa stayed up all night and rushed to Woot as soon as he heard his call, just before dawn. In the darkness Woot failed to recognize his brother and placed two eagle feathers in his hair. When the sun rose the people assembled and Woot realized with anger that he had been taken advantage of. He set fire to the village and left, together with his slaves. His wife, Ipopa, used magic to kill poultry and cause the millet to rot. Soon the people were threatened by famine. Then Nyimi Longa sent six envoys to Woot. They succeeded in rousing his pity and they brought back new seeds and poultry.

Here the code of M12 undergoes some minor transformations. The exile of the only son, the issue of incest, is the source of limited cultural differentiation: the Kuba and the Lele in fact belong to the same linguistic group. Within this differentiation, the character of the Pygmy presents two peculiarities: he belongs to an earlier people (according to the myth) than all those resulting from Woot's incest, and is radically distinguished from them by a rude mode of life and by physical appearance. The mythical function of the Pygmy is paradoxical: a sign *par excellence* of the discontinuity of the human species, he saves the dynastic continuity which Woot has decided to destroy by investing the firstcomer with divine kingship. The Pygmy's project is opposed to the will of the King, of whom he is the inverse symmetric image. The little man is a stranger (as a hunter-gatherer) to the cultivating civilization of which Woot is the culture hero. However, in M12 the Pygmy magisterially resolves the problem of a succession tainted with incest, but which Woot himself had wanted to be matrilineal (M10): he reminds Nyimilong that he is a uterine nephew. We shall see later (M13) that the Pygmies intervene in a second dynastic crisis, this time with a series of magical feats. Finally, it is a Pygmy who discovers the technique of gathering palm wine (M25); his intervention causes this precious drink to pass from the natural to the cultural order. M12 (iv) tells us that in the eyes of the Kuba the tree-born Pygmies appear as creatures in some way intermediate between nature (from which they emerge) and the culture in which they intervene unexpectedly after the fashion of the divine king himself, the drunken and incestuous demiurge: the Pygmy of M25 is the first drunkard in history.

Although the complex figure of the founder of kingship is enfeebled in M12 (iii), where the exiled sovereign is really no more than a benign food provider, this variant at least reminds us that Woot is the very source of life. Royal incest implies fecundity: Woot had nine children (the perfect number) by his sister Mweel.[38] M12 (ii) makes even more of this positive function of sin: isolated in the forest with Mweel, Woot discovers the symbols of divine kingship.

Achten's version for its part emphasizes the differentiation of men and animals, that is, the nature/culture opposition. Surprisingly, the transition from unity to cultural diversity appears here before the separation between the human and animal realms; this separation is one of the first consequences of Woot's anger in M12, in which the animals become wild at the same moment that Woot finally abandons the primordial village.

M12 (iv), Kuba: Woot's Incest and the Separation of Men and Animals (Achten[39])

After committing incest with his sister, Woot set off eastward with a large following. He decided that men would cease understanding one another. He magically changed the emigrants' language. Thus he created the Luba tribe. Until then, animals and men had got on very well. War began one day when the monkey Fum Mbombo stole the calabashes belonging to a drawer of palm wine. The man killed the monkey, then killed the leopard for taking the monkey's part. The animals thereupon left the village and began to populate the forest, the water, and the air. Only a few remained with men. After these events, men set fire to Buyengele, the primordial dwelling place, and Nyimi Longo founded a new village. It was at this time also that a niece of Woot was delivered of a sheep. Nyimi Longo's successor gave names to his subjects and their families to distinguish them from one another.

Cultural discontinuity and the separation of men and animals come about here in three distinct phases. The incestuous Woot contents himself with introducing a primary linguistic difference by separating the Kuba from the Luba in a world where animals live peacefully with men. In a second epoch, under Nyimi Longo (Nyimilong), the animal realm is separated from the human realm, at the same time subdividing into three zoological domains: the inhabitants of the forest, of the water, and of the air. Palm wine is at the root of the conflict between men and animals, as it is of the rupture between father and son in M9: it is through his overindulgence in this drink that Woot falls asleep naked and his sons insult him. In both cases, palm wine is a disjunctive term. It expels animals from the cultural order just as it introduces the first rift in the primordial society which had harmoniously united father and sons. But palm wine is also instrumental in cultural advance: on the one hand it leads to the matrilineal system and initiation, on the other it makes a definitive break between humanity and the animal kingdom.[40] The third sovereign completes the achievement of cultural discontinuity by introducing the finest distinctions and defining the concept of person (something generally attributed to Woot himself).

The discontinuous universe that Woot creates on fleeing from his people is also, according to a peripheral myth influenced by the Songo-Meno, that of sickness and death.

M12 (v), Kuba: Woot's Exile and the Origin of Sickness (Torday[41])

Woot (Woto) had three wives. One day he surprised the son of his twin brother Mweel (Moelo) with one of them. He complained to the young man's father and threatened to leave the country if anything like it happened again. Soon afterward, the nephew seduced his paternal uncle's second wife. The angry Woot went into exile. As a sign of repentance, his wives tattooed themselves. Woot agreed to return. But it was not long before he found his nephew with his third wife. Thereupon he left for good. Three of his brothers went away to search for him and never returned. Their descendants peopled the entire earth. The fourth brother, Etoshi, stayed in the village. After wandering in the forest, Woot reached the Lukenye River. He was sad at no longer having anyone to rule. He sang a magic song and the Pygmies (Twa) came out of the trees. At Etoshi's village, the first healer, who was also a sorcerer, invented sickness and death as a way of getting money from his clients. Hoping to escape from this evil doctor, Etoshi decided to emigrate in his turn with his followers. But the sorcerer managed to track them down. In vain the people used their clubs, swords, and spears against him: in the end they had to accept his company.

The table of kinship relations is completely aberrant. Far from being guilty, Woot is simply the victim of a mildly incestuous adultery: by lying with the wives of his paternal uncle, who are assimilated to "mothers," Woot's nephew commits nominal incest. The father-son conflict, the central theme of M9 and M11, reappears here in the form of a conflict between Woot and a paternal nephew (a classificatory son). Despite its unusual character, the first part of M12 (v) therefore brings together the two Oedipal *mythèmes* of the cycle. But the complete disappearance of the sister, whose name (Mweel) is assumed by a twin brother, makes us view this version as a prudishly toned-down rendering of the common Kuba tradition.

The second part of the narrative has the same purpose as the first, that of accounting for human diversity and migrations. But the explanation adds the crime of sorcery to incest. Sickness appears in the heart of Kuba country, soon spreading throughout the world. Into the linguistically diversified societies it introduces the principle of discontinuity in a natural form: death. Lévi-Strauss's proposed interpretation of epidemics is equally valid here: "The decimation of a particular population . . . is symmetrical with the general discontinuity of species."[42] In the case we are considering, the principle of discontinuity throws a particular light on the connection between sorcery, cause of death, and the breaking up of the original human community. But in our group of myths this breakup is, in its turn, accompanied by the creation of zoological, botanical, and geographical diversity (M12).

We can now interpret the theme of leprosy introduced in M12 (ii). This disease, which in Africa is often thought to be a consequence of incest, is here its cause. Woot, afflicted with leprosy, retires into the forest with his sister, who proceeds to give him numerous children; these children become the founders of tribes. Leprosy and the isolation it entails thus presage the future discontinuity of the human race, a discontinuity which we have decoded as a paradoxical transformation of incest. Tribal division is in its way a form of leprosy that isolates groups and condemns them to endogamy.

Although the exile of the incestuous father, at odds with his own people, inaugurates human diversity along the spatial axis, it also brings an end, along the temporal axis, to the succession of day and night. It seems as though the brutal separation of brother and sister entails an even greater cosmic peril than that introduced into society by their initial incestuous conjunction. In M10 it is not incest but rather its radical negation that leads to the disappearance of the sun, together with the definitive differentiation of the human and animal species, the animals being deprived by Woot of the power of speech: he drives them out of the primordial village at the same time that the sun disappears (M12). The division between the human and animal worlds (between which the royal ram maintains a mediating link) and the loss of primordial cultural unity are thus analogous to the separation of sky and earth, symbolized respectively by Woot and Mweel. M10, in which this cosmogonic code is clearly apparent, makes a point of correcting the totality of these extreme situations, which are seen to threaten men as they threaten the universe. Woot's daughter returns to her brothers with certain animals which bring back the vanished sunlight. This mediating action throws a bridge across the gulf created between nature (animal) and culture (human), sky and earth, incest and exogamy.

It is time to approach the cycle of patently cosmogonic myths and to show how they relate to the Woot cycle. But before returning to the origin of the world, let us first consider a myth awaiting us on the historic path taken by men after Woot's going. Reconstructing the routes followed in actuality by the Kuba subgroups after leaving the Atlantic coast to the north of the Congo River, Vansina describes them going up the Kasai River in the second half of the sixteenth century, some in canoes and others on foot, finally reaching the Plain of Yool. It was here that history refreshed itself, seemingly for the last time, from the distant source of the origin myths.

M13: The Kuba Chiefs in Conflict (Vansina, Denolf[43])

> After arriving in the Plain of Yool, the chiefs of the different Kuba tribes quarreled and decided to resort to an oracle to see who should be king. Each one would throw his hammer into the lake and the kingship would belong to him whose hammer floated on the water. The chief of the Bieeng had caused to be made for himself a hammer in very light wood covered with a thin coating of iron and copper. This man's sister stole it from him and gave it to her husband, Mboong, a chief of the Bushong. When Mboong threw this hammer into the water there occurred a series of miraculous events caused by the magic of the Pygmies. The water turned red, then yellow, then white; the trees shook; a crocodile came out of the lake, and the new king rode on its back. The Bieeng and the Bushong fought each other for many years. The other Kuba tribes dispersed.

Here we see completed, within the Kuba ethnic group itself, the process of fission and differentiation begun when Woot's exile caused the appearance of other peoples. One is not surprised to see M13 evoke M12 by taking up the theme of the imposed, and indeed fraudulent, succession. When the Bushong chief throws the fake hammer into the water, he cries: "Is there a spirit upstream, are there people downstream?"[44] Although Vansina does not comment on this saying, it is clearly a reference to the mythical separation of Woot and Mweel. The new king evidently wants to recover the lost unity; but far from abolishing the dispersion of peoples, his act aggravates it for many years. In fact, the Bieeng and the Bushong make war, while the Pyaang and the Ngeende emigrate to their present habitats.[45] It seems to have been accepted that the kingship imposed by the Bushong chief was effective over only a few Ngeende groups.[46] M13 therefore justifies the power struggle of the Bushong and the Byeeng, which it situates in the cycle of origin myths, at the same time closing the cycle with a perturbation of waters. This takes us back to an epoch before Woot, at the very beginning of the world. We shall now consider these cosmogonic myths, following the chastised sons of Woot down the path of the initiation school.

[CHAPTER FOUR]

The People of the Sun

M11, like M9, presents us with a father dishonored by his sons and permits the sovereign passage from myth to ritual. These two narratives have the explicit function of validating the initiation of young men. Woot's sons have to undergo for the first time a ritual chastisement for their lack of respect for the naked, drunken king (M9). The insolent son of M11 who got drunk with his mother without inviting his father to his quasi-incestuous libations was frightened by a lugubrious sound whose terrifying echo, likened to a leopard's growl, still threatens young men undergoing the initiatory ordeal: the novices have to go through a tunnel to the sound of a friction drum, while the mothers lament their sons' disappearance.[1] The outrage of the father, the central theme of Kuba mythology, is therefore counterbalanced on the ritual plane by the symbolic killing of the sons.

The parallel becomes closer when we know that Kuba initiation has the explicit function of breaking the excessively close bonds between young men and their mothers and sisters. The initiatory wall that separates the village from the bush where the novices spend a considerable time is primarily symbolic of Woot's incest: this is Vansina's interpretation, based on his firsthand experience of the initiation ritual. At the foot of the central post of the initiatory wall is a sculpture representing a woman in labor; this figure represents Woot's mother. Her name, "Wife of the Eagle," suggests she is joined to her son by an incestuous relationship, because the eagle is a royal emblem.[2] The statue is located in a small garden surrounded by a courtyard containing magical plants that prevent Woot from approaching. This primordial mother bemoans the fate which renders it impossible for her to make love without committing incest.

Again, according to Vansina, the "Wife of the Eagle" is identical with Kalyengl, the masked female personage who brings the novices into the world as they emerge from the initiatory tunnel. But Kalyengl is none other than Mweel, Woot's incestuous sister.

Thus, in conformity with the banal story of M11, the symbolism of initiation unashamedly transforms the incest of Woot and Mweel into an Oedipal relationship. The Kuba indeed say straight out that the most desirable women are those given to them by God and which they are forbidden to marry: their mothers and sisters.[3] Although given to others in conformity with the law of exogamy, mother and sisters remain the foundation of a matrilineal society constructed halfway between original harmony and incestuous regression.

The Ritual Killing of the Sons

The initiatory ritual (*nkaan*) of the Kuba, which is explicitly based on M9 and M11, deserves to be considered as a whole, and we summarize here Vansina's remarkable description.[4]

1. The young men spend several days in the middle of the village in a shelter entirely covered with raffia fibers. The ground is covered with the same foliage, which serves as a bed for the candidates. The candidates make themselves raffia loincloths and sing lewd songs. They are forbidden to raise their voices or to laugh, to go near women, to make fire or even to light a lamp, or to eat vegetables (food of feminine origin). After a successful antelope hunt has given evidence of the goodwill of the spirits of the forest, the elders build the initiatory wall. Between the palings (each of a different plant) they twine the ribs of palm fronds. The wall includes three triangular peaks (called "hills") topped with masks.* In the middle of the night the elders suddenly destroy the shelter in which the novices are sleeping. Just before dawn, they rush at the boys, shouting and blowing horns, and drive them into a ditch which has just been dug to the west of the village. The ditch is empty, but the youths believe it to contain the villagers' excrement. After this ordeal the novices run to the stream

*Vansina's account (1955:150) says: "The wall is composed of a framework of poles, all of different kinds of wood, on which palm ribs with their fibers loosely hanging are fastened. The wall is a long construction with three triangular peaks called 'hills.' The central peak is higher than the two others and reaches a height of about 22 feet." (R.W.)

to wash away an imaginary pollution, while the women, who are gathered at the eastern end of the village, watch the scene from afar, without being able to recognize the figures behind the early morning mist.

On the way back, a teacher tells the novices that two corpses are lying on the path. They have to pay several francs to be allowed to see the bodies, said to be those of a sorcerer and a lazy man. The candidates return home and eat a hearty meal. Their mothers[5] shave their heads and cover them with red powder. They put on their best clothes.

2. A drum calls the young men to the village square for a dance. Old initiates armed with sticks suddenly appear from the west and force the novices toward the east, where the initiatory wall is located. The novices pass through the barrier of foliage and are confronted by a masked man, *Nnup*. He wears a leopardskin kilt and brandishes a knife. He is symbolic of the king, and more particularly of Woot himself. The novices take off their clothes. Each rides on an instructor's back between Nnup's legs, ending up in a tunnel where he hears the frightening growl of the "leopard" (the friction drum). The women cry out, convinced the young men are being put to death. The novices pay for the right to see the friction drum; then they pass a nook where a man with a hammer pretends to be an ironworker. Finally, they fall into a ditch full of water, emerging from the tunnel between the legs of a second masked personage, Kalyengl, symbolizing both the original mother and Woot's incestuous sister.

The novices are reborn and take to crying like infants. Some old men wash them in the stream; then they take them to a nearby clearing where the young men find the raffia clothes they made in the first phase of initiation. They dress themselves. The two masked figures join them. Preceded by Nnup and followed by Kalyengl, they advance in single file while striking the ground with certain roots called *ngoontsh*, a name also applied to a weaver's baton. They cross the village from west to east, supposedly no more than their own ghosts, on their way to a distant land. Women bring them food for the journey. At the village boundary the two masked figures begin to dance; but they are driven away by the crowd, while the "ghosts" continue on their way. The teachers use their friction drums to prevent the people from following them. As night falls they reach a clearing where shelters await them. The novices sleep on the ground, in their raffia clothing.

The women believe that their dead children are going on a long journey through hostile territory.

3. The next day the young men, organized according to clan, build the huts in which they will live during their retreat. They get used to the routine of camp life. The novices learn riddles and songs. They have to observe a number of prohibitions. If they go to the palm grove to get wine, they must hide from women. Should they meet one, she is dragged off to the camp, where anyone has the right to rape her. Fathers steal chickens from their wives* and go to feed their sons after nightfall.

The novices make a brief reappearance in the village on the third day of their retreat, dancing and singing in the central square. They return to the camp in the evening and in the old days would remain there for several months.

4. At the end of their term of isolation, the youths are gathered behind the initiatory wall for a "hunt for the white chicken." One of them makes a noise like a chicken and runs round the village, the others pursuing him. The game is over when they catch him. On this day all the novices must eat chicken. The following night they leave the camp and obtain salt from a neighboring village (formerly they made it themselves). Dancing, they take the road to their own village, where the long-time initiates, accompanied by two figures masked as the Antelope and the Serpent, are waiting for them. The Antelope tries in vain to follow the dance steps. The Serpent attacks the novices with his tail; but the old initiates fight him off by throwing magic leaves at him. Carrying on this pretended combat, the group makes its entry into the village. The women mass along one side of the square to welcome the young men. The other three sides are taken respectively by the old initiates, the novices, and the Serpent. The youngest youth goes toward his mother; he gives her a packet of salt, which she accepts by dancing. The Serpent tries to intervene between them, but is chased away by the elders with their magic leaves. After giving the salt to his mother, the youth runs to his home. One after another, each of his companions executes the same "dance of the salt" facing his mother, his sister, or, failing either of these, his wife.

But it is no longer acceptable for them to go home. At dusk, they

*Commonly in Africa small livestock such as chickens are female property, and such would appear to be the Kuba custom. (R.W.)

are assembled on the public square where the old initiates encircle them with a hunting net; they dance within this enclosure. The next morning, the rest of the village gathers outside the net. A novice who plays the role of "chief policeman" bites the head off a live rat; this enables the first new initiate to get out. Other "policemen" carry out the same procedure on other rats to liberate all the novices. The young men have to eat this revolting meat, which belongs to the *nyetsh** category. They gather for the terminal rite behind the initiatory wall. The elders gather in front of them, on the side of the village, and throw them a flaming torch, which is received in silence. In contrast, the youths receive an extinguished torch with shouts of rejoicing. The initiation ceremony is complete.

On this complex ritual, which is closely linked with the origin myth, Vansina offers a sociological analysis. He argues convincingly that the mimed drama of symbolic death by the initiatory wall should be interpreted as a denial of incest; the specific prohibitions regulate relations with women, under the royal authority symbolized by the masked leopard figure, Nnup. One can also note, with Vansina, that the raffia palm evoked in the first sequence stands for the essence of the material culture: its fermented sap makes a highly valued drink, palm wine, while its leaves provide clothing and domestic furnishings. Esoteric exegesis, to which the Belgian ethnographer had access during his own initiation, throws light on several other important symbols. The earth of the initiatory tunnel is the skin of the royal leopard; the entrance represents this animal's jaws. The ironsmith hidden inside the tunnel is a double of Woot: after killing his children under his leopard aspect, he "forges" new men. The *ngoontsh* root with which the young men, dead to their old life, beat the ground during the rite of separation, symbolically evokes the baton of a loom which bears the same name: this ritual instrument has the function of driving women away.

In connection with the curious "hunt" which announces the novices' return to the village, Vansina notes that the chicken, in opposition to certain wild fowls, is the symbol of village social life (the chicken's feather is a royal emblem). Vansina explains that the "salt dance" is the high point of the novices' reintegration in society, because salt symbolizes the preeminent feminine activity of cooking. The gift of salt thus expresses the matrimonial order, the basic foundation of the

**Nyetsh* is the Kuba category of polluting and disgusting objects. (R.W.)

social order. The humiliating situation of the young men when they suddenly find themselves trapped in a hunting net then forced to eat rat (a repugnant animal) has to be related to a proverb comparing the hunting net to the dangerous royal authority.

The political structure is also revealed in elliptical form at the initiatory wall. The central peak ("hill") bears a mask of which the secret name is Woot. The two lateral peaks are occupied by effigies of Woot's two sons, who were the first to undergo initiation. But they also represent respectively the chiefs of the left and right sides of the village. Finally, Vansina observes that the novices are actors in a mythical drama: "they incarnate the Bushong (the dominant Kuba tribe) in search of Woot, the lost source of all fertility."[6] We will now try to integrate these findings with our earlier results, and go on to show that the symbolism of initiation is determined by subtle correspondences, the secret of which was not revealed by Vansina's teachers.

Incest, Labor, and Death

The temporary shelter wherein the novices gather in the center of the village is an ambiguous locality. On the one hand it is related to the symbolism of the raffia palm, that is, to the cultural order (the novives also make clothes in it). But on the other it explicitly represents Woot's sexual organs: the young men enter it backwards, commemorating the chaste act of Woot's daughter in covering the nakedness of her drunken father.[7] The raffia-covered shelter thus unequivocally recalls the original disorder caused by abuse of palm wine. The fact that the fibers used to make clothing and the intoxicating sap come from the same tree gives rise to an extended reflection on the meaning of existing civilization. This return to the origins occurs in a ritual central place, to which are subsequently opposed the west and east of the village, the respective directions in which Woot and Mweel emigrated after their incest.

The theme of incest which lies at the heart of the initiation ritual is directly related, in the myth, to the misuse of palm wine and the impertinence of the sons. But it is sometimes the father (M9) and sometimes the son (M11) who gets drunk or becomes implicated in an incestuous situation (M10, M11). After the evocation of M9 at the beginning of the ritual, it is not surprising to discover a projection of M10 and M11 on the initiatory wall, where the novices decode the cryptic reference to Woot's incestuous passion and find it like their own. For M11 told us that the first initiate was a young man who cut himself off from the world to drink palm wine with his mother. The ideological function of M9 as of M11 is to justify the punishment inflicted by the father. In the first myth, Woot in person finds himself in a scandalous situation (he is naked before his sons after overindulgence in palm wine); in the second, on the contrary, it is the impertinent son who (incestuously) misuses palm wine. M10 belongs to the same group, but this time it is Woot himself who commits incest. M10 really provides the framework for the ensuing scenes in the ritual drama when the novices set off in search of the lost father.

We have noted that the temporary shelter, symbol of Woot's naked genitalia, is built in the middle of the village. This ritual position suggests that matrilineality, the consequence of Woot's drunkenness, defines a social space at the extremities of which one finds the ditch of excrement (to the west) and the wall of incest (to the east). The center of this symbolic space recalls the original place where the primordial patrilineal society became matrilineal by a regressive process; the two poles mark the boundaries of the social order. In the west lies the *nyetsh* category, the repulsion inspired by real or metaphoric pollution; in the east lies the barrier of sexual prohibitions. This dichotomy confirms a thesis we have argued in respect to a neighboring tribe which is historically related to the Kuba, the Lele: the symbolic category of pollution and dirt must not be confused with that of prohibitions.[8] In the present case, this dichotomy seems to be of psychoanalytic inspiration: the anal zone in the west, the genital zone in the east. The west is weakly marked: the young men are taken there to be made fun of by the elders before symbolically dying in the east.

It all seems as if the cultural regression of these nonadults (even though some may be married) passes through an infantile phase which is the prelude to the annihilation of their earlier lives. Symbolic death and rebirth take place in the east, for this zone is devoted to creative activity and to the search for the father, whereas the west is the direction that saw the disappearance of Mweel, the original mother (M12 (ii)). The ithyphallic mask *Mboong a kwong* surmounting the left lateral peak of the initiatory wall represents one of Woot's sons equipped with an enormous penis.[9] It also symbolizes the novices, whose unbridled sexuality the initiation ritual is intended to socialize, under the sign of the father. This image evidently relates to M11, which condemns the incest of the son and the mother. The initiatory wall is, moreover, the barrier separating the one from the other. That is why one also finds there Woot's own mother (a transformation of Mweel), lamenting the fact that magical charms prevent her from copulating with her son.[10]

Nevertheless Woot, the source of all fecundity, infringes the prohibition. He is conjoined, in the form of the Nnup masked figure, with his sister Mweel, figured by Kalyengl. These two personages stand respectively at the entrance and exit of the tunnel that leads from the other side of the wall, into the bush. Woot kills the novices, then begets them anew with Mweel. Vansina sees clearly that this renaissance is a recreation of the incest of the culture hero (M10). The young men are in some way identified with the children of the incestuous couple.

The ritual drama unfolds entirely in mythical time and space. Dead to their earlier lives, reduced to the condition of ghosts, the novices cross the village from west to east. The masked figure Nnup (representing Woot) leads the march, and the masked figure Kalyengl (in which Vansina recognizes the image of Mweel) brings up the rear. After the incestuous union in the tunnel, the brother and the sister are separated by their own children; he stands to the east, she to the west, like Woot and Mweel in M12 (ii).

The ritual symbols we have been considering refer to the common tradition of the incest of the culture hero (M10). In contrast, the converse and complementary problem of M11, where the son (and no longer the father) behaves incestuously, is found on the other side of the wall. The results of paternal incest, discarded in the bush, the novices at least partially relive the situation of the hero of M11 who incurs his father's anger because he gets drunk with his mother. They have free access to the palm groves, they sing licentious songs; although they are forbidden to approach women, they evoke the image of the mother in lewd riddles and insults.[11] In the camp, sexuality is discussed without restraint. The young men have the right to fornicate collectively with any woman who strays among them.[12]

But M11 finally reestablishes the conjunction of the father and the son, after the latter has been separated from his mother. It is in this sense that one should interpret the role of the fathers as food providers in the ritual: they bring chickens to their sons, who are unable to eat vegetables, these being symbolic of female cooking. The reconciliation of fathers and sons, the liquidation of the Oedipus complex, is thus accomplished through a separation of the sexes. This is accompanied by generalized teaching on myth, technology, and social organization.

The chastised incestuous sons, thrown out of the village, leave in search of the original lost father, that is to say of their own identity. They discover it in labor. The figure of Woot as the teacher of technology dominates the initiatory scene. He is present in the tunnel of death and resurrection in the guise of an ironsmith who forges the new life of the novices.[13] Labor in general is given prominence in the sculpted figures hung on a nut palm planted in front of the central peak of the initiatory wall. Vansina says that the sculptures portray the following scene:[14] a parrot eats the fruits of the nut palm, while a trapped monkey tries to steal them; a man climbs on this tree to cut (gather) the nuts. His esoteric motto is "the courage of the cutter" because he defies the parrot, a dangerous bird whose feather symbolizes war, fear, and the royal power. The teachers explain to the novices that the nut cutter sums up all the material techniques invented by Woot. Labor is thus made to appear as virile, courageous, and necessary.

Let us recall M12: Woot leaves two corpses on his path to discourage pursuit, those of an idle man and a sorcerer. When the novices find these two corpses (as their wandering ancestors had done long ago) they are reminded of "the evil of black magic and the stupidity of idleness."[15] Vansina states that a legend, the text of which is unfortunately lacking, tells how seven men lost immortality because they were asleep at a crucial time.[16] Idleness is therefore punishable by death, like criminal sorcery. The one and the other compromise the work inaugurated by Woot. The corpse of the idle man he left behind him suggests that the Kuba see themselves as condemned to the untiring pursuit of a cultural project that is continually compromised and always unachieved. However, by a curious paradox, representation of heroic labor ("the cutter's courage"), like the converse image of idleness, is associated with mortal danger. A strange myth, which evidently belongs to the Woot cycle, teaches us that the instruments of labor are also the occasion of death.

M14, Kuba: The Nine Sons of Woot and the Origin of Death (Vansina[17])

The two youngest sons of Woot, Woot a shodik and Woot a pia, quarreled. The first had invented all pointed things (needles, thorns, boats, etc.). The second sharpened the iron objects produced by a third brother, Woot a Mboom anon. Woot a shodik wounded Woot a pia with an iron sword. He thereby introduced death and evil among men.

This short, enigmatic narrative plays on the formal properties of objects. The weapon used in the primordial murder* is a common creation of the three brothers, the conjunction of a universal form, comparable to the Platonic Idea, and an unformed substance (iron). The former belongs to the very essence of nature, the latter is the product of praxis. Woot a shodik, the creator of all pointed forms, is opposed to Woot a Mboom anon, the ironsmith, and to Woot a pia, the sharpener of tools. The first works at the level of universals, the other two collaborate in an enterprise of a technological order. Death results from this antagonism, as if the power of nature turns against the craftsman the weapon he has sharpened according to a model provided by Nature herself. Here we come across one of the major philosophic themes of Amerindian mythology, as decoded by Lévi-Strauss: death is the price of the transition from nature to culture. This narrative is the only myth to concern itself with this problem in a cycle of which the center of gravity is located elsewhere, in the following question: How do we explain the loss of a cultural Golden Age, the disappearance of the civilizing culture hero, and the irruption of incest in an ordered society?

In M14, the six other sons of Woot, all being engaged in creating the diversity of the landscape, seem little inclined to pursue their father's cultural labors. Three heroes out of nine are thus distinguished from the others. The total (a sacred number for the Kuba) is therefore simply the square of this trio.

The ironsmith grandly transforms raw matter, while the sharpener of tools introduces a universal dimension (the category of pointed things) into the authentically cultural creation of the first. The sharp-

*Vansina's 1955 account of the myth, on which de Heusch relies, does not explicitly say that Woot a pia's wound was mortal. More recently, however, Vansina has written of this myth that "Death came to the world when a quarrel between the last two Woots led to the demise of one of them by the use of a sharpened point." (Vansina, J., *The Children of Woot: A History of the Kuba Peoples*, 1978, University of Wisconsin Press, p.31.) (R.W.)

ener is in a mediating and dialectical position between nature (Woot a shodik) and culture (Woot a Mboom anon). But this mediating figure is vulnerable, exposed to death. In this philosophic perspective, Death has made his lodging in the place of labor, in the mythical workshop where nature and culture are tragically joined to define human destiny.

This interpretation takes us back to the very heart of the initiation ritual. For it is precisely beneath the sign of pointed things that the dangers inherent in human labor are therein presented. The cutter of palm nuts is threatened by the parrot's pointed beak.[18] Nature looms menacingly over man as producer. But the very tools of human praxis reflect this peril that derives from Woot a shodik, the murderous inventor of pointed forms. The superior order of craftsmanship inaugurated by the sons of Woot (if not by Woot himself) condemns man to limitation and death. On the initiatory path taken by the novices in their quest for the lost culture hero, the corpse of an idle man reminds them that the iron law of labor, the sole escape from the labyrinth of incest, sums up the human condition.

We can now better understand why the novices, banished by Woot's will from society, equip themselves symbolically with the pointed instrument of the weaver (the baton of the loom, represented by a long root called *ngoontsh*) as they leave the village, dancing the dance of the dead. The weaver's baton bears the same name as the plant;[19] the vegetable domain and the cultural domain thus find a common linguistic denominator among this class of pointed forms evoked by M14. The weaver's baton is a sacred object; it is forbidden to strike anyone with it. If it is the metonymic sign of weaving, that is to say of culture, it also probably has a phallic sense (which relates to nature), because the Kuba instructors teach that the baton-root is "a weapon intended to strike any women who dare to come near the novices."[20] This saying becomes clearer on recalling that the young men are authorized to fornicate with any woman found near their retreat. The weaver's baton is therefore, by its form and function, a privileged locus of articulation between nature and culture, at once symbolizing labor, love, and death. Accordingly, it is symbolically evoked—in the form of the *ngoontsh* root—at the moment when the novices, dead to their old ways, leave the village as ghosts to seek the trail of the long-lost culture hero: they are held to be about to make a long and perilous journey through the territory of hostile tribes.[21] This imaginary odyssey recalls the migrations of the Kuba who went eastward in search of Woot.[22] This mystical quest goes deeply into the ultimate meaning of civilization as the place where exogamy and labor are joined in opposition to drunkenness, incest, and idleness.

Death is the irreducible contradiction. It erupts among Woot's sons as the violent return of nature within culture, at the critical point where the craftsman imposes a definite form on matter. But it is also the punishment with which Woot, the culture hero, threatens the idle. It is easier now to understand why the monkey, a natural caricature of man, who in M12 (iv) tries to steal palm wine instead of working like men to obtain it, is caught in a trap set by the valiant cutter of palm nuts. One also understands why the novices make themselves new clothes from the fibers of a wild palm growing in the forest, near a stream:[23] they are purely and simply reinventing craftsmanship, the major expression of culture.

The parrot is an overdetermined sign. It opposes the naturally pointed form of its beak to the sharp weapon of the cutter of nuts. It is therefore one of the two terms of the fundamental nature/culture opposition. But it also explicitly symbolizes war, and in virtue of this meaning it also symbolizes, within culture, the opposition between labor and war. Lastly, the threatening parrot forces the laborer to pursue his task untiringly because it also represents, according to Vansina, royal power.

parrot	*cutter of palm nuts*
nature	culture
war	labor
king	subject

Other animal figures decorate the initiatory wall. A sculpted guinea fowl appears on the left side of the central peak. This representation corresponds to another found on the right side of the same peak, the Janus mask *Kaloongkaloong*. According to Vansina, this mask stands for the separation of village and bush.[24] The relation between the two figures is at once apparent. Kaloongkaloong, like Woot himself, is mediator between two worlds perceived as opposed and complementary: the guinea fowl, called "the chicken of the bush," is the explicit metaphoric representation of the condition of the novices, while its domestic homologue (the chicken) symbolizes village life.[25] Separated from social life as guinea fowl are from poultry, the young men are "the children of the forest spirits." The Kaloongkaloong mask expresses the same dualism while letting it be known that the initiatory wall is the locus of relation between bush and village. The symbolic figures adorning it relate partly to sexuality and partly to labor, confirming our earlier thesis that labor and exogamy constitute the two distinct levels of articulation between nature and culture.[26]

The language of feathers also has a political meaning. The guinea fowl expresses the internal dualism of the village, while the chicken expresses its unity. The feathers of the wild bird are worn by the chiefs of the left and right moieties,[27]* whereas the chicken's feather is a symbol of royalty.[28] In this perspective, the king, heir of the primordial culture hero, guarantees the ultimate unity of a society which has deliberately introduced a structural division between left and right into each village, to prevent the anarchic emergence of uncontrollable factions.[29]

The Initiatory Wall and the Universe

The birds draw us swiftly toward the world of myth. Describing the initiatory wall, Vansina reports two wooden figures representing a male and a female francolin.[30] These fowl of the pheasant family are "like the partridge but larger, with a longer beak and a wider wingspan" (Robert's Dictionary). The Kuba describe the francolin as a "chicken of the bush," just as they describe the guinea fowl, which is also a member of the pheasant family. The figures of the two francolins are found on a tree planted before the left peak of the initiatory wall: the male is caught in a trap, while the female flaps its wings nearby. The male, according to the Kuba instructors, expresses the condition of the novices undergoing the initiation ordeals in the bush; the female connotes the young women of the village, who are prevented from

*Every Kuba village is divided into two halves or moieties, one called *kombeen* and the other *kongweemy*. The moieties are associated respectively with right and left. Cf. Vansina, J., *The Children of Woot: A History of the Kuba Peoples*, University of Wisconsin Press, 1978, p.323. (R.W.)

approaching them. This superficial interpretation is enriched by a cosmogonic dimension since Vansina's informants add that the cock calls the sun while the francolin calls the moon.[31] The myth (M10) directly associates the cry of the cock with the sun, but it does not give him any nocturnal equivalent among the fowls. The ritual allows us to complete the symbolic system. The francolin relates not only to the night, but also to the primordial waters. The francolin's motto, "francolin of the rain of the water-god," is "like the praise-song of the origin of the world and the primal cataclysm."[32] The cock and the francolin therefore form a pair of oppositions which has other concordances:

cock	*francolin*
Woot	sons of Woot (novices)
village	bush
day	night
?	rain

If the system is coherent (which so far it has appeared to be), then one is entitled to guess that Woot and the cock are associated with the dry season as they are with the sun. The myth says so implicitly: if the millet rots when the angry Woot leaves his people (M12) it means that the wet season succeeds to the dry. The first messenger that Mweel sends to her brother is the tempest, whose appeal is rejected by Woot (M10).

The astronomical code is thus duplicated. The departure of Woot toward the east alternately brings on the wet season and the night. Let us consider the first alternative more deeply. Deceived by one of his sons who substitutes himself for the designated heir, Woot departs in a burning anger in a double sense (he sets fire to the village). M12 thus marks the culminating point of the dry season, before the rains begin (suggested by the subsequent rotting of the millet). For the Kuba, the very concept of time is rendered by the word for the sun.[33] This seasonal dialectic is projected in space since Woot is associated with upstream (and with east), Mweel with downstream (and west). Woot is at once the daylight and the burning sun of the dry season. The cock, a solar creature, in opposition to the francolin, a creature of night and rain, therefore symbolizes royalty; it is understandable that the myth makes a chicken basket the mystical container of a power that comes into operation just before dawn (M12).

Let us return to the singular "chicken hunt" that precedes the reintegration of the novices into the village. The domestic bird, impersonated by one of the novices, is here treated like a game animal, as is its wild homologue, the francolin, represented on the initiatory wall as caught in a trap. The novices, chickens of the bush, are in the process of passing into the category of chickens of the village; this change is effected in an intermediate zone between bush and village (they go round the village in the course of the chase). This is the explanation of the aberrant treatment inflicted on a domestic animal, as object of an imaginary hunt. The hunt expresses the ambiguous, unclassified situation of the novices, who have ceased being comparable to francolins as denizens of the bush without for all that becoming chickens—thoroughgoing villagers. Vansina sees clearly that the chicken connotes the village. He adds this valuable commentary: the pursuit and capture of the "chicken" symbolizes, for the initiates, at once the search for knowledge and the warmth of the sun; the forest is *cold* whereas the village is *warm*. These values are specifically masculine: "women do not eat poultry and the youngsters eat it only when they have acquired wisdom."[34] It is now apparent that the novices succeed in a multidimensional solar quest that associates the dry season, culture, knowledge, and manhood. On the cosmogonic level we suspect (and will establish in due course) that the serpent that opposes the final advance of the novices toward the village connotes humidity and the wet season.

The ritual throws new light on the latent cosmological code of the myth. By abandoning his people so as to punish them, Woot brings unending night upon them, according to M10 and M12. But we have already observed that a variant narrative, M12 (iii), has no mention of this eclipse. Taking account of the code just revealed, we can see that this event is mythically registered sometimes in its real form and sometimes in the metaphorical form of the chickens' death in the primordial village. When in M12 (iii) Woot offers poultry to his successor's emissaries in the same way that he restores the solar cock to Mweel's messenger in M10, he brings the eclipse to an end. In the same variant, the demiurge removes the terrible magical charm that causes the millet to rot (prolonging the wet season).

We can now therefore bring up to date the code set out earlier:

village	bush
Woot	children of Woot
chicken	francolin
sun (day)	moon (night)
dry season	wet season
heat	cold

The francolin sends us directly to the cycle of origin myths because this animal is associated with "the rain of the water-god" and the most ancient beliefs of the Kuba tell of an aquatic god (Ngaan) who is opposed to Mboom, the celestial god. The first is maleficent, the second beneficent. Each has created part of the world.[35] This cosmogonic cycle, unfortunately less richly represented in the ethnographic literature, is joined to the Woot cycle because a proverb says "Mboom in the sky, Ngaan in the water, Mweel downstream, Woot upstream."[36] We will now seek these correspondences through the examination of three new myths. Regrettably, we have only a very schematic rendering of the central cosmogonic myth, due to Vansina (M15) and two weaker versions (Denolf, Torday).

M15, Kuba: The Quarrel of Mboom and Ngaan (Vansina[37])

> "The myth tells how Ngaan and Mboom quarrel over a woman and after that Ngaan retires to the water (while) Mboom goes up to the sky. To avenge himself on Mboom, Ngaan invents evil and the pestilential animals. Nowadays no one believes in Ngaan anymore. All that remains of his cult among the people is an irrational veneration for serpents, tortoises, crocodiles, and other terrestrial beasts who were his particular animals."

In another work, Vansina presents a variant that transforms Ngaan into a son of Mboom. He produces eighteen children, all called "the bad children of Ngaan." Most of them are terrestrial animals (serpent, tortoise) or amphibians (crocodile, hippopotamus), but three men are also mentioned. "At first sight," observes Vansina, "it is not obvious why these creatures are called 'bad children.'"[38]

If we credit the motto cited by Vansina ("francolin of the rain of the water-god"), Ngaan, master of terrestrial water, also ruled celestial water. If the elliptical text of M15 portrays a truly dualistic division of the world, Mboom, associated with the sky, must also be associated with sun and fire. We thus obtain the following formula, which we shall provisionally adopt:

Mboom	*Ngaan*
sky	earth
sun and fire	terrestrial and celestial waters

But Torday's version of the creation of the world (M16) introduces a substitute for Ngaan, the master of rain: the Lightning.

M16, Kuba: Origin of the World (Torday[39])

Mboom (Mbumba), an enormous white personage, reigned over a world covered by water and plunged in darkness. One day he suffered from painful cramps and vomited the sun, the moon, and the stars. Under the action of the sun, the waters began to evaporate. Mboom began to vomit again. He then brought up nine animals: the leopard, the crested eagle, the crocodile, the small fish called *yo* (minnow), the tortoise, the lightning (a black animal, like the leopard), the egret (a species of white heron), the scarab beetle, and the goat. He then vomited a great number of men, of whom only one, Loko Yima, was white. The egret in its turn vomited up all the birds, except the kite; the crocodile vomited all the serpents and the iguana; *yo* vomited all the fish; the scarab beetle vomited all the insects; and the goat vomited all the horned beasts. The serpents then vomited the grasshoppers, and the iguana all the animals without horns (presumably quadrupeds). One of the sons of Mboom, Nyonye Ngana, vomited the white ants; he exerted himself so much in doing so that he died. In gratitude, the white ants buried their human begetter under some black compost which they dug up from the bowels of the earth and with which they covered the sterile sand banks. Another son of Mboom vomited a plant which produced all the vegetation. A third son succeeded only in vomiting the kite. The lightning-animal caused much damage on earth and Mboom drove him up to the sky. But men had no fire, so Mboom allowed the lightning to return to earth every now and again. Although suffering some damage to their property, men were able to get fire from trees struck by the lightning, among the first of which was the raffia palm (which provided tinder).

This lesson in phylogenesis produces a coherent taxonomy (however arbitrary from a scientific viewpoint) out of the primal darkness and waters. The sun appears and life springs up. Drought is the necessary condition of creation. Thus we discover that the regressive phase of the Woot cycle is the other side of the coin of this creator-inspired cosmogony. Woot, who like Mboom is master of the sun, in going away condemns the world anew to darkness and primordial humidity. Recall M12: at the moment when Woot leaves his people, not only does the sun rise no more but also the rivers overflow. M10 said the same thing in other terms, and in a minor key: Mweel sends the tempest in search of Woot. Darkness and humidity go together like daylight and dryness. We have already seen that the Woot myth encodes a double alternation, of long and short rhythms: of day and night, and of dry and wet seasons. The disjunction of Mweel and Woot threatens the one and the other and causes regression of the whole universe to the zero point of its natural history.

Vansina recognizes the connection between the ritual and the cosmogony evoked in M16: the spring where the polluted novices cleanse themselves symbolizes the primordial ocean.[40] In fact, there is a complete parallelism between the myth of world-creation and the cultural cycle of Woot. Just as God created nine fundamental animals, Woot begot nine children. From their creation, the animals are classified according to a phylogenetic order which clearly distinguishes one species from another. In contrast, humanity is just a teeming mass from which a lone individual emerges, white like the Creator himself. It is Woot's task to organize this mass by introducing cultural and linguistic discontinuity. Mboom had already brought into the confused human universe a primary order based on zoological diversity. M16 goes further. When the Creation was finished, God went round all the villages of men and told them: "Look at these wonderful things I have made. They all belong to you, but I forbid you to eat of such-and-such. All the rest, however, is yours to enjoy."[41] Thus the Creator set up the principle of clan division and totemic prohibition. In the course of the first (progressive) phase of his work, Woot refined God's pioneering cultural venture by establishing individual denominations;[42] during the second phase (made ambiguous by incestuous regression), he went on to a complementary demarcation of individual tribes, which thenceforth possessed distinct names and identities.

The resulting social organization can be represented by a triangle with Mboom at its apex because of his prior creation of animals:

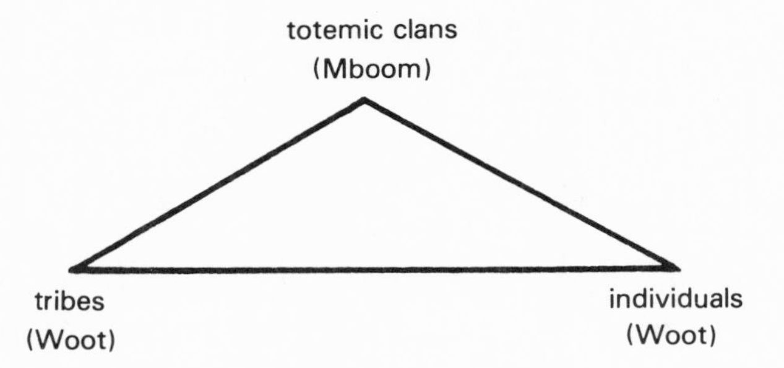

But the cosmogonic code of M16 considerably complicates the dualistic simplicity of M15. In the monotheistic perspective of M16, Mboom, as sole Creator, is equally above and below. However, the active principle of his creative work (the sun drying up the primal waters) remains located in the sky, to which Mboom returns after completing his labors on earth.[43] The waters and darkness in all probability represent the somber face of the aquatic Ngaan. Mboom brings forth from his body the sun and the night-brightening stars at the cost of a painful effort (which already sets a value on labor); he thereby inaugurates drought, permitting living beings to take possession of solid earth. But his work is imperiled by the lightning, which participates in both fire (of which men make use) and water (since lightning accompanies the rain). Mboom agrees to a compromise (the lightning can return to earth from time to time) which clearly represents the alternation of dry and wet seasons. For a primary dualism (archaic, according to Vansina) which opposes the sky (and fire) to the earth (and water) there succeeds a weakened opposition, but this time of a dialectical character. Mboom, the sole Creator, reigns at once over the earth (humid at first) and in a sky illuminated by the drought-bringing sun.

The first stage of creation consists in separating the dry from the wet through the action of the sun upon the earth. But the sky cannot remain entirely—or perpetually—dry without the total disappearance of humidity from the earth. The opposition of sky and earth, of sun and water, is surmounted by the mediating action of lightning, which brings down rain from above (not spelled out in the myth, but evidently entailed) and natural fire, the first source of domestic fire. In this monist vision, the initial, static opposition of high and low is made dialectical at the same time that the distance between the terms is lessened. It is not the blue firmament, the abode of the sun, but the nearer, airy sky that is periodically joined to the earth through the action of Lightning. This mysterious black creature, resembling a leopard, thenceforward participates in Mboom (sky and fire) and in Ngaan (earth and water). This dialectic makes men subject to the alternation of the seasons, just as the first part of the myth had delivered the world to the succession of day and night.

Even if, as Vansina believes, the concept of God has undergone an evolution from dualism to monotheism, this historical process does not abolish the structural character of the mythical universe. One can say only that in M16 the code of the seasons prevails over the geographic code peculiar to M15, the code that even today survives in condensed form in the saying "Mboom in the sky, Ngaan in the water, Mweel downstream, Woot upstream." The cycles of Mboom and Woot evidently come together on the cosmogonic level. On the temporal axis the spatial separation of Mweel and Woot, mediated by the return of the cock, symbolizes the alternation of day and night just as the separation of Mboom and Ngaan, mediated by the lightning-animal, symbolizes the alternation of the seasons. On the spatial axis, finally, the position of Woot (upstream) in relation to that of Mweel (downstream) reproduces in a weakened form the cosmogonic opposition of above (Mboom) and below (Ngaan).

In the same way, when the succession dispute breaks out among Woot's descendants (M13), the heir has to appeal implicitly to both Mboom and Ngaan. The hammer he throws into the lake relates to the former, for did not Mboom reveal the secret of metallurgy to Woot in a dream?[44] In contrast, the crocodile that emerges from the water and which the winner uses like a canoe is a creature of the aquatic Ngaan according to M15 (and the ancestor of all the reptiles according to M16). The apparent miracle which qualifies the crafty Mboong as winner of this fraudulent contest consists in the fact that the royal hammer, which bears the mark of the forge's fire, does not sink into the water of Ngaan. The wooden crocodile which adorns the initiatory wall therefore relates as much to the ultimate phase of mythical history as to the origin of the world.

It is not surprising that the Kuba king can cause the rain to fall, just as he can burn the earth if he comes into contact with it;[45] in the one case he represents Ngaan, in the other Mboom. He is "God on earth," as his title indicates.[46]

This mythology impregnated with the primal waters (of which both terrestrial and celestial aspects were under the jurisdiction of Ngaan in the archaic Kuba religion) curiously divides the domain of fire between several autonomous provinces: fire was first the sun, then lightning, then domestic fire. The fire of lightning is the original source of terrestrial fire according to M16. But this "natural" domestic fire is no longer used by men. For M17 tells us that Mboom revealed to a man called Kerikeri the secret of his "cultural" invention, so that men were thenceforth able to dispense with the lightning's ambiguous services.

M17, Kuba: Origin of Making Fire (Torday[47])

Mboom (Bumba) appeared in a dream to a man called Kerikeri and taught him the art of making fire by friction. Kerikeri kept the secret to himself. When all fires became accidentally extinguished, he sold flames at a very high price. The king had a beautiful daughter called Katenge. He promised her a seat on the council like a man if she succeeded in discovering Kerikeri's secret.* Kerikeri, to whom Katenge started to make advances, fell helplessly in love with her. One evening she went to him, after ordering the villagers to put out their domestic fires. The night was very dark. Katenge shivered and ordered Kerikeri to look for fire among the neighbors. The man returned with empty hands. In vain he implored Katenge to submit to his desire; she insisted that first he must make fire. Finally he agreed. He produced a flame by rubbing two sticks together. Katenge thereupon burst out laughing; she fled from the hut and made Kerikeri's secret public. Before this time, people had to rely on the lightning to reignite their fires if they went out.

*The *Katenge* (or *Katyeeng*) was, according to Torday, the name of a titled office in the highest Kuba state council, reserved for a daughter of a former king. The Katenge "wears on her waist a belt similar to that of the Nyibita ('minister for war') and in time of peace she has a bowstring wound round her neck. If war is declared, she hands this bowstring solemnly to the Nyibita; thus the decision, if there shall be an armed conflict, rests with this woman." (Torday, E., *On the Trail of the Bushongo*, 1925, Philadelphia, J. B. Lippincott: pp.122–123). The fire origin story is therefore, among other things, a "mythical charter" (Malinowski) for the *Katenge* office. (R.W.)

This curious "accident" which periodically extinguishes all the village fires evidently conceals an element of the cosmogonic code, the tempest. From this point of view, the situation evoked in the myth is the converse of the great fire (of the dry season) which ravages the primordial village on the day Woot avenges himself against the disapproving populace (M12). The two narratives may also be compared in regard to technological discoveries: one woman discovers the secret of making fire, another that of making salt. The latter operation is connected to the former, since salt comes from the ashes of aquatic plants. Furthermore, the first experience of salt is "burning": it is applied to a wound before it is tasted (M12). Fire and salt relate to cooking and conjugal life. This sexual connotation is indicated in a negative form in M17: making off with the secret of fire, Katenge also denies herself to Kerikeri, whom she has truly "inflamed."

Beneath the anecdote, which is taken with "a pinch of salt," a cultural and cosmogonic drama is played out. It seems as though the multiplication of domestic fires, cultural in origin, diminishes the intemperate power of tempest and lightning. Katenge's trick is an operation of advanced cosmic magic. It is no surprise to find this operation entrusted to the daughter of the solar king, because it makes the dry season return. Domestic fire fulfills a mediating function between the seasons, like the lightning for which it is the cultural substitute. But there is a lack of continuity between natural fire, the product of lightning, and the cultural fire of M17: the latter is given to Kerikeri by Mboom in person. Twice over, Mboom's work may be called "warming." At the beginning of time he first creates the sun, which dries up a part of the dark primordial waters; later, at the beginning of human history, he reveals the secret of fire. The sun and cultural fire (both issued from Mboom) are thus joined by secret cosmogonic affinities; the first is opposed to terrestrial waters (M16), the second to celestial water (M17); they are situated at the two extremities of a discontinuous series in which they appear as joint enemies of the wet season.

solar fire	lightning	domestic fire
(Mboom and Woot)		(Mboom)

Notice that the first cosmic mediation of lightning has left cultural traces in the making of fire: men formerly obtained fire from trees struck by lightning; the first of these was the raffia palm, which provided tinder (M16). The extremely rich symbolism of the raffia palm, veritable mediator between nature and culture, will be examined in a subsequent chapter. Let it suffice to note here that the raffia palm, which is associated equally with natural and with cultural fire, came out of a dried-up lake.[48]

Let us momentarily leave the theme of cosmic harmony and reconsider fire and cooking salt from a conjugal perspective. Salt, which we have just seen to be analogous to fire, is directly associated with a drama of adultery in a brief tale which would have little merit did it not once again link the technological discovery to a love relationship.

M18, Kuba: How the Preparation of Salt Was Discovered (Torday[49])

> Formerly, the Kuba used the ashes (of certain plants) to season their meals. A wife had just added this condiment to the water in which she was preparing to cook certain foods when she learned that her husband was paying court to another woman in the gardens. She ran out and began to pour abuse on her rival. The row went on a long time, so much so that when the wife returned home, she found the cooking water evaporated: there remained only a mass of grey crystals at the bottom of the pot. It was in this way that people found out how to make salt in its crystalline form.

The preparation of salt, which calls for excessive *cooking*, corresponds to a domestic crisis while M12 associates the discovery of saline plants with a catastrophic *fire*. Furthermore, salt is the symbol of cooking and of the conjugal union, as indicated by the final rites of initiation. The young men obtain salt in a distant village (formerly they took one or two months to make it themselves). They go on to perform a decisive rite of reintegration: the salt dance. The dance obviously marks the reintroduction of the initiates into the feminine world, wherein they thenceforward appear as adult men, infantile fixations (of an incestuous kind) having been destroyed by symbolic death. Salt, symbol of cooking, is the mediating term between the man (who has just made it) and the woman (who mythically discovers it and practically uses it).

Fire appears finally in an ambiguous form right at the end of the ritual. Two last ordeals await the novices before they can return home. The first suggests an unexpected twist, negating what has just been enacted under the sign of salt: trapped in a hunting net, the hunters (masculine food providers) are changed into game; the rat they go on to eat is an animal unfit for consumption, belonging to the category of disgusting things, *nyetsh*.[50] It seems, then, that in spite of the salt dance the new initiates are not yet ready to enter the culinary world in the dual capacity of masculine producers (hunters) and consumers. By eating rat they clearly situate themselves outside civilization. This interpretation is not incompatible with the somewhat abbreviated explanation offered by Vansina's Kuba teachers: "The novices eat a *nyetsh* thing to show they have reached such a state of purity that they cannot be polluted by a repugnant act."[51]

The terms of the culinary code distributed through the ritual form an easily reconstitutable symbolic structure:

excrement	chicken, salt	rat
(nonculinary)	(culinary)	(nonculinary)

Excrement, which appears at the beginning of the ritual, in the regressive phase, and the rat, which appears at the end (just before the definitive reintegration), occupy symmetrical and converse positions, respectively beyond and below cooking: they both belong to the category of impure and disgusting things (*nyetsh*).

Note also that reintegration into the female-ruled culinary world takes place in the course of a dance that the ungainly antelope (object and not subject of cooking) tries to imitate and which a serpent, driven off by the elders, tries to disrupt. The serpent, an earth creature, is like the aquatic animals in being a "bad" creature of the water-god Ngaan.[52] Furthermore, cooking fire is associated with Mboom, god of the sky and creator of the sun (M16 and M17). The struggle of the serpent and the elders restores the old dualist cosmogony in theatrical form: when Ngaan's animal tries to exclude the new initiates from the culinary world (which is also that of exogamy), the Kuba, who formerly called themselves "people of the sun,"[53] reenact the battle of sky and earth, of fire and water. The novices, "people of the tunnel,"[54] finally emerge from the cold, damp, terrestrial world of Ngaan to take on the warmth of life and the light of knowledge. But the old initiates, who have just removed the malign serpent from the initiates' path as these latter were dancing the salt dance (so facilitating their access to the village), have yet to give them fire.

Ambiguities of Cooking Fire

The elders and the novices find themselves confronting each other like enemies on either side of the initiatory wall, the former on the village side, the latter on the side of the bush. The elders throw over the fence a flaming torch, which the novices receive in silence. They next throw an extinguished torch, which causes shouts of joy. That same day the bush camp is burned down. This burning marks the end of the initiation. Vansina interprets this final episode in sociological terms: the burning brand is a declaration of war, the extinguished one signifies peace. Formerly, when a rebel village sought an armistice it sent a charred piece of wood to the royal court.[55] Nevertheless, there is once more good reason to relate the ritual to the myth. We know that lightning is the origin of natural fire, the first form of domestic fire. We suspect that a cosmogonic image is concealed behind the dialectic of war and peace. The acoustic code at once attracts attention: the novices receive in silence the flaming torch, which falls literally from the sky. If this fire is really an evocation of lightning (which we cannot be sure of), it would refer on one hand to the dangerous but necessary mediation of sky and earth (realized by atmospheric fire during the wet season), and on the other to the first phase of civilization, when man depended on conflagrations caused by lightning to obtain fire (M17). One can scarcely avoid reference here to the great lesson of Amerindian culinary mythology ("the acquisition of cooking fire demands a reserved attitude to noise"[56]) and then be astonished at finding this code reversed among the Kuba: natural fire (lightning) is received silently, even coldly, whereas its disappearance, heralding return to hearth and home, is greeted with joyous outcries. The opposition and complementarity of lightning (associated with the wet season) and cooking fire (associated with the dry season) are among the most original aspects of Kuba cosmology. In it the relations of fire and noise are peculiarly complicated. Let us consider them throughout the ritual.

In the course of their preliminary retreat in the provisional hut built in the center of the village, the novices, deprived of fire and light, must refrain from speaking loudly. Later, the return of fire (transmitted by the elders over the initiatory wall) obliges them once more to remain silent. There is nevertheless an apparent distinction between speaking softly and staying mute. The first attitude of reserve is necessary during the absence of fire in its cultural form (fire produced in the village), while the second would relate, if our hypothesis is correct, to the presence of fire in its natural and initial form. The series fire-and-noise therefore entails a third term: when an extinguished torch falls from the sky, the novices cry out. The system is therefore constructed in the following way:

absence of cultural fire	presence of natural fire	disappearance of natural fire
speaking softly	muteness	outcries

There is room for a fourth term, which must exist at least in a latent form: normal speech, which would be linked to the presence of cultural fire, to social life.

In this perspective, the "joy" evinced by the novices in the presence of the extinguished torch calls for a new explanation. It salutes the disappearance of lightning and the wet season. But these noisy exclamations are also cries for help, addressed to the sun as master of the dry season and of cultural fire. This dialectic also easily explains the transition from war to peace: the armistice offer from the elders signifies an end to the novices' seclusion in the cold, wet forest.*

This schema takes account of the strong opposition between silence and the outcries in the third column. But how to integrate the weak opposition between soft speech and normal speech suggested in the first column? Here the same dialectic is expressed, but within the confines of the village. Restrained speech is linked here with the aboli-

*Professor Luc de Heusch has asked me to add the following footnote to the text at this point: "Roy Willis me fait judicieusement remarquer que le dignitaire féminin chargé de représenter à la cour l'héroïne Katenge, responsable de l'introduction du feu domestique, est une figure complémentaire du chef de guerre (voir p.129). Cette observation va dans le sens de ma thèse: la ruse de Katenge (M17) qui met fin au règne de la foudre (et de la saison des pluies) signifie aussi le passage de la guerre à la paix. C'est donc bien un feu de foudre éteint que les novices accueillent dans la joie." ("Roy Willis has kindly drawn to my attention that the female office-bearer who represents at the royal court the heroine Katenge, the bringer of domestic fire, is a complementary figure to the war chief (see p.129). This observation is consistent with my argument: Katenge's trick in M17 which puts an end to the reign of Lightning (and to the wet season) also signifies the transition from war to peace. It is therefore most certainly the extinguished fire of lightning that the novices receive with such joy.") (R.W.)

tion of cultural fire and an impoverishment of social relationships (the novices are thenceforth separated from women). This weakening of speech heralds the end of the warm life of the village, homologous with the dry season. It is necessary to speak softly to inaugurate the reign of the fire of lightning (and of the wet season). Conversely, it is necessary to cry aloud to reintroduce symbolically into the world cultural fire and the dry season.

The myth on the origin of cultural fire (M17) lends support to our argument. When one man only possessed the secret of cultural fire, it so happened that tempests put out all the fires in the village. This heroic epoch of cultural fire was therefore one of excessive and particularly violent rain. Evidently nothing of the kind has happened since. It all seems as though, in making public the cultural secret of fire, the princess Katenge also brought to an end the intemperate rule of rain and lightning. Mocking the outwitted miser, she bursts out laughing and hastens to reveal his abused secret to the village. Her *noisy* expression of joy implicitly heralds the transition from the wet to the dry season, as do the ritual cries of the new initiates, triumphant at the end of their long quest for sun and fire.

In throwing the fire of lightning from the village into the cold, wet bush, the elders for the last time refuse the new initiates possession of cultural fire, as formerly the miserly Kerikeri had done. Thereafter abolishing the reign of this savage fire (by throwing an extinguished ember), they make available domestic fire, present in the absence of the other kind: this new fire is the solar fire of Mboom, projected into culture through the grace of Kerikeri's dream. It is not only the substitution of domestic for natural fire that is noisily acclaimed by the novices, it is also the return of daylight. The uproar that terminates initiation puts an end to the perilous eclipse brought on by Woot's departure; from this viewpoint, the ritual cries conjure up the disjunction of earth and sky; in this respect they fulfill the same cosmogonic function as the charivari* in other civilizations.[57]

But the ritual cries take us back again to another symbolic level, that of sexual relationships. Recall that at the beginning of initiation the elders *noisily* drive the novices toward the ditch of excrement as a sign of protest against the incestuous situation of these latter, a

***Charivari*, a cacophonous "serenade" made by beating pots, pans, and trays and used to express popular derision of incongruous marriages, or the like, in some West European countries and especially in rural France. Also, chiefly in the United States, "shivaree." (R.W.)

situation resembling that of the hero of M11, who secretly drank palm wine with his mother in defiance of his father. In the first place, then, the cries denounce unacceptable sexual conjunctions. Or more exactly, as Lévi-Strauss emphasizes in a general comment on the symbolic value of the charivari, they are opposed to the "disjunction, through a reprehensible union, of partners virtually intended one for another by their position within an established network of alliances."[58] One notices at once that a relation exists between this aspect of ritual noise and its cosmogonic function: it is after Woot's incest that the sun becomes separated from the earth. In both cases, it is cries that reestablish normal matrimonial and cosmogonic conjunctions which are indispensable to social and universal order, as Lévi-Strauss has made clear for the Amerindians. The parallel goes yet further, because—as in America—ritual noise (in the form of the charivari) removes the danger of a "world gone rotten" (too wet) which would result from the definitive disjunction of the sun and the earth.

But the diachronic duplication of cooking fire sets up a novel situation by comparison with the Amerindian symbolic systems:[59] if our hypothesis is correct, silence is obligatory on the evocation of lightning, that dangerous mediator between sky and earth and source of wild fire. In contrast, the ritual introduction of cultural fire (the sun) at the end of a long ritual night calls for outcry.

The composition of the Kuba and Luba codes reveals two neighboring types of opposition between silence and noise. The reader will remember that a hero associated with rain and lightning, Mbidi Kiluwe, introduced the Luba to culturally superior customs relating to fire, with cooking attended by silence and numerous prohibitions. The same people employ the charivari to drive away a drought-bringing monster, the rainbow, which is the enemy of rain.

Kuba:	RITUAL SILENCE nondomesticated fire of lightning	RITUAL CRIES cultural solar fire
	wet season	dry season

Luba:	SILENCE culturally superior fire brought by lightning-hero	CHARIVARI rainbow
	wet season	dry season

If we take the two *mythèmes* together, the opposition between cries and charivari within the category of noise emerges as significant in two respects: ritual cries (Kuba) bring about the conjunction of sun and earth and inaugurate a beneficial dry season, while the charivari (Luba) separates sky and earth and puts an end to a maleficent dry season. In contrast, silence serves the same purpose in both cases: whether associated with a dangerous, precultural cooking fire (Kuba) or a supercultural royal fire (Luba), it guarantees a moist mediation between sky and earth.

In passing from the Kuba to the Luba, that is from a positive solar mythology to a negative mythology of the rainbow, a number of thematic inversions appear:

Kuba mythology	*Luba mythology*
Dry season valued	Dry season devalued
Incestuous and drunken culture hero (Woot)	First king drunken and incestuous (Nkongolo)
He goes east to exile	He is murdered in the west
Loss of primordial cultural unity	Establishment of political unity
Installation of matrilineality	Restoration of patrilineality

In the first case, the hero's incest is the cause of a decisive cultural change; in the second, it marks a prior stage of civilization. Despite these divergencies, however, the question remains in both cases of, on the one hand, the advent of exogamy and, on the other, the separation of sky and earth and the alternation of the seasons. Although the Kuba take the part of the sun against the rain, the Luba that of the rain against the rainbow, it becomes increasingly obvious that the two symbolic systems are not independent of one another. We shall soon discover that Lunda mythology plays a truly pivotal role between them.

The Virtues of the Bull-roarer

It remains to examine several complementary aspects of the Kuba acoustic code. M11 presents a father, a noisy ghost, in which one can easily recognize the alternative image of Woot the Leopard,[60] whose threatening growl is ritually conveyed by the friction drum hidden in the tunnel. The instrument designed by the hero of M11 to frighten his incestuous son suggests the bull-roarer,* although the latter does not appear to figure in the Kuba ritual arsenal. However that may be, mythic bull-roarer, friction drum, and leopard's growl are identical. Torday reports a brief legend (M19) which attributes the invention of the friction drum to a king who surprised one of his wives in the act of adultery. He killed the offending man with his sword. When people became anxious about the disappearance of the guilty person, the king contented himself with saying "the village leopard (i.e., the friction drum) has eaten him." Since that time human sacrifices have always been carried out to the sound of this instrument.[61]

M19 is therefore simply a transformation of M11. The second myth puts an end to an adulterous situation, the first to a quasi-incestuous one (an excessive conjunction of son and mother). The bull-roarer (or its equivalent, the friction drum) is therefore, as in many other parts of the world, a terrifying instrument associated with death and the disjunction of sexes and generations.

Let us compare its low throbbing with another continuous but this time high-pitched sound: the soft whistle that Woot in person emits in M12 when discreetly summoning his successor. He expects his elder son, but another son appears; the people make no protest against the illegality of the procedure. The soft whistle therefore connotes a legitimate conjunction, notwithstanding Woot's anger. To the light whistle that determines the transfer of power just before dawn is opposed the throbbing of the friction drum in the initiation ritual: the latter is nothing other than Woot's cry as he punishes his disrespectful sons, driving them out of the village and symbolically plunging them into night.

An episode of M10, which we have thus far neglected, should be interpreted in the light of this code. When Mweel sends the woodworm to her incestuous brother in an attempt to bring back daylight to the village, the envoy bores a hole in the rock behind which Woot is sheltering; he finds Woot asleep, but the cry of the leopard awakens him.

**Bull-roarer*, a term used to describe an instrument, usually of wood and with a hole in it, which is made to emit a low-pitched, throbbing noise by rotation at the end of a cord or string. The use of bull-roarers has been reported for many tribal societies, typically in association with initiation ceremonies. (R.W.)

We know that this cry is the equivalent of the bull-roarer's throbbing. It should therefore prove an obstacle to the conjunction of Woot and Mweel. And indeed Woot refuses to return to his sister as the messenger asks him. Nevertheless he agrees to restore the daylight, and he makes available the calls of the birds that herald the dawn. Later we shall discuss the place of the Kuba bull-roarer among the "instruments of darkness"* peculiar to initiations in Central Africa. It suffices for the moment to establish that myth and ritual evoke similar cosmogonic situations. Woot's exile plunges the world into eternal night, emphasized by the growl of the leopard, the friction drum, or the bull-roarer.

Minor Royal Bestiary and More about the Night

According to Vansina, the Kuba royal bestiary includes several "noble" animals reserved for the sovereign. This category comprises one domestic animal, the ram, and several wild animals: the black genet cat (*mbiidy*), the civet cat (*shim*), and the pangolin.[62] The king is alone in possessing several flocks of sheep. The carcasses of all "noble" wild animals have to be given to the king as a gesture of homage.

The translation of the terms *mbiidy* and *shim* as proposed by Vansina presents a problem. So also does the selection of these animals for special status, a matter which Vansina also finds puzzling. The word *shim* is evidently similar to the Luba term *nshimba*, which appears in M10 with the doubtful meaning of "wild cat" (Denolf). Remember that Woot gave a piece of meat wrapped in the skin of an animal of this name to the dog sent by his sister Mweel. Daylight would return if the skin became white, night would continue if it got black. *Shim* or *nshimba* therefore relate to an animal with two characteristics: its mottled coat (light and dark) readily connotes the alternation of day and night, and the species includes a dark variety that

*"Instruments of darkness" (*Les instruments des ténèbres*) is the title and subject matter of the fourth part of Lévi-Strauss's *Du miel aux cendres*. In his discussion of musical instruments peculiar to the period of spiritual "darkness" between the anniversaries of Christ's death and resurrection, Lévi-Strauss draws substantially on the work of Van Gennep (Van Gennep, A., *Manuel de folklore français contemporain*, 1947, Tome I, Vol. III, Paris, Picard: 1209–1215). (R.W.)

connotes the night. It is precisely in these terms that the problem is posed in the myths. When the dog infringes an alimentary prohibition in M10, the skin becomes entirely black, so preventing the sun from rising. M12 (iv) (Achten) takes up the same *mythème* in another context. Woot, having just gone into exile with his following in an easterly direction, goes to sleep in a wood. At cockcrow he makes out the markings on a "wild cat" skin and exclaims: "The day is at hand, let's go!"[63] In other words, the animal called *shim* or *nshimba* has the same significance in the visual code as the cock has in the auditory code.

Let us try to establish its identity. Van Avermaet's dictionary translates the word *nshimba* as "genet cat." This designation is also that of Bouillon, who cites a significant Luba proverb: "The *nshimba* who walks at night, the night which creeps away along its [the animal's] path."[64] This allusion to the nocturnal habits of the genet is congruent with the function of this animal in the Kuba myth. The genet cat (*genetta*, a genus represented by four species in Zaïre) belongs, like the civet cat, to the *viverrinae* subfamily of carnivores. Its body is "decorated with numerous more or less defined patches, on a light background," but there also occur "dark specimens in which the background coloring approaches black and in these cases it is hard to make out any patches and rings [in the coat]."[65] The black genet (which should probably be identified with the term *shim* rather than the term *mbiidy* in Vansina's inventory) is, therefore, as much by its habits as by its coloring, apt to signify night in the Kuba code—or more precisely, the absence of daylight.

Should we therefore permutate Vansina's proposed translations and conversely discover the civet cat behind the term *mbiidy*? Unfortunately, the Luba evidence does not confirm this hypothesis: according to Van Avermaet's dictionary, *m-bidi* designates the serval cat. However, our thesis is supported by a Luba authority, Sendwe, who translates *mbiidy* as black civet.[66] Furthermore, Bouillon renders the term "serval cat" as *nzuji* for the Luba, so casting doubt on Van Avermaet's translation.[67] In translating *mbiidy* as civet cat, we in no way change the bestiary of noble animals established by Vansina, since we find in it both black genet and (black?) civet. These two animals are zoologically very close. The civet (*Civettictis civetta*) is a viverridous* carnivore, larger than the genet, which is represented by the form

*Of or belonging to the civet family, which includes the genet. (R.W.)

congica Cabr. The coat, of a greyish color which sometimes appears as yellow or light green, is dotted with numerous black patches which form more or less regular clusters; completely black individuals occur quite frequently.[68]

Thus the civet and the genet, members of the same subfamily of nocturnal carnivores, equally meet the conditions required by the myth for signifying the alternation of day and night as regulated by Woot; at the same time they include a dark variety suitable for representing the disappearance of the sun. Evidently, the genet and the civet symbolize the king's absolute power over the daylight.

As nocturnal wild animals, the royal genet and civet are opposed to the diurnal and solar ram.

ram	black civet and black genet
village	forest
day	night

In the absence of data, we are unable to account for the solar properties of the ram among the Kuba. Perhaps it is the well-known pugnacity of this domestic animal that makes it apt to signify the ardor, the "burning" character (*paam*) of the sovereign. The ram is united with royalty by a link of natural contiguity: he is of royal blood. For M12 taught us that Woot's niece bore a sheep during the cataclysm which accompanied the hero's departure. This brutal association of the human race and the animal world is a monstrous consequence of incest. Incest is perceived negatively as a regression into nature and positively as the inexhaustible source of fecundity. The ram is the sign that divine kingship articulates itself on to nature and obtains from it the obscure powers that the Kuba themselves compare to sorcery.[69]

This domestic animal, which bears witness to the presence of nature in the very heart of the village, has its symmetric and converse homologue *in the forest*: this is the pangolin. To explain the pangolin's presence in the Kuba royal bestiary it is necessary to refer to the ideology of the Lele, which we have discussed elsewhere. This curious, scaly mammal, which, like human beings, bears a single young, is a mediator between the natural and the cultural realms.[70] One can reasonably assume that the Kuba, whose culture and language are closely related to those of the Lele, share this belief. On this assumption, the pangolin appears as the second term in a system of oppositions that also includes the ram. They are both points of royal articulation between nature and culture. The ram is situated inside culture, the pangolin inside nature. The ram, a domestic animal descended from a woman of royal blood, is a metonymic representation of royalty, while the pangolin, a wild animal with fecundity comparable to that of a woman, is a metaphor of it. Both attest that divine kingship is the institution that overcomes the contradiction between nature and culture: the king, master of the social order, is also identified with a spirit of nature.[71]

The other oppositions forming the symbolic system coexist harmoniously in the person of the sovereign. He participates at once in Ngaan and Mboom because he has the power to cause the rain to fall just as he would burn the earth if he sat on the ground or walked across a field:[72] the heat of the sun and the cool of the rain are joined in this being who is beyond nature and beyond culture. He is comparable with the sun, but also with the moon. "The king and the moon, it is said, have the same powers. . . . In the absence of the moon, the king may not show himself."[73] While the myths we have considered make Woot the master of the sun, one narrative, of which unfortunately we have only a brief summary, tells us he was lost for nine days at the time of the new moon; when he came back, the moon reappeared in the night sky.[74] In this lunar function Woot is no doubt accompanied by Mweel, for even today the sister of the Kuba king possesses magical charms which relate to the moon; while her brother may not leave his hut during the new moon, it is quite acceptable for her to go out provided she covers her head.[75] Life and death are, as it were, suspended during this time, when, it is said, women do not go into labor nor do men die. There could be no better way of saying that human life is one with the movement of the heavenly bodies, which the king and his sister rule absolutely, after the example of Woot and Mweel. And, in this dark night when the king is in peril and time ceases to exist, how is it possible not to think of that zero point in Earth history when sun and moon shine no more in the cold primordial waters destined for annihilation?

The Kuba royal bestiary establishes a new link with the Luba epic. The very name of the celestial hero of M1 gives him at once the qualities of a hunter (Kiluwe) and a black civet (Mbidi). Thereby is explained the pains taken to emphasize the dark color of the stranger-prince and his descendants, in opposition to Nkongolo the Red. Mbidi

Kiluwe is situated entirely on the side of night, whereas Woot, the solar hero, momentarily plunges the world into the shadows of an eclipse, the end of which is heralded by the mottled coat of a kind of civet cat and the cries of the animals of daylight.

[CHAPTER FIVE]

Palm Wine, the Blood of Women, and the Blood of Beasts

The Luba epic (M1) has evident historical connections with the foundation myth of the Lunda empire, the hero of which is, like Mbidi Kiluwe, a wandering hunter who marries a faraway princess. This celebrated narrative, of which we possess several versions, each worthy of consideration, unites in a single story the typically Kuba theme of conflict between father and sons over palm wine and the typically Luba theme of the foundation of a new dynasty with newly codified customs. The semantic relations we have established between the Kuba and Luba mythical cycles, starting from the familial code, are consolidated here under the sign of palm wine, examination of which was deferred from the preceding chapter.

We begin with a version recorded in 1927 by the colonial administrator Duysters at the court of the Lunda sovereign, the *Mwaant Yaav*, whose rule today is confined to an important chiefdom in the west of Katanga in Zaïre. We shall employ the spelling "Mwata Yamvo," which is general in the ethnographic literature, just as we also use the term "Lunda," which ought properly to be written "Aruund."[1]*

M20: Foundation Myth of the Lunda Empire (Duysters[2])

A. *The origins*

Formerly the ancestors of the Lunda (Aruund) lived in peace, scattered in small familial communities. They knew the arts of

*The nuclear Lunda or *Ruund* (also spelled *Aruund*) occupy the districts of Kapanga, Sandoa, Dilolo, and Kolwezi in the southwest of Zaïre's Shaba province. According to Crine-Mavar, their social system is distinguished by bilateral kinship and the absence of clans, and by a state structure headed by the *Mwaant Yaav*. (R.W.)

pottery, mat making, the making of hunting nets, and ironworking. They were ignorant of warfare. The country around them was deserted. The first chief, Mwaku, was succeeded by his son Yala Mwaku. When the latter died, at an advanced age, the Lunda had become very numerous. The chiefly power was passed to one of his sons, Konde. This last had three children: two sons, Chinguli and Chiniama, and a daughter, Lueji. One day, Konde was weaving mats. Beside him he had a pot of cloudy water to moisten the fibers. His sons questioned him impertinently, accusing him of spoiling the palm wine instead of distributing it. "Is water wine?" retorted Konde, angrily.

Thereupon the sons insulted their father, calling him a liar. But Lueji took his part. Konde cursed his sons and their descendants; he disinherited them and announced that his daughter would succeed him. When he came to die, he entrusted the bracelet, symbol of power, to his brother Sakalende, instructing him to transmit it to Lueji. Konde was buried in a riverbed. Sakalende called the important people (*tubungu*) together and they ratified the deceased's decision. Lueji's brothers submitted to her authority.

B. *The strange hunter*

One morning, an important man who went to draw his palm wine found his calabash empty. He followed some footprints and came upon several men busy cutting up an antelope. They spoke a strange tongue. He observed them for a while from a distance, then, as they did not appear savage, decided to approach them. One, who seemed to be the chief, a tall and handsome young man, introduced himself with these words: "I am a hunter called Chibinda Ilunga." He offered the other a piece of meat.

Judging himself recompensed, the man recounted his adventure to a companion, who made contact in his turn with the strangers. Chibinda Ilunga gave him a basket of meat for the princess Lueji. The princess then sent a deputation of three notables who were charged with inviting the hunter to the court. Chibinda agreed to go with them. He offered Lueji the antelope he had just caught. The princess caused beer (or palm wine?[3]) to be brought. But Chibinda refrained from touching it. His followers explained that their chief was prevented by a ritual prohibition from eating or drinking in public. Lueji then had a hut built into which her guest could retire. Impressed by the beauty of the young woman and the respect shown her by her subjects, Chibinda Ilunga rendered homage to her by offering the ritual greeting due to a sovereign. He introduced himself as grandson of the first Luba king, Mbidi Kiluwe. He said he had left his native land near the Lualaba because his brother Ilunga, the reigning king, jealous of Chibinda's hunting prowess, had insulted him by alleging that he never made war. He had left with several families, crossing the Lomami and then the Lubilash, and passing through unoccupied country.

Overcome by his charm, Lueji invited the young man to spend some time with her. He soon married her. At first the stranger-prince and his two brothers-in-law got on very well. When Lueji retired to the ritual hut reserved for women during their menstruation, she took off the bracelet and deposited it in the sacred basket; during her retreat her brothers and her husband addressed the ritual salute to this basket. One day, coming out of the hut, she called the elders together, sat on a leopard-skin, and made a long speech. She recalled the fall from grace of her brothers and expressed displeasure that they refrained from rendering homage to Chibinda Ilunga. She then solemnly handed the chiefly bracelet to her husband. It was thus that power passed to the Luba stranger. The two brothers preferred exile to submission. The new king passed his time hunting and did not think of making war. Men were less numerous, because many Lunda had followed Chinguli and Chiniama in their migration. It was alleged that Lueji was sterile. She gave her husband a second wife, Kamonga, who bore Chibinda's successor, Naweji.

When Chibinda died, at the end of a rather long and peaceful reign, he was buried on the right bank of the river at the very place where he had his first encounter with the notables. Naweji made Lueji his first wife. Kamonga became queen mother (Lukonkesha). Fighting against the Kaniok, who threatened his country, the new king fortified the capital and created the powerful military and political entity of the Lunda empire. He died during a campaign. Lueji had to pay dearly to buy back the royal bracelet from the enemy. She designated a son of Naweji as successor. At his installation, the son expressed his intention of making conquests. Immediately numerous neighboring petty chiefs submitted to him. Lueji died at a very advanced age. The king then designated among the female descendants of Konde a lady who would replace Lueji, with the title of *Swana murunda* (heiress of love).

The king mustered the warriors and considerably extended the empire.

M20: Foundation Myth of the Lunda Empire (variants)

1. *Pogge's version*

Pogge, one of the first explorers of Lunda country at the end of the last century, summarily records the same mythical events while introducing some details not found in the preceding version.[4] The chief Konde, who is here designated by the royal title Yamvo (Yaamv), makes fun of his sons by making them taste the cloudy water that they have taken for palm wine; they quarrel with their father and immediately flee for fear of punishment. The narrative omits the menstruation episode. The epilogue contradicts Duysters's account, claiming that Chibinda Ilunga prosecuted many victorious campaigns.

2. *de Carvalho's version*[5]*

The chief Yala (Iala) had two sons by his first wife Konde (Condi), Chinguli (Quinguri) and Yala (Iala), as well as a daughter, Lueji. The sons were lazy and drunken; they despoiled the people. Under the influence of drink, they one day mistook for palm wine the milky-colored water in which their father was dampening vegetable fibers. They insulted the old man, accusing him of spoiling a drink they were obliged to beg for. They beat him and left him in a pool of blood. Returning from the fields, Lueji took care of her father with the help of his followers; she concealed her anger lest her brothers finish the old man off. But she did tell his close relatives. Yala was dying and the people were gathered at his bedside. He made his last wishes known: he ordered that his daughter succeed him and he authorized her to hand on the sacred bracelet to the man she loved. Lueji found favor with the people because of her wisdom. The elders urged her to choose a husband. But no one succeeded in gaining her heart.

Then the Luba prince Chibinda Ilunga came along. Some female servants of Lueji saw him approaching with his followers at

*For an English translation of de Carvalho's version of this myth see V. W. Turner, "A Lunda Love Story and its Consequences," *Rhodes-Livingstone Journal*, 19 (1955), 1–26. (R.W.)

sunset, while they were bathing. They came out of the water in a hurry and hid themselves to observe the strangers. Chibinda Ilunga, who had noticed them, spoke to the women. The boldest of them undertook to inform her mistress, but she advised Chibinda not to cross the river, which was guarded by sentries. The strangers camped on the right bank. The servants praised the handsome stranger to Lueji. Her curiosity aroused, Lueji sent food to the hunters, inviting them to visit her the following morning. These orders were carried out. Lueji also caused the great stone on which her father used to sit to be deposited by the river. When Ilunga came to visit her, Lueji invited him to sit by her while his companions were taken to the huts prepared for them.

Lueji asked Chibinda to teach her people the use of the bow, because hunting with traps, the Lunda custom, was proving unsuccessful although the country was rich in game. Chibinda agreed. Lueji, who had fallen in love with the stranger-prince, made him stay in the courtyard of her own hut, for fear that a servant girl might also fall for him. After some time Chibinda decided to send the ax he had brought with him to the Luba king, his elder brother. In so doing he wanted to inform his compatriots that he had decided to live in Lunda territory. Lueji was deeply moved by this gesture, but she delayed the messenger's departure, fearing that Chibinda might later regret a hasty decision. However, there was a growing affection between the two young people. Chibinda caused shrubs to be planted near the stone where Lueji had welcomed him. In gratitude, Lueji had the ground about the stone cleared and beaten and it became the special place of their meetings. Every afternoon they conversed there while drinking palm wine. Finally Lueji called a council of her close relatives and told them of her intention of marrying Chibinda, who had been brought to her by her father's spirit. The council ratified her choice. Then Lueji sent messengers to the Luba court, bearing Chibinda's ax. Lueji also asked the Luba king for eventual military assistance against Chinguli, whose anger she feared. The deputation was favorably received by her powerful neighbor. But he sent back the ax and advised his younger brother to entrust it to one of his own officers. He also sent gifts of ivory and iron weapons to his future sister-in-law.

The marriage took place when Lueji was pregnant. The eldest dignitary solemnly handed the chiefly bracelet to Chibinda, enjoining him to unify and build up the country his son would rule. When the child was born, he was called Naweji (Noeji).

Lueji then handed over power to Chibinda. She prostrated herself before her husband and obliged those about her to do the same.

Chinguli refused to submit. He left the country with his followers. Chibinda gave Lueji five more sons. At his death, he was buried on the right bank of the river, at the place where he had camped on the night of his arrival.

3. *Van den Byvang's version*[6]

Chinguli, Chiniama, and Lueji are the children of Yala Mwaku and of his first wife Konde. As in Pogge's version, the father is at least partly to blame for the initial quarrel. Yala Mwaku did not wish to reveal the secret of the drawing of palm wine to his sons. He made fun of them by making them believe that the cloudy water in which he was moistening mat fibers was wine. Chinguli went so far as to strike his father. Van den Byvang mentions two different versions of the transmission of power to Chibinda. According to the first, when Lueji welcomed Chibinda she offered him wine. But the noble stranger said he could not drink in public. Then Lueji had a shelter made for her guest. Impressed by the refined habits of the stranger, she offered him the royal bracelet. According to the second version, Chibinda appropriated the bracelet when the indisposed princess placed it in the ritual basket. However that may be, Chinguli decided to emigrate; according to some informants, Chiniama had already left the country when his sister took power; but other informants agree with the official court historian, Duysters's principal source, that the two brothers emigrated at the same time after refusing to recognize the authority of Chibinda Ilunga.

4. *Peripheral version from Kahemba region* (Struyf[7])

The chief Konde (Konda) became drunk while drinking palm wine in the company of his wife Kamonga and his children. He retired behind the hut. Chinguli found his father naked and left him in this state. His sister Lueji (Na Weji), however, covered her father with a mantle and washed him. On awakening, Konde disinherited his son in favor of his daughter. Konde was fighting the Chokwe tribe. To bring an end to the conflict, the two chiefs decided to submit themselves to a test. Decorated with their insignia of office, they took turns crossing the river in a canoe. Konde went first and arrived safely on the other side. But an aquatic animal snatched the regalia of the Chokwe chief. The quarreling between the two people became more bitter and Konde was murdered. Tyanza ya Koola succeeded him during Lueji's minority. The Chokwe were eventually beaten and forced to pay tribute.

The Luba hunter Chibinda arrived in the country and sent a dish of meat to the queen Lueji; the queen sent him two calabashes of palm wine in exchange. The next day she invited him to a great drinking party. But her period suddenly came on; obliged to retire, she ordered that homage be paid to the stranger in her absence. Chinguli refused to do this. He emigrated westward with a party of Lunda. Lueji had four children by Chibinda. They founded numerous clans.

5. *Peripheral version from the Kazembe chiefdom, Luapula region* (Labrecque[8])

The king Konde had three sons, Kingudi, Chinyama, and Lyulu (or Dyulu), and a daughter Lweshi (or Lweji). According to the patrilineal tradition, the eldest son should have succeeded his father. But Kingudi and Chinyama quarreled with Konde, who drove them away and disinherited them in favor of Lweshi. Some days later, the old king died; he was buried beside his ancestors Nshimaweshi Kantanje, Mwaku, and Yala.

The ministers gathered to debate the succession. Many were uneasy about the deceased's decision: "How can a woman effectively govern a country as big as the Lunda?" They proposed to entrust power to Lyulu, the youngest son. Finally a compromise was agreed on: Lweshi was proclaimed queen, but Lyulu was charged with helping her in the tasks of government. Lweshi was intelligent. She gave proof of wisdom and firmness. For many years she refused to marry, for fear that her authority might be compromised. When she had her period, Lweshi took the sacred bracelet from her arm and entrusted it to Lyulu, who ruled in her place during the five days of retreat.

Lyulu had just died when a Luba prince, Kibinda (Chibinda) Ilunga, belonging to the family of Mbidi Kiluwe, presented himself at the Lunda court, accompanied by a band of hunters. They had ventured far from their native land. Having followed the trail of an antelope to the shore of a small lake at sunset, they decided to camp there. They were surprised by some women who had come to draw water and who alerted the men. The men then went to see the hunters, to get some meat. Struck by the impres-

> sive stature and noble appearance of the chief of the band, they invited him to accompany them to see the queen. As soon as she saw the handsome stranger, Lweshi declared to her people that she was choosing him as her husband, causing general stupefaction. The great men of the kingdom were summoned to the court. Kibinda presented himself before this reticent assembly in the following terms: "I am Kibinda Ilunga; I come from the country between Lake Kisale and the Lualaba River. My eldest brother, Ilunga Walwefu, is the Luba chief of Lake Upemba. He is a great warrior; with his bow he dominates the neighboring tribes and destroys the enemies who try to resist him. As for me, I prefer hunting beasts to hunting men. Our common father is Kalala Ilunga, conqueror of the country of Nkongolo. I am a prince of royal blood and my kingdom is the immensity of the forests and the plains rich in game."

Familial Constellations

The first part of the epic is singularly reminiscent of the Kuba cycle about Woot. A violent conflict erupts between the original father and his sons over palm wine; the father disinherits the sons in favor of a daughter. The familial code thus faithfully reproduces that of M9, of which the explicit function is to validate the matrilineal system. The peripheral version collected by Struyf in Kahemba territory simply restores the Kuba myth. But M20 by no means endorses the matrilineal system. The new order of succession established by the old chief Konde is transformed anew into patrilineality by the mediation of a hyper-exogamic matrilocal union, which in its turn reproduces a Luba *mythème* (M1): in both cases a stranger-prince, a hunter of great charm who comes from afar, makes ready a new dynastic order and introduces a refined culture. The two heroes are furthermore linked by a close genealogical tie, since Chibinda Ilunga introduces himself as the grandson of Mbidi Kiluwe. The familial codes of M9 and M1 are therefore superimposed on M20. Duysters's version in particular insists on patrilineality since three generations of chiefs succeed from father to son before Lueji. The same notation appears in the peripheral version obtained from the court of the chief Kazembe of the Luapula valley.

The epic therefore begins with a crisis in the constituted patrilineal order, as in the first part of M1 (Burton's version). M20, like M1, reveals as problematic the situation created by the conjunction of father and daughter. While this *mythème* (correlative with the father-sons disjunction) is used by the Kuba to found matrilineality, it is incapable of any positive development in the Lunda epic, not only because the complementary conjunction between brother and sister is compromised by the arrival of a stranger, but also because *Lueji is sterile.* On this point, Duysters's version is confirmed by Biebuyck: "Contrary to what is customarily claimed, Tibind (Chibinda) had no children by Rweej (Lueji)."[9] Biebuyck thereby gives the lie to de Carvalho's version, of which the very emphasis is suspect (Lueji supposedly having six children by Chibinda). One may well suspect that de Carvalho's informants, like those of Struyf, have sought to disguise a monstrous defect in their heroine. In fact, our accounts hover around three interpretations: between the versions of Duysters and Biebuyck, which proclaim the *definitive sterility* of Lueji, and those of de Carvalho and Struyf, which show her as fecund, there is a third, intermediate version collected by Turner among the Ndembu.

M21, Ndembu: The Menorrhagia* of Lueji (Turner[10])

> Lueji (Luweji Ankonde), co-foundress of the Lunda dynasty, retired to the hut reserved for women during their menstrual periods, first having handed her royal bracelet to her husband Chibinda Ilunga, for fear this precious ornament should "lose its whiteness" (become impure). She remained there for many days. The people became anxious about her prolonged absence and prepared a magical medicine. She recovered quickly and soon bore a child. This long menstruation is called *nkula*. This is also the name of the ritual which, since these events, has been applied to women suffering from menstrual disorders. The red feather of the *kalong'u* parrot, which figures in the ritual, evokes the blood of Lueji.

Struyf's version displaces sterility on to a woman of the ascending generation, Lukonkesha, Lueji's maternal aunt. Kamonga, Konde's widow, had a young, sterile sister called Lukonkesha who looked after Kamonga's children. The title *Lukonkesha* exists to this day at the

*The term *menorrhagia*, excessive or long-continued menstruation, seems more appropriate to the severity of Lueji's condition than the milder indisposition implied by de Heusch's *menorrhée* (*menorrhea*). Menorrhagia is also Turner's term (1968:58). (R.W.)

Lunda court, where it is borne by a high-ranking female dignitary who is "the mother of the left side" in opposition to the *Swanamulanda*, who perpetuates the memory of Lueji and is known as "the mother of the right side."[11] According to Biebuyck's informants at the court, Lukonkesha (Rukonkesh) commemorates the second (fecund) wife of Chibinda Ilunga, the one Lueji gave him when she discovered her own sterility. The version of the Lunda of Kahemba (Struyf) therefore inverts the function of Lukonkesha while maintaining the fundamental opposition between a sterile "mother" and a fecund mother.

Symbolism of royal "mothers" at the Lunda court:

Lukonkesha: fecund mother (second wife of Chibinda Ilunga)	Swanamulanda: sterile mother (Lueji)

Struyf's version of the myth:

Lukonkesha: sterile "mother"	Kamonga: fecund mother

To this duality corresponds a bipartition of ritual space. The capital is laid out in the form of a tortoise along an east-west axis. The royal palace is built in the middle of the western half of the "tortoise's back"; the quarters of the two "mothers" are found side by side in the eastern half, adjoining the "head" of the tortoise.[12]

It is evident that the dualism of maternity refers to a complex cosmogonic code. For the moment let us dwell upon this strange personage Lueji, a passionate young woman who failed to achieve motherhood, or achieved it only with difficulty. Labrecque and de Carvalho make Lueji an untamed virgin whose heart remains unmoved until the arrival of the prince charming: Lueji rejects all suitors for many years. She is thus characterized by a provisional refusal of maternity, which other versions transform into definitive sterility. In Labrecque's version, Lueji reigns with her young brother, Lyulu; despite the father-sons conflict, the brother-sister conjunction has therefore been provisionally retained. Other versions, however, confirm this situation more discreetly: Chinguli and Chiniama submit to Lueji's authority. Labrecque indeed justifies the prolonged virginity of the princess by the fear of seeing this fragile harmony broken: "She (Lueji) knew that once she was linked to a prince-consort . . . her authority could no longer be shared with her brother Lyulu, but divided and possibly destroyed. . . ." One sees a curious solution outlined here which the myth itself presents as a compromise between the wish of Konde, who disinherited his elder sons Chinguli and Chiniama, and the desire to maintain patrilineal succession. But this compromise is unworkable because it obliges Lueji to remain virgin. . . .

Provisional virginity like the sterility of the queen assigns a zero value to the initial *mythème* (father-daughter conjunction). The Luba and Lunda epics are therefore based on the same familial armature:

M1 (Burton's version):	M20:
Father-son(s) disjunction/father-daughter conjunction:	
Mbidi's father wants to deprive him of power in favor of his daughter Mwanana.	Konde quarrels with his sons and makes Lueji his heiress.
Brother-sister disjunction, preceding or following a matrilocal, hyperexogamic marriage:	
Mwanana drives away her brother Mbidi, who marries Mabela and Bulanda far away.	The brothers leave Lueji, who has just married the stranger Chibinda.
Disjunction of brothers-in-law:	
Mbidi quarrels with his brother-in-law, Nkongolo.	Lueji's brothers refuse to recognize the authority of their brother-in-law.
The matrilocal marriage of the hunter hero creates a situation which is strained or devoid of matrilineal sense:	
Kalala Ilunga, Mbidi's son, is brought up with his maternal uncle Nkongolo and enters into conflict with him.	Lueji is sterile; the maternal uncles are absent.
Father-son conjunction, inaugurating divine kingship:	
Kalala Ilunga rejoins his father and kills his maternal uncle. He founds the Luba dynasty.	Chibinda has a son; the latter founds the Lunda dynasty.

The provisional situation preceding the accession to power of the stranger-hunter could develop into a matrilineal order analogous to that imposed by Woot in M9 or to that enjoyed by Nkongolo and his sisters in an excessively incestuous mode in M1. In more ways than one, Lueji and Nkongolo have something in common. Both are autochthonous sovereigns of countries visited by a stranger-hunter who founds a new dynasty. On the familial level, their situations are inversely symmetrical: Lueji lives with her brothers as an untamed virgin; Nkongolo lives incestuously with his sisters. An aberrant sexual relation is opposed here to an absence of sexuality, which is just as abnormal. But in both cases the *mythème* connotes sterility. This is the very kernel of the Lunda epic, this episode about menstrual blood, which is so shocking to African sensibilities and which is defined through the ensemble of variant accounts. Menstruation is effectively situated at the critical point where sterility enters into the procreative function. The Ndembu, who provide M21, which transforms menstrual blood into menorrhagia, believe this blood has to coagulate to nourish the fetus.[13] From this perspective, the variants can be placed on the following scale:

discontinuous sterility (menstrual blood)	danger of continuous sterility (menorrhagia)	definitive sterility

To this more or less lengthy period of sterility there corresponds, in this myth, a rupture of a sociological kind: menstrual blood endangers the continuity of political power just as it suspends fecundity. According to Duysters, Lueji hands the royal bracelet to her husband after her indisposition; she provisionally entrusts him with power each time she retires to the hut, according to information obtained by Bastin.[14] Certain informants of Van den Byvang claim that the hunter took the bracelet while the indisposed Lueji was secluded in the ritual hut. This account resembles a variant of Struyf's version, in which Lueji's husband one day slipped the bracelet onto his wrist and was unable to take it off; Lueji removed it with a magical remedy and forbade her husband to touch it again. In apparent contradiction, however, she thereupon told Chinguli to greet Chibinda with the salutation reserved for chiefs. Chinguli refused and went into exile.[15] Happily, Duysters's version articulates the two *mythèmes*. When Lueji transmits the royal bracelet to her husband on leaving the ritual hut, she provokes the departure of her brothers and a numerous following: emigration thus prolongs the menstrual flow on a historical plane, causing the collapse of many huts.*

What is then the symbolic function of the hunter-prince in the face

*Because they are no longer occupied. (R.W.)

of this catastrophic situation for the dynasty and the whole country? M21 goes far toward providing the answer: this narrative says that Lueji had to undergo the rite of *nkula* to end menorrhagia (i.e., sterility). But the *nkula* ritual introduces the fecundity theme in the guise of a hunter. Dressed in animal skins and holding a bow and arrows, the female patient executes the hunters' dance.[16] Turner comments that a woman who is incapable of bearing children is necessarily turned into a man. This summary explanation deserves developing, especially since the red symbols deployed in *nkula* explicitly recall the historical links that joined the Ndembu to the Lunda empire.[17] Hunting, in the eyes of the Ndembu, is a particular mode of sexual activity: the feminine curve of the bow complements the phallic form of the arrow, and the term for the latter (*nsewu*) also denotes bridewealth.[18] Furthermore, the hunter is expected to have an intense sexual life. One recalls here that M20 makes much of the physical attraction exerted by Chibinda Ilunga. In its strong version, the Lunda epic brings together a sterile princess and a hunter who should be a provider of children just as he is a provider of food. The blood spilled in the hunt is indeed analogous in Ndembu symbolism to the blood of childbirth. The marriage of Lueji and Chibinda therefore has the function of overcoming the fundamental opposition between sterility and fecundity which is encoded in two sorts of blood:

menstrual blood	*blood of the hunt*
absence of life (sterility)	birth (fecundity)

But the fecundity brought by the hunter is balked by menorrhagia, the phantom haunting the ritual hut. This continuous menstrual flow, which is Lueji's secret sorrow, also expresses the impossibility of crystalizing the matrilineal system outlined by Konde after his dispute with his sons. Among the Ndembu the "red" symbols of *nkula* are related to the matrilineal principle that governs kinship.

Lunda (M20)	*Ndembu* (M21)
definitive sterility of Lueji breakdown of matrilineal model	Lueji cured of menorrhagia matrilineality

If most versions show us Lueji shut in the ritual hut in bondage to her sanguinary biological condition, it is because fear of menorrhagia dominates the scene. In the menstrual cycle, the sign of biological periodicity, the Lunda paradoxically discern the danger of a continuously sterile and nonperiodic nature. Here, further parallels emerge between Lueji, the untamed virgin whose periods threaten to go on forever, and the incestuous Nkongolo. For is not menorrhagia, the dialectical negation of the principle of discontinuity governing menstruation, a new form of the maleficent rainbow? This equivalence, first suggested by Paul Jorion during one of our seminars at the University of Brussels, allows us to take account of the thematic similarities and divergences which both bring together and separate the Luba and Lunda epics. In both cases the mythical scene is occupied in whole or in part by an exiled hunter who marries a foreign princess matrilocally. Mbidi Kiluwe has been humiliated by an aggressive sister, Chibinda Ilunga by a brother who reproaches him for not making war (Duysters's version). Both heroes are gentle and civilized men. Chibinda arrives in a small chiefdom governed by a pacific virgin who has two violent brothers; Mbidi strays into a kingdom of which the violent master has two incestuous sisters.

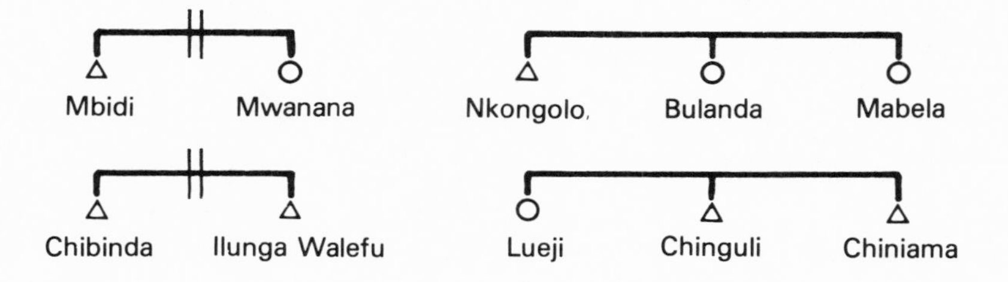

This double inversion bearing on the sex of the associates already suggests that the Lunda epic is a reformulation of the Luba epic: the amorous virgin Lueji is a transformation of the incestuous and hateful Nkongolo. The duplication of the brothers (Chinguli and Chiniama) corresponds to the duplication of the sisters (Mabela and Bulanda). Both pairs are called on to separate themselves from the autochthonous sovereign: Bulanda and Mabela betray Nkongolo, Chinguli and Chiniama abandon Lueji. The Lunda queen, like the first Luba king, is ignorant of the customs of divine kingship introduced by the prince charming: Lueji, like Nkongolo, has a hut built for her guest where he can drink and eat without fear of being observed (Duysters's version). It may be objected that the resemblance between Lueji and Nkongolo ends there because the relationship with the stranger-prince is positive in one case and negative in the other. But have we not just established that the meeting of Lueji and Chibinda, like the meeting of Nkongolo and Mbidi, expresses the opposition between sterility and fecundity? The maleficent menstrual blood temporarily separates Lueji and the hunter. Struyf's version introduced this fundamental opposition from the very beginning: Lueji has her (calamitous) period the very day that she invites the stranger to drink with her. Finally, the sterility of Lueji has a parallel in the "hole of Nkongolo," which connotes the same symbolic category. It will be recalled that this expression applies precisely to sterile women (p. 24). We must now look again at this logic of forms, already outlined in respect of the Luba epic. Nkongolo quarrels with his guest about a question of opening: he reproaches the guest with never laughing (Orjo de Marchovelette's version). We have seen that this theme relates directly to the refined eating habits of the stranger-prince who refrains from taking refreshment in public. This reserved conduct defines Mbidi by a prohibition affecting the mouth, which should now be compared with the sexual prohibition that separates Lueji, for a more or less prolonged interval, from her guest:

Mbidi	*Nkongolo*
mouth closed	mouth open (he is ignorant of royal customs)
Chibinda	*Lueji*
weakened form of closed mouth	sexual orifice too open

Nkongolo is a being who is "opened" above; he eats and drinks in public; he even drinks "like a hole" (Verhulpen's version). Lueji appears as someone who is "open" below; she is the "flowing woman" of certain Amerindian myths.[19] It is remarkable that a Luba myth, which diachronically follows the epic of state foundation, allows us to understand how mythical thought envisages the possibility of substituting a higher natural orifice for a lower one in the same physiological context, that of menstruation.

M22, Luba: Origin of the Mediums of Mpanga and Banze, Guardian Spirits of Divine Kingship[20]

Here is how Mpanga and Banze became the guardian spirits of divine kingship (*bulopwe*). During the reign of Kalala Ilunga there lived a famous diviner called Mbayo wa Kubungwe. The founder of the new dynasty sent to him a certain Kamazi Banze to obtain a *mboko* calabash containing white clay and other ritual ingredients. He offered two women and two slaves in exchange. The diviner gave the sacred calabash to the royal envoy. On the way back, the envoy met a woman called Mpanga Maloba. He wanted to spend the night with her, even though all sexual relations were forbidden to one in possession of the calabash. Mpanga warned him of this, reminding him that he stood to lose his life. She told him that in any case she could not be approached sexually because she was having her period. But Banze infringed this double prohibition. At the place where they died a pond appeared, with wild fruits floating on its surface, fruits similar to those the woman had gathered earlier (apparently to give herself magical protection). The local inhabitants deposited the precious *mboko* calabash in a sanctuary. Mpanga and Banze were transformed into spirits. They returned to their native land, on the other side of Lake Upemba, where they possessed two female mediums. The mediums were transported to the edge of the magic pond, which became a renowned place of divination. Before these events there were no mediums in Luba country: until then diviners consulted the spirits of the dead beside water. Afterward men would interrogate Mpanga and Banze about the causes of female sterility.

Kalala Ilunga soon learned what had happened. The priestesses were enrolled in the exclusive service of the king and his family. It was forbidden for anyone to approach the magic pond. The king, who observed this prohibition himself, always consulted the mediums through emissaries. The two women attached to the cult also provided him with the white clay needed in ritual. At each new moon, possessed by the spirits, they hung themselves by the feet from the *mumo* (fig) tree: then menstrual blood flowed from their eyes and fingernails.

In the absence of sufficient information we shall not attempt a complete exegesis of this strange tale that transforms a scandalous couple into guardian spirits of royalty. We restrict ourselves to situating the priestesses' tears of menstrual blood along a comparative scale.

Nkongolo	*mediums of Banze and Mpanga*	*Lueji*
bleeding head turned skywards	bleeding head turned downwards	bleeding genitalia

Each of these in some way monstrous personages possesses part of the sacredness of power. Banze and Mpanga keep the ritual white clay and reveal the causes of sterility. This semantic reversal of menstrual blood goes with the inversion of the personages, hung head downward in the sacred tree.[21] The head of Nkongolo relates to the sky and the sun (see p. 37). The heads of the mediums are poised between sky and earth; the vulva of Lueji, given over to menstrual blood, is situated at the lowest point of all, in the perilous shadow of the ritual hut where men may not go. This obscure retreat is analogous to the night of the new moon, the time when the two mediums of M22 have their periods. There is therefore reason to believe that the temporary eclipse of Lueji signifies the disappearance of the moon, a point we shall return to later. To complete the comparison with M1, let us note that the tragic heroes of M22, like Nkongolo, are associated with terrestrial waters and move from one lake to another. Like Nkongolo, they find themselves mystically associated with the divine kingship of Kalala Ilunga. The female mediums of Mpanga and Banze open up the possibility of transforming Nkongolo into a bleeding woman, sterile source of royal power in the Lunda dynasty. In this connection it is worth noting that Nkongolo in his rainbow form is sometimes thought of as an androgynous being or as a couple devoid of descendants.[22]

It begins to look as though this menstrual blood has a cosmic dimension. But before dealing with this problem, it is necessary to go further into the transformations of the familial code. The Lunda epic effectively displaces the barbaric violence of Nkongolo and the hatred he bears for his hunter-guest on to Chinguli and Chiniama. De Carvalho's version in particular blackens the portrait of Lueji's two brothers, who are shown as patricidal sons. We find an echo of this somber note in one of the rare narratives reporting the sequel of the adventure, and here we see Chinguli put to death by his uterine nephews.

M23, Lunda (Kahemba Region): The Exodus of Chinguli (Struyf[23])

After refusing to pay homage to his brother-in-law Chibinda Ilunga, Chinguli went away to the west, accompanied by a large following. He was a violent chief, ill-mannered and barbaric. On the way he stabbed many women to death, despite the protests of his uterine nephews. Outraged by this massacre, the nephews ended up shutting their uncle into an enclosure, where he received very little food. Emaciated and feeling his end to be near, Chinguli summoned his son Kasanji, whose mother was an Imbangala woman. He gave him the insignia of office after disinheriting his nephews.

This myth comes from a peripheral region where invading Lunda have imposed their rule on matrilineal peoples. M23 justified the existence of patrilineality among the conquerors. The bloody Chinguli, impious son of Konde, here finds himself transformed into the restorer of the very family order that he has helped to demolish in his country of origin (M20). The general familial code that we outlined earlier is verified and completed diachronically:

Father-sons conflict (M20)
(crisis of the patrilineal order)

Brother-sister disjunction (M20)
(critical situation without resolution)

Conflict of maternal uncle and nephew (M23)
(crisis of the matrilineal order)

Father-sons conjunction (M23)
(restoration of the patrilineal order)

Considering M20 and M23 together, we discover the entire kinship code of the Luba epic (M1); we also discover in the murder of the maternal uncle the converse and complementary *mythème* of the patricide on which M8 founds *matrilineality* among the Luba-Hemba. In dying of hunger, the barbarous Chinguli finds himself in the situation of alimentary deficiency characterizing the society of Nkongolo, whose two sisters are called "poverty" and "a little meat" (Colle's version). In this respect Chinguli is opposed to Chibinda, the provider of game, as Nkongolo is opposed to Mbidi the hunter. The putting to death of Chinguli by his uterine nephews replicates the tragic end of Nkongolo, killed by Kalala Ilunga.

The Lunda epic (M20 and M23) thus emerges from the Luba epic through a vast transformation. Nkongolo and Lueji, characterized by lack of food, the rudimentary form of eating habits, sterility or incest, occupy homologous positions in relation to a hunter-prince, Mbidi or Chibinda, whose roles are interchangeable. In the Luba epic Mbidi brings the meat of the hunt and introduces refined alimentary customs, but he does not found the empire. He limits himself to mediating between a primitive cultural order and a new civilization. He fills an initial natural deficiency (hunger and sterility) by cultural means (hunting weapons, ritual fire). Chibinda, his homologue in the Lunda epic, finds himself in a comparable situation: his hunting is successful, he gives an heir to the sterile Lueji, but the stranger Chibinda does not create the State, any more than Mbidi did. In setting himself up with his hosts, he even brings about a demographic impoverishment, emphasized in Duysters's version: Chibinda spent his time hunting and gave no thought to warfare. "After the departure of Chinguli and Chiniama numerous huts collapsed and entire families took the road into exile. Lueji's people were no longer so numerous."[24] Naweji, Chibinda's son, was on the defensive and it was not until the hunter-hero's grandson (Yaav Naweji) took power that the epoch of conquests began. The hunter-hero is not a warrior. In Labrecque's version, Chibinda proclaims it himself: "My elder brother, Ilunga Walwefu, is the great Luba chief of Lake Upemba. He is a great hunter of men; with his bow he overcomes the neighboring tribes and exterminates enemies who try to resist him. As for me, I prefer hunting beasts to hunting men."[25] This opposition between hunting and war, to which we shall revert, is also present in the Luba epic, which successively introduces two heroes, a father (Mbidi Kiluwe) and a son (Kalala Ilunga), respectively devoted to these distinct activities. The warrior, who pursues Chibinda's enterprise on another level (that of the hunt for men), no longer belongs to the myth but rather to the history of the Lunda.

The center of the mythical scene (the court of Lueji or of Nkongolo) is in both cases the place where the hero marries matrilocally. Although the Luba hunter soon leaves this central place to return to his native land while his Lunda homologue stays where he is, it should be noted that Chibinda's corpse is symbolically returned to the country of the east when he is buried on the right (eastern) bank of the river (Duysters's and de Carvalho's versions). The mythical center is affected by a grave familial crisis that is always resolved by the installation or restoration of an original, compromised patrilineality. But matrilineality is realized for a time to the west of the place where patrilineality appears as an autochthonous value: with Nkongolo for the Luba, with Chinguli for the Lunda. It would seem then that matrilineality is to patrilineality as the west (the earth) is to the east (the sky). A Chokwe adage confirms this spatial arrangement: "East, the morning sun, the side of Mwata Yamvo. West, the evening sun, the side of Chinguli."[26]

In the Lunda as in the Luba epic, a river separates the mythical center from the country of the east whence the hunter comes; in de Carvalho's version, the messengers warn Chibinda that he may not cross it until dawn, although he arrived there as the sun was going down. This feature suggests an association between the hunter-hero and the sun, reversing that found among the Luba (Mbidi has a lunar connotation). But before going more deeply into the cosmogonic code, let us try to conclude this analysis.

Divine kingship emerges in a central place that is the scene of a confrontation between brothers-in-law. The stranger-hero arrives to restore the patrilineal order (Lunda) or to bring the promise of its installation in an incestuous and pseudomatrilineal society where the stranger is undesirable (Luba). Matrilocal marriage is therefore thought of in myth as the mediator between the matrilineal system and the patrilineal system (where it is equally abnormal). The first cannot be thought of mythically without recourse to the second, and vice versa. In one way or another, the myths present patrilineality as progressive; it puts an end to an uncouth original culture in which the refined customs of divine kingship were unknown. Even where kingship emerges within the matrilineal system, as in the Kuba case, the myth presents the existing situation as the outcome of a cultural regression (drunkenness, incest); the father complex always dominates the mythical scene. This dialectic reflects contradictions in thought as much as in practice, for matrilineal and patrilineal societies exist side by side in Central Africa. The two models are found within Luba culture, the eastern Luba being matrilineal, the western patrilineal. As to the kinship system of the Lunda of Katanga, it is marked by nondifferentiation of filiation. Vansina employs the term "bilateral" for this mode of unilineal descent.[27] Biebuyck says that the existing "ambilateral" system was preceded by a primitive matrilineal system;[28] he seems to base himself on the myth, the historical value of which is highly questionable. Present-day juridical practice evinces "a certain preponderance of the male line."[29] In fact, the royal power seems to have been transmitted for several generations from father to son, or from elder to younger brother. The mode of succession becomes complicated from the sixth incumbent after Chibinda Ilunga: Naweji II was the son of the daughter of his predecessor.[30] This "bilateral" model of filiation is undoubtedly presented by the myth because the old Konde transmits power to the son of his daughter Lueji. But it is nonetheless evident that it is in no way a function of the myth to justify such a mode of filiation, which appeared very late in royal history.

The matrilocal marriage of the hunter-hero, the mediator between the matrilineal and patrilineal systems, is marked by a further anomaly: contrary to custom, it is the woman who seduces. The love-struck sisters of Nkongolo, like Lueji, take the initiative and invite the reserved stranger to stay with them. Taking up this theme in *Du miel aux cendres* [*From Honey to Ashes*], Lévi-Strauss discovers "a relation of equivalence between a rhetorical transformation and a sociological transformation" in the Amerindian myths. The transition from the *mythème* "seduction of a woman by a man" to the *mythème* "seduction of a man by a woman" should be interpreted as a movement from the proper sense to a figurative one.[31] In other words, "in indigenous thought, the seduction of a woman by a man belongs to the real order, the converse happening in the order of symbolism or the imaginary."* We shall endeavor to find out how far this proposition is true for the Luba-Lunda world.

The Mystique of Hunting

We have seen that hunting can be a metaphoric image of fecundity. When the untamed virgin Lueji asks the handsome stranger to supply

*In the Weightmans' translation of *Du miel aux cendres* this passage is given rather a different sense, appearing as: ". . . in native thought, the seduction of a woman by a man belongs to the real world, and is the reverse of a symbolic or imaginary procedure." Claude Lévi-Strauss, *From Honey to Ashes* (translated from the French by John and Doreen Weightman), 1973, London, Jonathan Cape, p. 164. (R.W.)

her with game, the myth obviously alludes to real hunting while expressing amorous passion in a veiled form. But the metaphor (desire for children) is nullified because Lueji remains sterile. Only the literal sense subsists: Chibinda is a provider of meat. In the Luba epic, in contrast, the economic activity of the stranger-hunter, drawn by the charms of the two young women, is much less marked than fecundity. The figurative sense of hunting prevails over the literal sense. Even the hunting weapon becomes the symbol of paternity: before leaving his two pregnant wives, Mbidi gives each a "curiously fashioned" arrow (Burton's version) which is to ensure that his children will be recognized when they present themselves to him. Bulanda is soon delivered of a son (Kalala Ilunga), while Mabela has twins. This gradation in the intensity of the figurative sense calls for elucidation.

This apparent weakening of the metaphor corresponds to the emergence of a second and stronger figurative sense. Do not forget that the hunter-hero brings not only fecundity but also and above all divine kingship. It is precisely through the intermediary of the less prolific spouse that divine kingship is instituted; it is the only son of Bulanda, and he alone, who has the task of transforming the imperfect culture of Nkongolo into a superior civilization; the birth of twins to Mabela simply expresses the power of nature.

The double marriage of the hunter-hero therefore corresponds to a duplication in the metaphoric sense of the hunt. The more prolific wife relates to a primary figurative sense (fecundity); the less prolific wife is the bearer of divine kingship. This second metaphor seems richer than the first because it truly expresses the ideological function of the myth: it takes account of the magico-religious legitimacy of power, the ultimate source of all fecundity.

Most Lunda versions take no account of the second figurative sense (divine kingship) of hunting; only the versions of Duysters and Van den Byvang also mention the refined alimentary habits of the hunter, who is above all—and most often uniquely—a provider of meat. In Struyf's version Chibinda, far from secluding himself, drinks palm wine in the company of Lueji and her people, like a chief devoid of manners. De Carvalho is content to dwell at length on the literal sense: Lueji desires that the hunter supply her people with meat, and for a long time she conceals her amorous passion, being unsure of Chibinda's sentiments. The primary figurative sense (desire for children) is therefore expressed here after the literal sense (desire for meat), which

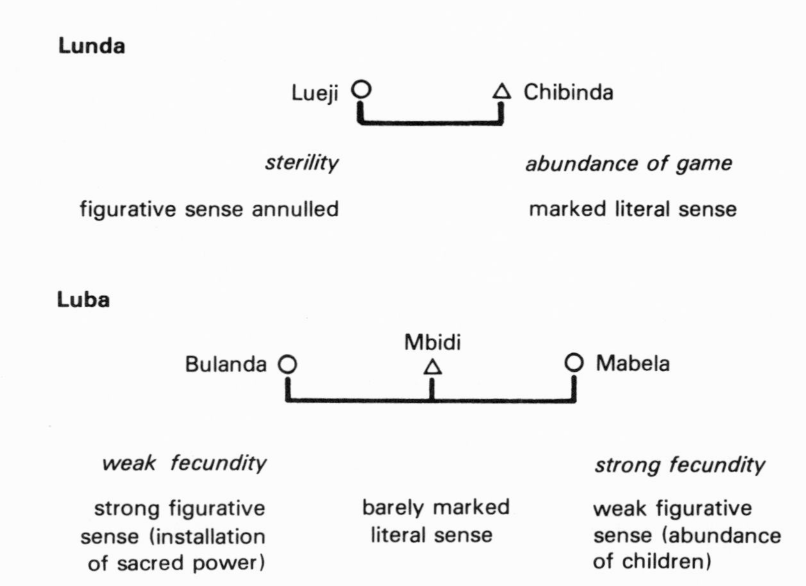

remains dominant. All versions, moreover, join in acknowledging that the literal sense is positive (the brothers-in-law collaborate in the hunt) while Lueji's marriage remains sterile and provokes a mass emigration. In one way or another the figurative sense of hunting is compromised.

The passage from Mbidi to Chibinda can therefore be interpreted as a weakening of the two metaphoric senses of the hunt in favor of its literal sense (desire for meat). By merging Chibinda and Mbidi and comparing their respective marriages, we obtain a continuous series of terms marked by a greater or lesser degree of fecundity.

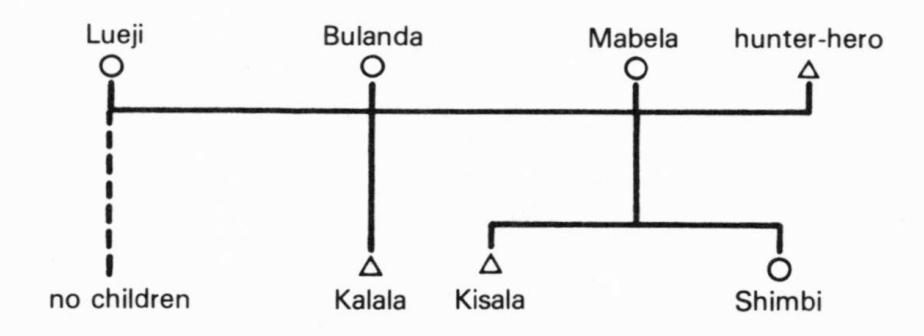

The first figurative sense (desire for a child) increases but is destroyed at both extremes: Lueji's lack of children is homologous with the birth of twins to Mabela. Kalala, in whom the second figurative sense is dominant, is finally opposed to his half brother Kisula, a *stupid giant*. The potency of nature (twins) like its impotency (sterility) is opposed to the divine kingship introduced by the medial relation (uniting the hunter and Bulanda). The Luba-Lunda mythical system therefore includes three seductive women, differently open to the figurative senses concealed under the guise of the hunter: Lueji and Mabela relate to the *natural* figurative sense of the hunt, Bulanda to its *cultural* figurative sense (foundation of divine kingship). This bipartite division recalls the hypothesis of Lévi-Strauss relative to the duplication of wives in mythology: "The duality of women is not a simple pair, but a polar and oriented system."[32]

In the Lunda epic, the unique marriage of the hunter with Lueji obliterates the strong image of the civilizing hero; the mythical system preserves only the literal significance of hunting, which is much poorer than its figurative sense. The myth makes no mention of the culinary precautions peculiar to divine kingship, which ceases to appear as a new value brought in from outside: it inheres entirely in the royal bracelet that the princess has received from her own father. Chibinda is merely a mediator between the ancestor Konde and Konde's grandson. De Carvalho's version illustrates this weakening: the hero manifests his intention of divesting himself of the chiefly symbol he has brought from Luba country. However, a Luba myth that we shall examine later reveals that the second metaphoric sense has not completely disappeared. Therein it is said that Chibinda "hunts the secret of hunting and the quality of chief." However that may be, Mbidi much more clearly imposes a new style on the Luba dynasty. Giving a second wife to Chibinda belatedly establishes the bigamy indispensable to the installation of the symbolic values of hunting, but these values then emerge at the weakest level: procreation. Chibinda begets an heir who belongs entirely to history and who is no more than a faint mythical copy of Kalala Ilunga.

Blood of Beasts and Blood of Women

The symbolism of the hunt cannot be understood in isolation, being just one province of the semantic domain of blood. Here we find the first opposition: Chibinda, who sheds the *blood of beasts* in abundance, enters into relation, through the mediation of palm wine, with a sterile queen characterized by the loss of *menstrual blood.* Recall that in at least one version Lueji is obliged to retire because of her indisposition at the moment when she is welcoming the hunter (Struyf); most of the other versions make a point of Lueji's periodic retreats.

The blood shed by men in the hunt and the menstrual blood of women are opposed as fecundity to sterility. In the heart of the natural order, where both are equally situated, the hunter and the indisposed woman occupy inverse positions. While the Lunda sources are remarkably impoverished in this matter, the symbolism of blood has been closely studied by Turner among the Ndembu, who belong to the same culture area. The Ndembu distinguish three kinds of blood, all connoted by the color red: 1. the blood of hunting (*mashi awubinda*), violent and beneficent; 2. maternal blood (*mashi amama*), good and pacific, evoked in several rituals concerned with reproductive disorders and notably in the *nkula*; 3. the blood of homicide, circumcision, and war (*mashi awubanji*), associated with courage and transgression, and calling for ritual purification.[33]

We need to reinterpret the second category, that which defines the blood of woman, in relation to two kinds of blood shed by man. For menstrual blood must not be confused with the blood of childbirth that nourishes the fetus. In the *nkula* ritual, the first does not become the second except through a transformation that brings in the blood of the hunt. It will be recalled that the female patient, who is dressed in animal skins and carries a bow and arrows, is identified with the hunter.[34] The bleeding feminine condition, obstacle to reproduction, makes of the patient a wounded game animal. She can only escape from this unhappy state by turning herself into a hunter. The maleficent menstrual blood and the beneficent blood of childbirth are opposed as animal and hunter. One can therefore write:

$$\frac{\text{indisposed woman}}{\text{pregnant woman}} = \frac{\text{game animal}}{\text{hunter}}$$

Turner himself clearly distinguishes, in another text, menstrual blood (*mashi awambanda ejima*)[35] from the maternal blood of parturition (*mashi alesumu amama*). But he fails to observe the existence of a ternary structure of blood, in which childbirth is situated halfway between menstruation and the beneficent hunt.

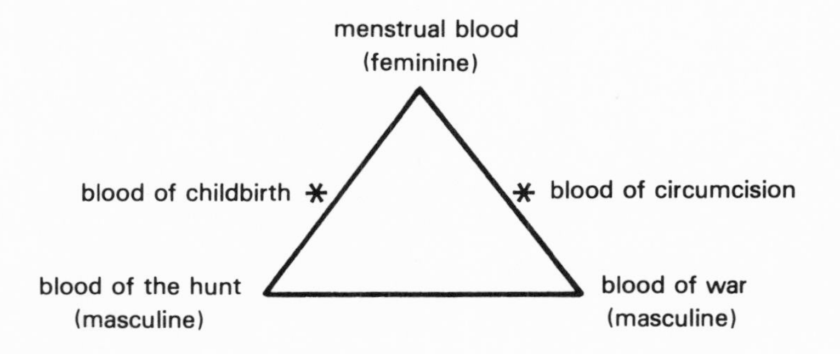

The three terms inscribed at the angles of the triangle are opposed in pairs as follows:

hunt (animal victim)	war (human victim)
hunt (animal victim, fecundity)	menstruation (human victim, sterility)
war (masculine victim)	menstruation (feminine victim)

The opposition between hunting and war is explicit in the Lunda foundation myth, as much from the diachronic viewpoint as from the synchronic viewpoint. Chibinda, the dedicated hunter, is opposed not only to his warlike descendants but also, in Labrecque's version, to his brother, the Luba king, who reproaches him precisely for never fighting. Chibinda describes himself with the words, "I prefer hunting beasts to hunting men."

Let us examine the figurative senses of these various terms. We have seen that menstruation connotes sterility, as the hunt connotes fecundity and the emergence of divine kingship. But the Lunda epic can be said to stifle at birth this metaphorization of the hunt, as though the myth were solidly fixed to the menstrual pole: not only does the hunter-hero fail to give Lueji children, but his reign is also marked by demographic loss. In contrast, the warlike successors of Chibinda have the task of creating or aggrandizing the State: Naweji,

Chibinda's son, establishes the powerful military organization of the empire, and his own son proclaims his desire for conquest at his installation (Duysters's version). The ritual of royal installation requires the new sovereign to undertake a victorious campaign before founding his capital.[36] War, the third pole of the triangle of blood, therefore realizes in the Lunda epic the metaphoric function normally devolved to the hunt. The "hunt for men" is in some respects no more than a transformation of the "hunt for beasts." The one and the other are capable of taking on similar figurative senses that are equally opposed to the metaphoric values of menstruation.

	hunting	war	menstruation
figurative sense	fecundity divine kingship	conquest foundation of the State	sterility, lack of people, primitive political organization

Hunting, like war, connotes the enlargement of the social group, in the one case by natural reproduction and in the other by conquest. As a sign of fecundity, hunting also signals the emergence of divine kingship, State foundation effectively realized by war. But hunting and war also constitute an insurmountable opposition in Luba-Lunda thought. M1, like M20, shows that the transition from one to the other can occur only along the diachronic axis: the warrior-hero succeeds the hunter-hero. Thenceforth among the Lunda each new king inaugurates his reign with a ritual war. This hunting/war opposition no doubt means that the magico-religious aspect of sovereignty has to be distinguished from its politico-military aspect.

Bleeding Heads and Bleeding Genitals

The blood of war and menstrual blood are respectively related to specific parts of the human body. The Ndembu war chief brandishes the bleeding heads of enemies killed in combat during the *kutomboka* triumphal dance.[37] The warrior-hero of the Luba epic, Kalala Ilunga, decapitates his enemy Nkongolo. The bleeding head of Nkongolo in M1 and the bleeding genitalia of Lueji in M20 therefore express the symbolic opposition and complementarity of war and menstruation:

war	*menstruation*
masculine head	feminine genitalia
bleeding	bleeding
(Nkongolo)	(Lueji)

The Luba myth M22, in which we see two women bleeding from the head as though from the genitals, is good evidence that we are dealing with a veritable symbolic transformation whereby war, finally conceived as a hunt for heads, relates to menstruation. One cannot avoid referring here to the troubling parallel between this code and that of several Amerindian peoples who "unite in the same narrative the origin of scalping and of menstruation, or render . . . the first menstruation responsible for the taking of the first head."[38] However that may be, the Ndembu code provides us with unexpected confirmation of a major hypothesis: Lueji, associated with menstrual blood, is a transformation of Nkongolo, who dies beheaded. In this perspective, circumcision should relate directly to our foundation myths. And indeed, the semantic analysis undertaken by Turner allows us to situate the blood shed by the novices in attaining manhood precisely halfway between menstrual blood and the blood of war. The Ndembu openly recognize that "the blood of the novices" belongs to the category of "blood of homicide."[39] But furthermore, "the novices are implicitly treated like brides at their first menstruation."[40] The reddish gum of the *mukula* tree (*pterocarpus*), under the sign of which the *nkula* ritual, as well as circumcision, is situated, is associated in these two contexts with desire for the rapid coagulation of blood. During the initiatory retreat, the novices are considered the "wives" of the principal officiant. Ndembu circumcision thus makes the young boys pass from feminine sterility to the virility of the wounded warrior.

The Lunda foundation myth (M20) expresses the ternary structure of the "blood" category as we have already elucidated it.

Substituting Nkongolo for Lueji, Mbidi Kiluwe for Chibinda, and Kalala Ilunga for Naweji, this triangle of blood also takes us back to the Luba epic. But only Nkongolo is described as "red," in opposition to the "black" Mbidi and his warrior son. However, among the Ndembu the category "red," connoted by the *mukula* tree, *mukundu* clay, and other signs, itself forms part of a larger code including "white" and "black." The ternary principle that we have discovered in the Ndembu

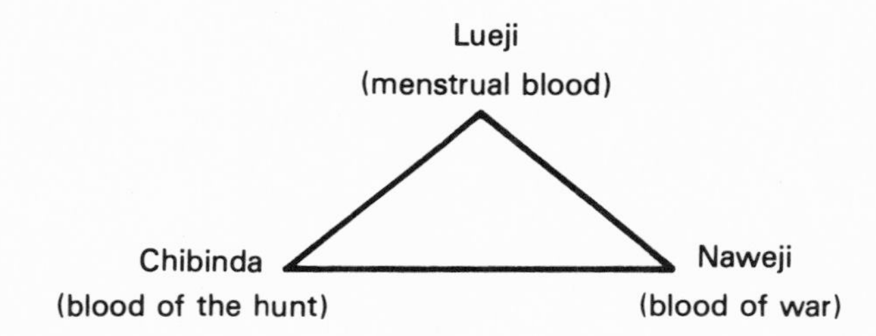

blood rites and in the Lunda epic is also present in the construction of the general color code described by Turner.[41] But according to Turner, the triad can be reduced to a binary black/white system displayed along different axes:

White	*Black*
purity	absence of purity
good	evil
absence of bad luck	bad luck
life	death
friendship	sorcery
make visible	obscurity, night
etc.	etc.

Turner observes that in many rites "black" symbols are absent; to use them would be tantamount to invoking death, sterility, sorcery. Therefore red/white is the only active opposition, the first color sometimes taking on the malign significance of black. That is why Turner considers red to be an ambivalent symbolic category in Ndembu thought, with white being positive and black negative. The Ndembu say explicitly: "Redness acts both for good and ill."[42] For example, menstrual blood is "black" while the blood shed by a hunter is beneficent and associated with whiteness. Sperm is blood "purified by water," that is, "whitened."[43]

Contrary to what Turner thinks, these examples in no way support a reduction in practice of the initial ternary structure to a binary system. We shall endeavor to take account of the "ambivalence" of red while honoring the triad educed by Turner himself but thereafter abandoned at the cost of a logical contradiction: for if red is substituted for black and is operative in a binary system in which the other term is white, it cannot without grave confusion be equally associated with white. Red is an autonomous symbolic category, and the color triad should be taken seriously. We shall show it to be founded on a double opposition, all the elements of which Turner provides without drawing the necessary conclusion: red and white are together opposed to black insofar as they both connote "activity"; but red and white are opposed to one another as "preservation and continuity of life" (white) is to "danger" (red).[44] Therefore it seems desirable to abandon the idea of an "ambivalent" red category inside the color triangle.

But there is a preliminary problem. To what "signified"* does red relate when free of all allegiance to white or black? We shall begin by eliminating all kinds of blood symbolically associated with white or black and, in particular, menstrual blood (black) and the blood of the hunt (white). Only the blood of homicide and war now remains of our initial triangle of blood. However, Turner notes incidentally that war and peace are opposed as red is to white, and that these colors are both opposed to black, the category of death and negativity.[45] There is little about war in Turner's researches into symbolism. The *wubanji* ritual intended to purify a man guilty of killing a fellow tribesman, a lion, or a leopard, and the *kutomboka* dance executed by the war chief at the presentation of the heads of enemies killed in battle, are briefly mentioned during a preliminary analysis of the circumcision ritual.[46] In this study we learn that "the blood of homicide is a mark of courage," the affirmation of a transgression calling for admiration. The Lunda myth M20 has familiarized us with the idea that war takes on an original and positive value; this is evidently the converse of the negative value of the crime of sorcery (which belongs, according to Turner, to the black category), just as it inverts the diverse values of peace and social harmony connoted by the white category. War clearly defines the red apex of our triangle, while the white apex signifies peace and social harmony and the black apex sorcery.

It remains to specify the positions of the "ambivalent" red terms, whether turned toward white, or black. The infertile sperm of impotent men is situated like, menstrual blood, along the axis uniting red and

*"Signified" (*signifié*) is the term originally proposed by de Saussure to denote the conceptual component of a sign (or symbol) and is opposed to its complement, the concrete image or "signifier" (*signifiant*). Ferdinand de Saussure, *Cours de Linguistique Générale*, Paris, Payot, 1949, p.99. (First edition, Geneva, 1916.) (R.W.)

black since it is made of "blackened" blood, conversely to fertile sperm, which is "whitened" blood.[47] The blood of the hunt is "ritually associated with white symbolism"[48] like the blood of childbirth; the *mudyi* tree with its white bark notably connotes the close tie between a mother and her infant.[49] But we have seen that the blood of childbirth is expressly described as menstrual blood that has coagulated round the fetus.[50] It should therefore be inscribed on another axis joining menstruation, situated between red and black, and the hunt, situated between red and white. We have already explained the reasons for localizing circumcision in a semantic field including menstruation and war within the red subsystem. The more general position we are now adopting confirms this position because Turner's informants say that the blood of the uncircumcised "lacks whiteness" in the same sense as does that of indisposed women.[51] These two modalities of blood should therefore be situated along the axis joining red and black. Finally the position of menstrual blood between red and black is identical to that of a fourth kind of blood of which we have not so far taken account, the "blood of sorcery."[52]

The category black includes at least one positive but suspect value in sexual passion (*wuvumbi*), a door opening onto fertility (white) but also onto the disorders of adultery.[53] It should therefore be inscribed between white and black. Turner notes on this topic that during girls' initiation the old women blacken the vulvas of the novices with the black sap of certain trees to increase their sexual attractiveness;[54] it is remarkable that the most notable bark used for this purpose comes from the *mudyi* tree (*Diplorrhyncus mossambicensis*), the most important *white* symbol: it connotes milk and the maternal breasts, the mother-child relationship, matrilineage, femininity, and the like.[55] The black powder obtained by pulverizing its bark nevertheless has the property of "blackening" the vulva, which thereupon becomes an "ambivalent" sign evoking "sexual lust and adultery (which sometimes lead to murder and sorcery)."[56] That is why particularly dark women are especially desirable as mistresses, but not as wives.[57] In this connection Turner evokes the Wagnerian concept of mortal passion. It is precisely this kind of passion that Lueji experiences for the stranger-hero, a passion that upsets the harmony of the autochthonous group and leads to sterility.

We thus verify that our first red triangle (shadowed in the scheme above) constitutes a subsystem (as it were, a reduction) of the triadic

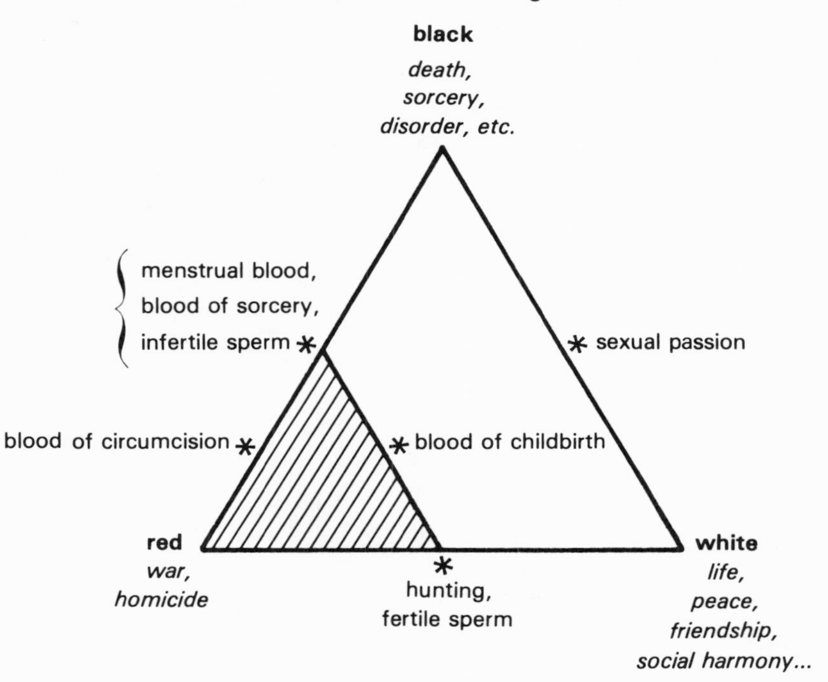

structure which also includes white and black. The category red, which immediately suggests blood, is the richest and most complex because it relates to the principal masculine activities of hunting and war and to the reproductive function of woman. It is this basal triangle that we find in the myth, while the initiatory teachings appear to emphasize the general color code. It will be seen that there is no hesitation about evoking the black category in these teachings. Suffice it to note here that the novices of the *mungonge* and *chiwila* religious associations are taught about "the mystery of the three rivers," respectively white, red, and black. The first, the oldest, is "the trunk to which the red and black rivers are attached like branches," according to the very words of one of Turner's informants. The red river signifies the couple and copulation; the black river, the youngest, evokes death. A riddle, the esoteric sense of which is explained in *mungonge*, makes the meaning of the principal river explicit: it makes white water the metaphoric image of sperm.[58] The ancient white water that "flows straight toward the initiatory shelter" must therefore be the river of life that is fed by the river of blood and is eventually polluted by the black river. Only the white and red rivers come from God; the red river is dangerous and it is forbidden to talk about it in the village. This belief is also found among the Luba: in the other world (Kalunga) there flows an immense river of clear water with its source in the Creator's palace, but as it gets further from its source it becomes red and bitter and ends up, before falling into the ocean, in a dark valley where bad people who have died endure a miserable existence.[59]

Turner gathered only fragmentary information about the complex symbolism of *mungonge* initiation among the Ndembu. What he did obtain nevertheless fits very well with the description of the Pende ritual that we owe to de Sousberghe (and which we shall examine later). The Pende myth of origin about *mungonge* would be inexplicable without referring to the Lunda-Ndembu color code.

M24, Pende: Origin of the *Mungonge* Male Religious Association (de Sousberghe[60])

> Men had sent *kimunga*, the vulture that eats palm nuts (*Gypohierax angolensis*), to search the sky for white kaolin (*pembe*), the symbol of peace and benediction. But on the way back he rubbed his belly with kaolin. He did not have enough for his whole body, and that is why the back and wings of this bird are black today. All he could offer men was the red earth, *ngula*, color of blood and war, which has left some traces on his plumage. That is why initiation into *mungonge* is bloody.

This myth transposes onto the plumage of a bird that would deny palm nuts to men the (fluvial) system of three colors proper to the initiatory symbolism of *mungonge* among the Ndembu. The western Lunda, from whom the Pende have borrowed this institution, evoke the same bird in this ritual chant: "Chimunga, we asked you for *pembe*, and you came back with *ngula*."[61] De Sousberghe observes that this bird, which is foreign to Pende folklore, plays the role of messenger between the world of the dead and the world of the living among the Lunda. It is indeed the dialectic of death and life, night and day, black and white that *mungonge* teaches in a ritual form wherever it is found. Red, expressly evoking the blood of homicide, complements the two fundamental colors in the feathers of *kimungu*, a bird of ill omen that should have brought peace but came back with war. We shall ascertain that *mungonge* also articulates with the Lunda foundation epic (M20), to which it is time to return.

The Temptations of Palm Wine

Next to blood, palm wine occupies a prominent position in M20. This valued drink is indeed the occasion of the quarrel between Konde and his sons; it is also a mediator between Lueji and the stranger-hunter. Chibinda, who begins by draining the calabashes belonging to one of the princess's important followers, is not looking for trouble: he gives meat in exchange and so comes into contact with Konde's daughter.

Let us go more deeply into the first matter. In one way or another Konde abuses palm wine, whether in reality or in appearance (in the eyes of his sons), so provoking a familial and dynastic crisis.

Struyf's version	*Van den Byvang's version*
Konde gets drunk and is shamelessly naked	Konde keeps the secret of making palm wine to himself
Pogge's and Van den Byvang's versions	*Duysters's and de Carvalho's versions*
Konde makes fun of his sons by letting them think cloudy water is palm wine	The sons reproach their father for abusing palm wine

Struyf's version, collected in a peripheral region near the Kuba, purely and simply reproduces what happened to Woot (M9). Let us begin by asking why palm wine recurs so persistently as a cause of discord in Kuba and Lunda mythology. Drawing the sap of the raffia palm by means of a calabash placed under an incision in the trunk is more like gathering wild produce than it is like agriculture, even though the trees are planted near the villages. Here nature shows herself to be generous. Without demanding much effort, she dispenses a highly valued intoxicating drink. But furthermore, the Kuba also obtain useful products from the raffia palm. The foliage serves to make ropes, while leaves, branches, and trunk are used as building materials.[62] Palm trees are individually owned and belong to those who plant them.[63] We have seen that this tree symbolizes the whole culture in the initiatory ritual (see p. 113). A myth explains its origin.

M25, Kuba: Origin of the Raffia Palm (Torday[64])

> At the time of creation, a great lake contained palm wine. People helped themselves to the wine at will. Then one day a woman urinated in the lake. She was surprised by a man, who reproached her for her antisocial act. Very soon the lake dried up. Four unknown kinds of shrub began to grow in the basin. Some years later they had become a forest. A Pygmy had the idea of making a hole in one of the trees in the hope of discovering the vanished palm wine, but the sap did not flow. Then the Pygmy saw a man in a dream who advised him to persevere. The next day he cut the tree again. This time a thin trickle came out. After a few days, a large vessel had filled with palm wine. The Pygmy returned to the village in a drunken state and caused a lot of trouble. He was taken before the king, and told him secretly of the reasons for his disorderly conduct. The king sent a man to check on what the Pygmy had said. When this was confirmed, the king caused the palm tree fruit to be harvested and the seeds distributed throughout the country. Since then the Kuba avoid drinking palm wine alone. They always invite friends to join them.

This narrative is of great interest because it shows how natural palm wine was lost through the indecency of a woman, then rediscovered on the cultural level. When palm wine was as abundant as water men apparently used it with moderation: the first drunkenness occurred with the first drawing by incision, which provides only moderate quantities. The myth teaches how palm wine passed from the order of the continuous (nature) to the discontinuous order of the cultural. This break introduces delay and labor where abundance formerly reigned. But the patient collection of palm wine, which henceforth has a certain agricultural form, brings with it the danger of extreme and antisocial behavior. That is why the Kuba decided it should no longer be consumed alone, but always in the company of others. M9 has already taught us that the solitary drinking of palm wine is a cause of disorder: when Woot becomes drunk and takes off his clothes his sons make fun of him. Palm wine carries the same value in the

Lunda epic: no matter what version, the dispute of father and sons is always associated with a situation that is really—or could seem to be—an excessive solitary consumption of palm wine that is not shared or is denied to others.

Palm wine therefore expresses in a new mode the fearsome power of nature, which had formerly dispensed wine liberally. In this respect, palm wine suggests parallels with Amerindian honey.[65] It is situated, like the honey that is easily transformed into an alcoholic drink, between natural products that are collected and agricultural produce in the strict sense. More exactly, the reign of nature seems to extend itself into the arboriculture that has palm wine as its object. It is easy to understand why it gives rise to such wide-ranging reflections. Palm wine is the mediator between nature, to which it formerly belonged entirely, and culture, which now regulates its production and consumption. In the Lunda epic, the exchange of game for palm wine leads to the meeting of Lueji and the stranger-hunter. Withdrawn from the natural realm, it becomes preeminently suitable for social exchange. It frequently accompanies matrimonial transactions in Central Africa. But its abuse exposes the culture to a regressive process: in a Kuba myth (M11) a son refuses to offer it to his father and isolates himself to drink with his mother. Palm wine is therefore also a mediator between incest and exogamy.

That being the case, Chibinda's ceremonial consumption of palm wine presents a paradox: the hero withdraws into a hut to drink alone and unobserved. This custom, of Luba origin, was faithfully observed at the Lunda court at the end of the nineteenth century.[66] The customs of divine kingship curiously take us back to a dangerous situation: solitary drinking, associated with drunkenness and incest in Kuba mythology. The incest theme is absent from the Lunda myth but it recurs in royal practice. The hyperexogamic marriage of the stranger-hero is transformed in subsequent generations into an incestuous "passion" that de Carvalho, who is so prudish about Lueji's menstruation, is pleased to describe with some exaggeration: the king would summon his sisters, aunts, and nieces to his "harem."[67] Whatever the truth of that, we know from a reliable source (de Sousberghe) that the paramount chief of the Lunda of the old district of Kwango, the Mwata Kombana, had to have sexual relations with a full sister at the time of his installation.[68] The sacredness of power is founded at least partially on this symbolic regression that situates palm wine in a circular structure in which royalty rediscovers the natural order beyond culture.

Nature	*Culture*	*Royalty*
solitary drunkenness	exchange of palm wine	solitary consumption
incest	exogamy	ritual incest

If palm wine makes its appearance only in the Kuba-Lunda culture area, it is because it properly belongs to the western region of the savanna civilization.[69] According to Denolf, the raffia palm was unknown in the east of Kasai.[70] Neither does it occur in Ndembu symbolism, which seems to substitute mead for palm wine. Mead (*hydromel*) is considered a "wild" or "violent" drink (it is hard to find an exact translation for the English term "fierce" used by Turner) in opposition to maize beer, which is soft and feminine.[71] This single indication relating to an intoxicating drink made from honey does not allow us to reconstitute the whole ideology. But it confirms our initial suggestion that palm wine occupies the same semantic space in Central Africa that honey does in America.

Menstrual Blood and the Rainbow

It is a risky undertaking to assemble the scattered cosmogonic elements in the Lunda epic into a coherent whole. We have established that Lueji is a metaphoric transformation of the rainbow, concretely personified by Nkongolo in the Luba epic (M1). The feminine menstrual blood of the heroine flows downward, whereas the masculine rainbow reaches toward the sky. These two natural phenomena beyond man's control are felt to be threatening: the first as concerns fecundity, the second cosmically. Menstrual blood prevents the formation of the fetus, just as the rainbow stops the rain. The vulva of Lueji inversely restores the bleeding head of Nkongolo. Since Nkongolo's head is in a relation of homology with the sun, it is tempting to believe that conversely Lueji's vulva is a lunar figure. Does not the periodic retreat in the hut, insisted on by the myth, evoke the moon's monthly disappearance? The female mediums of M22, mythical figures intermediate between Nkongolo and Lueji, strengthen this hypothesis because in their case the onset of menstruation coincides with the darkness of the new moon. A people with close historical links with the Lunda, the Chokwe, explicitly assimilate the moon to woman and the sun to man.[72] Further, the Chokwe give the moon the name of *Kakweji,* which is semantically close to that designating the Lunda heroine. If the inversion in relation to the Luba myth is coherent, the hunter-hero and his descendants should be assimilated to the sun among the Lunda.

The sparse information relating to Lunda royal symbolism does indeed bear witness to the solar character of the kings descended from Chibinda Ilunga: "All Lunda know that the sun symbolizes the *Mwaant Yaav* (*Mwata Yamvo*)."[73] The beneficent sun is opposed to the maleficent moon. To quote Crine-Mavar, the sun is to the moon as the sovereign is to great disasters: "the *Mwaant Yaav* protects his subjects, wards off calamities; the sun succeeds the moon, night, and death."[74]

The Lunda queen mother who perpetuates the memory of Lueji, the *Swanamulanda*—does she therefore symbolize this moon, dangerous if not maleficent? Unfortunately it is impossible to answer this question with certainty in advance of the publication of the definitive results of Crine-Mavar's long field researches of recent years. In 1957 Biebuyck was able to observe the protocol of the Lunda royal council at the capital, Musumba: the *Swanamulanda*, venerated as the mother of the nation, sat to the right of the sovereign, while the *Lukonkesha*, the king's symbolic mother, sat at his left.[75] According to an old report of de Carvalho, the two queen mothers would live side by side in the eastern half of a symbolic space with the form of a tortoise having its head to the east and tail to the west.[76] The royal palace would occupy the center of the western part. The huts serving as retreat for high-ranking women during their menstrual periods would be built at a place corresponding to the hind legs of the "tortoise." The queen mothers would therefore disappear periodically toward the west for several days.

It seems likely that this symbolic geography relates to the apparent movements of the moon. But if this is so, the queen mothers should disappear for several days *toward the east*, after the moon's cyclical movement whereby it appears to move in this direction, reappearing in the sky to the west of the point where it disappeared. These astronomical deductions lead us to suggest reversing the east-west axis in de Carvalho's schema. This rotation through 180 degrees restores the solar king's palace to the eastern half from its incongruous location by de Carvalho in the western half. Such a conclusion might seem rash were it not for a recent report by Lucas which, without the author being aware of its implications, has confirmed the validity of this ethnographic rectification. The plan of the capital drawn in 1964 by Gubbels locates the quarters of the two army chiefs (which in de Carvalho's schema correspond to the tail of the symbolic tortoise) *in the east and not in the west.*[77] Such being the case, the queen mothers would live in the western half of the capital, as we have suggested; when they have their menstrual periods they disappear eastward, like the moon, to reside in ritual huts in the region representing the tortoise's hind legs.

This correction allows us to recover the cosmogonic meaning of the topography. However, the reason why this sacred space takes the form of a tortoise remains obscure. In the course of his field inquiries Lucas was unable to discover the significance of this representation, on which de Carvalho offers no comment. But according to Marie-Louise Bastin, the slow movements of this animal evoke the majesty of chiefs among the Chokwe; the song of the young tortoise is intoned in honor of nubile girls; its shell is used to contain "medicines" of all sorts, especially hunting charms; and when placed in the roof of a hut it protects against lightning.[78] Baumann says that this talisman is effective against excessive rain.[79] In these various ways the tortoise is an apt symbol for the new dynasty founded by Chibinda Ilunga, hunter and bearer of fecundity. The cosmogonic character of the shell with which the capital is identified possibly relates to the solar king's ability to command the lightning and its destructive powers.[80] To these observations should be added a brief cosmogonic text from the Lunda of the Kahemba region, that we owe to Roelandts.[81] This valuable document reveals the existence of a fundamental dualism opposing the lightning to the rainbow on one side and the rain to terrestrial waters on the other.

M26, Lunda of Kahemba: Origin of the World (Roelandts)

The primordial serpent, Tianza Ngombe (or Chinaweshi), the mother of all things, divided up the world with the lightning,

> Nzashi, her husband. The latter set himself up in the sky with the sun, the moon, Venus, and the stars; his urine became the beneficial rain. Tianza Ngombe, on her side, had the earth and the rivers. When the thunder rumbles in the sky, Tianza Ngombe responds in the waters and the rivers become swollen. Tianza Ngombe bore a son, Konde, and a daughter, Naweshi. These two united incestuously and had three children, among them Lueshi (Lueji). At the confluence of two rivers Lueshi met Chibinda Ilunga, the tireless hunter with the long hair who was a master of his art and became chief.

The presence of the heroes of M20 in this cosmogonic narrative authorizes its insertion in the mythical ensemble we are concerned with, even though it comes from a peripheral Lunda region. The Chokwe, who know Tianze Ngombe under the name of Chanza Ngombe, identify him with the rainbow (Nkongolo), a fearsome aquatic spirit.[82] The Lunda-Chokwe cosmogony is therefore founded on the grand opposition between the rainbow serpent, master of terrestrial waters, and the lightning-animal, master of rain and storm, which belongs to the armature of the Luba epic (M1). If the hunter Chibinda Ilunga is really a solar hero, as suggested by Lunda royal symbolism, he belongs to the world above, ruled by the lightning, in opposition to the world below connoted by the rainbow serpent. But the serpent is now seen to be the most remote ancestor of Lueji; a tradition collected by Biebuyck[83] at the court of the Lunda sovereign gives Lueji a primordial ancestor called "Chinawezi," whose name is no more than a slight phonetic transformation of the serpent Chinaweshi of M26. Crine-Mavar furthermore tells us that the installation ritual causes the new sovereign to participate "in the nature of the chthonic serpent-god Chinaweezi."[84] We know that this ritual occurs in the dry season. Leaving the capital, the designated heir is carried on a man's back over the Kalanyi River at a time when the waters are at their lowest. He would lose his title if he came into contact with the water. On the opposite bank he is led into an enclosure by the chiefs of the land (men of Lueji), who remind him that they are the true owners of the country. They awake him in the middle of the night and oblige him to light a fire.[85]

These fragmentary items of information do not allow a complete exegesis. But at least one can say that in crossing the river the future king goes in a direction opposite to that taken by Chibinda when he met Lueji. He quits the terrestrial domain bequeathed to the queen by the primordial aquatic serpent Chinaweezi and so finds himself at the zero point of human, and perhaps even of universal, history. Separated from terrestrial water, the domain of Chinaweezi, and brought to the fire, is the future king not identified with Nzashi, master of lightning and rain, who draws the sun and the stars on high? The new ritual fire, lit in the middle of the night on the farther bank, is plainly a fire heralding the sun; we shall see presently that throughout the area of Lunda expansion the nocturnal fire lit during the culminating phase of the *mungonge* ritual expressly connotes the light of the sun; among the Pende it is identified more precisely with Venus (see p. 190). The hyperexogamic union of Chibinda and Lueji, which is played out again in the sacred theater of royalty, now appears as hierogamy, a marriage of heaven and earth. By correlating the cosmogonic code of M26 and the familial code of M20 we obtain the following metastructure: a solar king, master of lightning, comes from afar (from the sky, like the Luba hunter-hero) to meet the granddaughter of the rainbow serpent, the master of terrestrial waters. As in the Luba epic (M1), a river separates the realm above from the realm below.

Hypothetically, we provisionally suggest the following cosmogonic division:

Chibinda	*Lueji*
solar fire	terrestrial waters
lightning and rain	rainbow serpent
wet season	dry season
fecundity	sterility
sun	moon

A fragment of the Lunda epic (M20, Struyf's version), as yet unexplained, becomes clear once we realize that Lueji's family is protected by the spirit of terrestrial waters. Konde, the heroine's father, struggles with a Chokwe chief for power. He crosses a river in a canoe without incident, while an aquatic animal that is not described but could well be Chinaweezi grabs the insignia of his rival (see p. 150). The very name of Lueji's father asserts a relation with terrestrial water and reptiles, for "Konde" means the little crocodile *osteolaemus* according to a tradition recorded by Biebuyck.[86] Further, in Struyf's version the mysterious Tyanza ya Koola (Tyanza from the Lunda country of origin), who is said to have reigned during Lueji's minority, is evidently the rainbow serpent (Tianza Ngombe) of M26.

This first rainbow dynasty practices incest like the family of Nkongolo among the Luba: during four generations, up to and including Konde, Lueji's father, the sons and successors of Chinaweezi marry their sisters.[87] In both cases the advent of a stranger-hunter marks the transition from incest to hyperexogamy and heralds the transformation of a rudimentary culture into a more refined civilization. But the Roelandts manuscript tells us that the ritual union of the Lunda chiefs with their sisters is inspired by the converse mythical model provided by M26 (the incestuous union of Konde and Naweshi). Lunda divine kingship, like its Luba homologue, therefore realizes a dialectical synthesis of its two historical sources, which are really symbolic expressions of complementary aspects of the universe.

If we compare the cosmogonic material in the Lunda and Luba epics, we find that the change in sex of the rainbow serpent entails another modification: the masculine moon is associated in M1 (Luba) with fecundity and the wet season, while in M20 (Lunda) the same heavenly body, now feminine, is situated on the side of the rainbow, sterility, and the dry season, with the sun connoting the beneficent power of the royal hunter. The rainbow is an invariable semantic complex, whereas the moon and sun are unstable signs. Hostile brothers-in-law in the Luba epic, a sterile couple in the Lunda, sun and moon always connote the double opposition drought/rain, sterility/fecundity. But the change in sex of the moon entails a permutation of their respective domains:

Luba (M1)		*Lunda* (M20)	
Nkongolo /	Mbidi	Lueji /	Chibinda
(sun)	(moon)	(moon)	(sun)
drought /	rain	drought /	rain
sterility /	fecundity	sterility /	fecundity

This structural instability of the moon partly resolves the difficult exegetical problem presented by Luba popular beliefs. It will be recalled that these beliefs suggest a capricious moon of fluctuating moods, sometimes related to Nkongolo and sometimes to Mbidi, midway between life and death (see p. 53). Indeed, the moon can be associated as much with the dry as with the wet season; like the sun, it is not linked in any necessary way to either form of seasonal periodicity.

The cosmogonic symbolism of the Chokwe reproduces the Lunda code in all respects: in it the beneficent sun is associated with a mythical *hunter* called Samuhangi, represented in a mural painting as "armed with a club and gripping the solar disc."[88] Long ago this hero revealed the secrets of hunting magic. Through an association that is now familiar, he is venerated both by hunters and by sterile women. Like hunting and fecundity, divination is placed under the sign of the sun. More fortunate than the physicist Joseph Plateau, who was permanently blinded by the solar glare while studying the retinal persistence of its image,* the Chokwe diviner fearlessly contemplates its symbolic likeness while probing into the unknown: he finds the answer he needs by scrutinizing a mirror placed at the bottom of a small basket and partly covered by a waxen rosette representing the sun at its zenith.[89] The circular form of the winnowing tray (*lwalo*) also symbolizes the beneficent sun; placed at the top of a pole, it has the power to stop torrential rain.[90] The Chokwe sun is thus also, like the Lunda king, the master of the wet season.

*Joseph Plateau (1801–1883) was a nineteenth-century Belgian physicist whose major discovery was the persistence of retinal images. He became blind in 1843. (R.W.)

[CHAPTER SIX]

Animals with Eyes of Night

The Mungonge *Religious Society*

The Lunda sun-king is immortal. His corpse is entrusted to the *Achudyaang* association and submitted to a mysterious ritual of "resurrection."[1] This important religious society, more usually known under the name of *mungonge*, is represented throughout the area of Lunda expansion, notably among the Ndembu and Luvale of Zambia, the Chokwe of Angola, and the Yaka of Zaïre.[2] Among the Lunda proper, the term *mungonge* (*mungony*) is applied to the ritual dance performed by the *Achudyaang* when they celebrate the foundation myth.[3] Turner considers that this association has the dual function of preventing the spirits of the departed from troubling the living and of imparting a religious mystery to the young men.[4] White disputes the first point. Among the Luvale the funeral function is of secondary importance, while the rites of initiation are a constant preoccupation. These rites create a mystical communion with the dead and the initiates acquire a new and indeed superhuman nature.[5] The initiatory process is fairly uniform. The "ancestors" and their helpers take hold of the novices and cut and bruise them during a night of ordeals, in the course of which one or more men mounted on stilts make mysterious appearances. The admission of the neophytes after their ritual death is marked by an alimentary rite: brought at dawn to a sacred enclosure, they are given some boiled cassava through a gap in the palisade.

Some idea of the complex significance of the ritual can be gained from the information, albeit incomplete, obtained by de Sousberghe among the Pende of Kwango in southwest Zaïre, notwithstanding his exclusion from participation in the rites themselves.[6] Thanks to this capital text, we can attempt to outline the symbolic structure without any pretence of direct access to these well-guarded secrets.

There seems no doubt as to the institution's Lunda origin. Although de Sousberghe states that the *mungonge* society is no longer a funereal association, the only occasion it appears in public, apart from initiations, is in connection with deaths among its membership.[7] Furthermore, the initiation itself establishes "close relations with the dead."[8] The society is exclusively masculine but, as commonly elsewhere, it has a feminine counterpart (*chiwila*) about which virtually nothing is known. In the ceremony described by de Sousberghe, the symbolism of the moon and the sun is especially striking. The candidates are symbolically slain at night by hyena-men operating under the sign of the maleficent moon; their resurrection occurs with the return of daylight. The initiatory ritual eloquently underlines the cosmogonic oppositions we have already elicited from the Lunda myths:

sky	earth
day	night
sun	moon
life	death
abundance of food	shortage of food, or famine

Men on stilts appear at the crucial moment, at the end of the night of ordeals. Just before dawn, they wave on high a torch expressly representing the morning star that presages the benign return of sunlight. These impressive figures, called *Mbongo*, ritually achieve the cosmogonic goal that has eluded so many builders of mythical towers: reuniting heaven and earth so as to become immortal like God or the sun.

The *mungonge* songs oppose the low, night, and death, to the high, sunlight, and life. The terrestrial animals and birds evoked in the songs are associated with obscurity. The *kwanji* bird (the hornbill, *Bycanistes*) makes its nest in the hollow of a tree trunk. The nesting female is shut in there behind a wall of dried mud and fed through a tiny aperture: if the male is killed, the female starves to death.[9] The blue pheasant *kolomvu* (*Corytheola*) is called "a denizen of dark places";[10] the pangolin is "an inhabitant of hollow trees";[11] the aardvark "disinters the corpses of Kalunga" (the underground world of the dead), whereas the men on stilts "walk in the sky; they have added (sticks) to their heels."[12] The whole world of terrestrial animals is associated with darkness in this splendid invocation that the Pende address to their ancestors to ensure success in hunting: "Deliver unto us, we men with eyes of light, the beast with eyes of darkness!"[13] This world lies under the sign of the moon. The sun, introduced by the Mbongo stilt-dancers, is opposed to the hyena-moon in the organizer's opening address to the candidates when the ceremony begins.

In this context we have a minor disagreement with de Sousberghe. The text emanating from the Lunda *mungonge* is as plain as can be: "Who are thy grandfathers? My grandfathers are the sun of Ilunga (*Kasai ka Ilunga*) and the hyena of Ilunga (*Chimbungu cha Ilunga*)."[14] And the Lunda commentators state unequivocally that the hyena is a metaphoric image of the moon. However, de Sousberghe inexplicably gives a completely different interpretation of the very similar Pende formula. According to de Sousberghe, the term *kasadi* (or *kasai*) does not simply represent the sun but "the light appearing by day in the sun, at night in the moon," while the hyena (*Chimbungu*) is the symbol of darkness and night.[15] But this is contradictory, and clearly the Lunda interpretation, equating the "hyena of the sky" with the moon, is correct. This reading is moreover confirmed by Cordemans: "They call the sun *kasala k' ilunga* . . . , the moon *chimbungu ch'ilunga* (hyena of ilunga)."[16]

This celestial hyena has a terrestrial counterpart in the initiatory ritual of the Luvale and Chokwe: a personage walking on four feet and called by the name of this animal precedes the band of the dead that comes to torment the novices.[17] On consulting Roelandts's copy of a Pende initiatory sketch (*khata*), there can be no further doubts as to the identity of the mythical hyena: it shows, on the upper left-hand side, a circle with the words "*Kasali ka Ilunga* (sun)," and on the upper right an identical circle inscribed "*Chimbungu ka Ilunga* (moon)."[18] We are far from exhausting the complex symbolism of these esoteric drawings, but it is noteworthy that, according to Roelandts, they specially evoke the union of the hunter Chibinda and Lueji and the resulting dispersion of peoples. The *mungonge* ritual therefore takes us back to the foundation myth of the Lunda empire.

But one difficulty arises: the absence in M20 of any figure comparable to the Mbongo stilt-dancer, the herald of sunlight. Even the sun itself is not directly evoked in the myth. To what other myth can this strange personage refer? A piece of information kindly provided by Bastin gives us a clue. In the Chokwe ritual, the single stilt-man

Mbongo wears a conical straw hat, with a tuft of feathers from the *kumbi* bird dangling by a string from its tip.[19] But this bird, which in reality has elongated, stiltlike legs, plays a key role in the foundation myth of *mungonge* among the Lunda. The bird in question is a small black stork with a white belly, the *Sphenorhynchus Abdimii*,[20] whose name also designates the sun. The Luvale term for this creature (*londakumbi*) is even more significant, because *londa* comes from the archaic verb *ku-londa*, to follow.[21] Horton, to whom we owe this information, explains that the stork *londakumbi* is often seen flying high in the sky toward the setting sun (*likumbi*). Here is how this solar bird came to be directly responsible for the *mungonge* dance.

M27, Lunda: Origin of the *Achudyaang* Funerary Association (Crine-Mavar[22])

A Lunda group, the Amalas, consisted of two moieties, the Amalas Ankul (vomiters of wet earth) and the Amalas Achaan (vomiters of dry earth). During the reign of the first Mwata Yamvo (king), the women belonging to the wet-earth moiety went to a pond to dry it up so they could gather the fish. They exhausted themselves in vain at this task. Then two birds, *nkumb* (the stork *kumbi*) and *kaaz*, came and perched on the bank. The beating of their wings soon dried up the pond. But during their efforts some feathers fell out of their wings. The women gathered them up and stuck them in their hair. They also used them to adorn their ankles. Thus attired, they returned to the village and told of their experience. The men stripped the women of their feathers and hid them in a solitary hut. When the village chief died, the men dressed up in these feathers and danced in imitation of the two birds. The men of the other moiety came running and were initiated during the ceremony. So the funerary association was born.

There are multiple correspondences between the stilt-man (Mbongo) of the ritual and the stilted bird of the myth. The former is either adorned with the feathers of the solar stork (Chokwe) or bears a torch explicitly identified with Venus, heralding the sunrise (Pende); the latter follows the setting sun, thus resembling the evening star. Our little crepuscular stork is doubly a bird of fire. In the myth, it dries up a pond by beating its wings so as to provide the women with food;

in the ritual, Mbongo brandishes fire in the sky as the converse sign of vanished water. We thus have the formula:

$$\text{celestial fire} = \text{terrestrial water}^{(-1)}$$

The *kaaz* bird that accompanies the stork is unfortunately not identified. But in any case the pair cause terrestrial water to disappear by a natural method that men transform into a cultural means (the dance) to affirm the victory of the sun and life and to procure an abundance of food. The mythical stork, associated with the setting sun, comes down from the sky to help women threatened with starvation. The stilt-man Mbongo conversely rises up from the darkened earth toward the sky to bring men a message of hope and a promise of nourishment: a common tradition of the Pende and Lunda teaches that "the *mungonge* came into existence in a time of hunger in order to procure an abundance of food."[23] Among the Yaka in particular, *mungonge* is celebrated to ensure the success of collective hunts.[24] The Pende ritual thus enacts the Lunda origin myth in complementary terms:

M27 (Lunda)	*Pende ritual*
Solar bird of evening comes down from sky to earth (= evening star).	Stilt-man rises up from earth toward sky with the fire of Venus, morning star.
Disappearance of terrestrial water.	Reappearance of celestial fire.

The Lunda initiatory ritual practiced by the *Achudyaang* follows the myth of origin more faithfully, because the initiates mime the dance of the aquatic birds who dry up the pond. The term *mungonge* (*mungony*) means this realist choreography.* But the luminous elements of the myth (sun, Venus) are present there under a form different from that found among the Pende: the old initiates and the neophytes who are to undergo symbolic death gather *at dusk* around a great fire which has supposedly been stolen from the village.[25] This crepuscular fire probably relates to the mythical image of the stork which follows the sun high in the sky *shortly before sundown*. Lunda initiatory ritual reaches its climax under the sign of the sun trium-

*The primary meaning of the term *mungonge* (or *mungony*) is, appropriately, "bird." (R.W.)

phant: the supreme moment in the reintegration of the novices after their night of ordeals occurs when the sun shines at its zenith. The novices then cast off the clothing of banana leaves and take on new names "associated with their future ritual apparel."[26] There could be no better way of proclaiming the solar nature of the members of the funerary brotherhood, who, like the king, are promised a new being, the metaphysic of which remains obscure. On the earthly plane this mystical rebirth in the *Achudyaang* society promises nourishment, since "this change of state is followed by a feast that includes an abundance of goat meat and mutton presented by the village chief."[27] Similar celebrations mark the end of *mungonge* initiation among the Pende. In both cases the myth illuminates this ritualized gastronomy.

This last theme merits closer investigation. At dawn on the second day, the novices take part in a curious chicken hunt that recalls an episode in the initiation of young men among the Kuba (see p. 123). Armed with bows, they rush in a band to the village and gather before the huts of the new initiates' mothers. Each time, the door opens sufficiently to allow the escape of a chicken, which one of the initiates kills with an arrow. The slaughtered birds are hung on a line of strings attached to a pole that two men carry on their shoulders. The poultry is ritually eaten the same day, constituting the final course of a long banquet.[28] A similar episode occurs in the Yaka *mungonge*.[29]

This bogus hunt that occurs at dawn evidently represents metaphorically the return of the sun and nourishment. Transformed into game, the ritual chicken is, as it were, the inverse image of the birds killed by the hunter Kalumbu, who was the originator of *mungonge*, according to the Lunda-Chokwe of the Kulinji region.

M28, Lunda-Chokwe: Origin of *Mungonge* (de Sousberghe[30])

Kalumbu killed many birds, among them the *ndua* (the touraco, *Musophaga Rossae*), the *kolomvu* (the blue pheasant, *Corythaeola cristata*), the *mukuku* (the coucal, *Centropus grillii*), and the *nkwanji* (the hornbill, *Bycanistes*). A time of famine followed. The hunter's wife, Nankoy, got hold of the feathers from the birds her husband had killed and, without his knowledge, made herself a hat (*gayanda*) from the feathers and went dancing with it in the neighboring villages. In this way she obtained food. She did

> the same thing several times, being careful to hide the feathers in an anthill on her return. Astonished by this unexpected influx of comestibles, the husband spied on his wife and surprised her one day with her headdress of feathers. He killed her to obtain the hat. He buried her in the anthill and tried out the dance for himself.

In the ritual, the *Gayanda* hat is worn by the master of ceremonies, who thus represents the mythical hunter in person.[31] It is apparent from the beginning that the ritual quest for the sunlight (heralded by the morning star) and the quest for nourishment go together: the birds' feathers serve as a ritual instrument for getting food. But we need to take account of an apparent paradox. Two of the species cited are already known to us as associated with darkness and night: the *kwanji* and the *kolomvu*. The red feathers of the *ndua* situate it on the side of death: after preliminary instruction the new members of *mungonge* return to the village, each with a touraco feather in his hair.[32] In our opinion de Sousberghe is in error when he interprets this feather as "the sign of success in the ordeal." In fact, the initiates wear this feather for several days, while their bodies are covered with red powder. The powder was brought to men by another bird of ill omen, the vulture that eats palm nuts (see p. 176). In connection with this myth, de Sousberghe himself notes that the color red signifies blood and war.[33] That is why the officiant who most directly symbolizes death in the Luvale *mungonge* bears the very name of the touraco (*nduwa*) and wears one of its feathers in his hair.[34] Among the Ndembu, all those who have shed blood (hunters, murderers, circumcisers) do the same.[35]

A fourth bird cited in M28, the coucal, known to the Pende as *kulukulu*, sings at night, some time before dawn. The coucal "on the edge of the forest" and the cock "on the edge of the village" seem to call to each other as they announce a new day.[36] In the general perspective that concerns us here, the coucal appears as the nocturnal and wild homologue of the cock, the solar bird.

All the birds in this myth are therefore associated with darkness (the *kolomvu* and the *kulukulu*), with hunger (the *kwanji*), or with death (the *ndua*), whereas the stork *kumbi* of M27, although associated with the dusk, bears the light of Venus. The respective bestiaries of the two foundation myths of *mungonge* undoubtedly form a system of oppositions. The transformation of M28 into M27 is easily made out:

M28	M27
birds as objects of a masculine hunt	birds as subjects of feminine fishing
woman deprived of feathers by her husband	women deprived of feathers by men
feathers serve culturally (in the dance) to obtain food (agricultural products)	feathers serve naturally (beating of wings) to obtain food (products of fishing)

We can now account for the paradoxical function of birds in M28. The auspicious, food-providing stork of the twilight in M27 is replaced by various birds of darkness and ill omen who herald famine. To remedy this situation it is necessary to use their plucked feathers as a dress. In contrast, the Venusian stork intervenes actively, using a natural method to overcome the cultural impotence of the women. The feathers shaken from his wings serve as much to ward off hunger as to ward off death. M27 therefore has a stronger figurative sense than M28, which remains entirely at the alimentary level.

Alimentary and cosmogonic references are included in the ritual of aggregation, which consists of a meal (the "meal of the night") taken *at cock-crow*, after the symbolic death. The new initiates take turns in seizing with their teeth a ball of cassava presented to them on the end of a stick by an invisible person concealed behind a palisade.[37] This curious procedure suggests that the novice, who is precluded from using his hands, is treated as an animal "with eyes of night" before acceding to the community of men of light. This interpretation is confirmed by an odd detail which has so far remained unexplained. An underground tunnel connects the interior of the enclosure to the outside (where the recipient stands). He is told to plunge his arms into the tunnel and "catch the rat inside." The officiant waiting at the other end winds a noose round the hand (as though it were caught in a trap) and makes incisions on it: the resulting scar, which is in the form of a cross, is the badge by which initiates recognize one another. It is then that the novice is offered the piece of cassava pudding. The fact that this food has been mixed with red earth suggests it is impure and, in a sense, like the flesh of the rat the neophyte was supposed to hunt before being caught himself in a metaphysical trap. This ritual of aggregation is comparable to the final phase of the circumcision ritual. Here also the seclusion of the new initiates ends with a repugnant meal: they eat raw meat.[38] After the "meal of the night" the new adepts of *mungonge* truly find themselves in a state intermediate between death and life, nature and culture: dressed in leaves, bodies stained with red earth, they parade through the village with heads held low. They are given presents by close relatives and join briefly in the villagers' dance. Then suddenly, on a bizarre signal something like the howl of a whipped dog, they flee into the bush and trade their garments of leaves for woven loincloths. Then they are ready for a first initiatory lesson. They are not really reintegrated into village life until the day of the curious chicken hunt that we have already discussed.

This symbolic search for the sun marks the attainment of a privileged religious position. In particular, the initiates benefit from a special funerary ritual. This ritual is conducted by the master of ceremonies (*Gayanda*), who wears a hat and a mantle of feathers; significantly, the feathers come from the birds of darkness enumerated in M28. Gayanda, decked in his finery, repairs to the home of the dying man and places magic grasses all round the edge of the hut roof.[39] Accompanied by other initiates, he attends the sick man in his last moments. Immediately after the man's death, Gayanda climbs on the roof, removes the truss of straw at the top, and covers the hole with his hat and his mantle of feathers. He recovers his apparel as the funeral party moves toward the grave. After the interment, he cuts off part of his mantle and sticks feathers in the earth of the grave. The feathers that allowed the heroes of M28 to overcome famine also ensure the passage of the dead to a new life in the beyond. A feather of a cock and that of a hen, solar birds, are added to the feathers from the birds of darkness; a ball of white clay, symbol of light, is placed above the head of the corpse.[40] Several days later the deceased's hut, around which the initiates gather in festive mood, is burned down. This complex ritual reveals the metaphysical sense of the foundation myth: repletion after fasting is the metaphorical image of a veritable rebirth of solar man. That is why the gravediggers throw cassava and millet into the half-filled grave.

Fire and the solar stilt-man constitute an indissoluble combination in all the *mungonge* rituals. These two elements are united in the person of the Pende torchbearer. Among the Lunda, the chief of the ritual, the *Samazembi*, perched on stilts, comes and goes around a fire in the initiatory enclosure.[41] The Chokwe call by the very name of the supreme being (Kalunga) the two ritual fires burning in the enclosure, their flames supposedly reaching the sky.[42] The present paucity of information precludes our making explicit the connection between these fires and Venus. However, the star of morning and evening is present in the Chokwe ritual in a veiled form: the stilt-man Mbongo wears stork feathers on the top of his headdress. In Chokwe thinking, Venus is the wife of the sun.[43]

We have not exhausted the riches of the cosmogonic code of M27 in noting that it symbolizes the succession of days and nights. It is evidently no accident that the beating wings of the solar bird *dry* up the waters of a pond where the women belonging to the *wet earth* moiety go to fish. The mythical bipartition of primitive Lunda society (dry earth/wet earth) does not appear to relate to any real institution. But it could well connote the alternation of the seasons in quasi-totemic terms. A myth of the twilight, M27 also takes us back to this time of the year when the rain-swamped lands do not lend themselves to fishing. The drying action of the two birds suggests a change of season. The seasonal calendar of the Lunda and related peoples is unfortunately not well described, but we know at least that the Lwena, who are consummate fishermen, build temporary huts near dams where they stay for several weeks, catching fish as the waters recede from the flooded plain.[44*] This item of information, owed to a manuscript note of White's, shows that the method of fishing by "drying," the subject of M27, occurs at the beginning of the dry season.

In consequence, we are led to propose a new thesis: in drying up the pond where the women of the "wet earth" moiety have exhausted themselves, the stork and his mysterious companion bring an end to the wet season; in one and the same cosmic gesture, they inaugurate both night and the dry season. To confirm this hypothesis, the identification of the companion of Venus in M27 is crucial. The lack of information is once again an obstacle. In general, ethnographic reports on the constellations associated with seasonal changes in the Bantu world

*The Lwena people of Angola are, according to White, the same people as those known in Zambia as Luvale. See C. M. N. White, "The Balovale Peoples and their Historical Background," *Rhodes-Livingstone Journal*, 1949, 8, p.27. (R.W.)

are lamentably deficient. To the best of our knowledge, only Jacqueline Roumeguère-Eberhardt has interested herself in this problem in southern Africa. In an invaluable study of Venda symbolism, she observes that the dry season, the time of harvest, is introduced by the heliacal rising of Sirius.[45] If the *kaaz* bird in the Lunda myth could be identified with Sirius, or with any constellation associated with the beginning of the drought, the cosmogonic sense of the myth would be much clearer. The Venus-stork, wife of the sun, burns like a torch of life in the nocturnal sky dominated by the hyena-moon; she prefigures the daily resurrection of the royal sun, and is its veritable annunciation. But with the *kaaz* bird who accompanies her, the stork also connotes the annual rhythm of the seasons, with their associated economic activities. M27, the myth of abundant feminine fishing, completes the foundation myth of the kingdom (M20), with its abundance of male-provided game. Venus collaborates in fishing (in the form of a long-legged bird), while Chibinda, the solar hero, is a hunter.

M20	M27
sun	Venus + an unknown star (? Sirius)
masculine hunt	feminine fishing

Venus, mistress of fish, and the Sun, master of game, remedy a shortage of food in different and distinctive ways. The hunter-hero of M20 brings nourishment to Lueji, heiress of the aquatic serpent; and the helpful birds of M27 join in the fishing of the women of the wet earth. The comparison can be continued on another level: the transmission of the *mungonge* ritual from women to men is analogous, *mutatis mutandis*, to the transmission of divine kingship from Lueji to Chibinda.

If indeed the foundation myth of the State and the origin myth of *mungonge* form a symbolic whole that includes the sun, the moon, and Venus, it should be possible to pursue this deductive game further, even at the very real risk of constructing an imaginary myth. The Venus-stork succeeds the sun at twilight and twinkles on high until the sun's return. Husband and wife, the sun and Venus harmoniously control the succession of day and night. But Venus appears in the double role of morning and evening stars. The first aspect alone is evoked in the Pende ritual, the second in the Lunda myth (M27). The morning star is the promise of agricultural produce (symbolized by cassava in "the meal of the night"); the evening star brings fish. This duality of Venus allows us to encode the transition from the wet to the dry season (evening aspect) and the converse transition (morning aspect) without forgetting its general meaning of abundant food. The evening star is allied only in appearance with the night, the domain of the hyena-moon, symbol of sterility and famine. In the heart of darkness Venus proclaims the eternity of the sun. The following schema shows her semantic position midway between day and night and as homologous articulator of the seasons.

	night		day	
Moon		Venus		Sun
	Evening star (dry season) fishing		Morning star (wet season) agriculture	

The cosmogonic duality of Venus corresponds to a dialectic of the elements: the evening star makes water disappear (M27), the morning star is materialized by fire (Pende ritual). It also seems likely, although we are unable to demonstrate it, that the duality of Venus is projected in the two marriages of Chibinda, the one sterile, the other fecund. It may be recalled that we have already been led to formulate this hypothesis in connection with the two wives, of differing degrees of fecundity, of the Luba hero Mbidi Kiluwe (see p. 52).

Venus therefore mediates between day and night, as between the seasons. The ritual context of *mungonge* clearly reveals the existence in the Lunda culture area of a triad Sun-Moon-Venus with the last term playing the dominant role, like the moon in Luba cosmogony: for the Lunda, Venus articulates the longest periodicity with the shortest. The evening star proclaiming the end of the day also connotes, on the mythical plane, the end of the wet season. Conversely, the moon is held to bring the rain among the Luba (see p. 51).

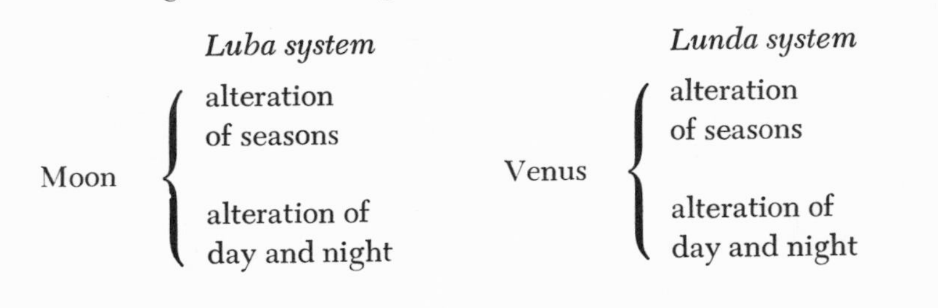

The principal difference between the Lunda and Luba systems is in a permutation of sex and in the role of the moon. In the Lunda epic (M20), the lunar heroine is sterile, the (solar) hunter-hero is fertile; in the corresponding Luba myth (M1) the masculine moon (which we have identified with the hunter-hero) brings fecundity to the sisters of the infertile rainbow. Correlatively, Venus is the wife of the moon for the Luba, while for the Lunda she is the wife of the sun. The sun, associated with the rainbow and drought, is maleficent for the Luba; associated with the wet season, the sun is beneficent for the Lunda.

The giant stilt-man of *mungonge* (Mbongo), who joins sky and earth under the sign of Venus, allows the initiates to dream of immortality without suspending the succession of the seasons. This ritual personage again evokes the Chokwe spirit Samuhangi, who is seen in mural paintings, gripping the sun and carrying a club on his shoulder.[46] A spirit of hunting and fecundity, Samuhangi establishes a new structural link between the solar hunter Chibinda Ilunga (M20) and the *mungonge* ritual with its Mbongo giant. Samuhangi, like Mbongo, also draws our attention to a fragment of the epic of the Lunda of Kazembe.

M29, Lunda (Luapula Valley): Variant of the Myth of the Cosmic Tower (Cunnison[47])

> When the Lunda king was away from his capital with the object of punishing two rebellious chiefs who would not pay tribute, a terrible fire broke out in the quarter of the ironsmith Lubunda. Because he refused to denounce the arsonist, Lubunda was condemned to build a tower that would reach the sun. The edifice collapsed several times, killing Lubunda's men. Lubunda himself fled.

In this short myth, inserted in a historical chronicle, we again come across a familiar theme: a hecatomb is associated with the destruction of a tower intended to join sky and earth (and, according to M6, guarantee immortality). The impossible conjunction of high and low is allied here with an attempt to bring together terrestrial fire (of which the ironsmith is the master) and the celestial fire of royalty. To be able to interpret this fable correctly it would be necessary to know the myths of the forge, but to the best of our knowledge these have never been collected. However, the figure of the ironsmith occurs in an esoteric design (*khata*) of *mungonge* reproduced by Roelandts and recopied by de Sousberghe.[48] The sequel of the narrative merely allows us to guess that the dramatic ascent of Lubunda was at the origin of the discovery of copper: when the first miniature crosses* made their appearance in the country it was said that the exiled ironsmith had made them. An expedition was sent to search for him. These events are said to explain the foundation of the Lunda kingdom of Kazembe.

When the Lunda king personally orders the ironsmith to take hold of the sun it is evident that he is derisively inviting him to rival the king's own power. We suspect that the discovery of copper is an alternative form of the quest for light. However that may be, the mythical ironsmith fails where the *mungonge* stilt-man brandishing the torch of Venus succeeds, as does the hero Samuhangi, who seized the sun without difficulty.

These diverse representations are evidence of the permanence, in the culture area we are concerned with, of the longing for a hero who will unite the luminous sky and the somber earth. The *mungonge* initiation, like the resurrection ritual of the solar king, allows us to conclude that this project can also be interpreted as a quest for immortality. It all seems as though the *mungonge* ritual brings an unexpected solution to the cosmogonic riddle of the myths in affirming, against all dialectical argument, the possibility of suspending time for men, under the sign of light and abundance. As a faithful wife of the sun, the star of evening and morning symbolizes the permanence in the sky of the solar principle, the victory of life over death. It is probably to this grand cosmogonic conception that we should relate the tradition according to which the Pende built several high towers of stone in their country of origin, the High Kwango.

The Paka tell the following story: Samba, the queen of the Pende, wanted to build a tower up to the sky near the salt mines that she had just taken over. When the edifice was complete it collapsed "through the fault of the Koshi people." Many men died in this catastrophe and

*Small cruciform copper ingots originating in the Shaba (Katanga) region of southeast Zaïre were widely used as trade currency in south central Africa in the later Iron Age. See Brian M. Fagan, "Early trade and raw materials in South Central Africa," in *Pre-Colonial African Trade*, R. Gray and D. Birmingham, eds., London, Oxford University Press, 1970, pp.30–38. (R.W.)

Samba wished to punish the Koshi. But the Koshi, in alliance with other peoples, put the Pende to flight.[49]

This myth, which is but a variant of M6, is common to many peoples of Central Africa. According to Grévisse, the term *Kaposhi* designates the tower itself; there was a kind of intertribal brotherhood between the peoples whose dispersion went back to these events (the Kaonde, Lwena, Lamba, Lala, Chokwe, etc.). "Even today," says Grévisse, ". . . the stranger is warmly received when he says he is a 'Mwina Kaposhi.' "[50] According to the Bemba foundation epic (M32), the tower was built at the very court of Mwata Yamvo; the collapse of this fabulous monument gave rise to the many wanderings forming the exodus of the hero Chiti Mukulu (see p. 229). The cosmic tower is here a symbol of the sons' rebellion; that is doubtless why the Lunda proper, faithful subjects of Mwata Yamvo, "obstinately refuse to be Bena Kaposhi."[51] We are here in the presence of an authentically African version of the Babel myth. The theme is far too deeply incorporated in the Luba and Lunda symbolic systems to be explained away in terms of hypothetical Christian reminiscences. But the first evangelization experienced by the Kongo civilization of the Atlantic, from the end of the fifteenth century to the eighteenth, may perhaps explain the appearance in the Paka myth of the surprising image of a *stone* building. We know that the Bantu have only exceptionally, at Zimbabwe, in Southern Rhodesia,* built monuments in durable materials. Would not a Paka chief compare the traditional construction of a Pende queen with the towers of existing churches?[52] In the east of our mythological domain, in contrast, the Bemba epic retains the image of a tower made of tree trunks.[53] The legends of the Sanga and neighboring peoples explain the construction by the desire to seize the moon,[54] while the Lunda myth associates it, as we have seen, with the quest for the sun (M29). But in this region a new cosmogonic image springs up; in radical opposition to the Tower of Babel, its chimeric project always doomed to failure, the triumphant figure of the giant gripping the fire of the sky (Venus or sun) imposes the theme of human glory, of the initiate with eyes of light. The exoteric information we possess allows no deeper penetration into Lunda metaphysics. The latter would seem to possess great coherence, because the solar symbolism also furnishes one of the major keys to the circumcision ritual.

*Now the Republic of Zimbabwe. (R.W.)

The Sun, Venus, and Circumcision

In the whole area of Lunda cultural influence, the circumcision ritual (*mukanda*) is governed by an identical schema. The best description, Turner's among the Ndembu, is dominated by sociological preoccupations to the exclusion of a complex cosmogonic symbolism; and the literature on neighboring populations does little to clarify the latter. The materials available for comparative analysis are therefore much less rich, from the perspective adopted in this book, than those used in studying the initiation of young men among the Kuba. It should be noted in passing that although the social function of the ritual is the same in the two cases (breaking infantile links with the mother, endowing adolescents with manly status), circumcision is absent from Kuba initiation. Without denying the evident differences between one ritual and another, we shall endeavor to bring out the symbolic vocabulary common to the whole culture area.

A myth which exists in simplified form among the Chokwe and their neighbors[55] explains the origin of the institution among the Ndembu in the following manner.

M30, Ndembu: Origin of Circumcision (Turner[56])

> A woman and her son were together gathering the grass the ashes of which are used to make salt. A sharp leaf (belonging to another species) accidentally cut the penis of the young man, who lay on the ground writhing with pain. Fearstricken, the mother brought her son back to the village. Some men declared that he should be separated from women. They brought a razor and completely removed his foreskin. They applied medicines to the wound, which healed in a few weeks. The same treatment was applied to other youths. People found these circumcised penes to be beautiful and the custom became general.

This apparently trivial narrative has the distinction of making two points: 1. The original wound was inflicted by a piece of sharp vegetation and not by a knife; it relates indirectly to cooking because the incident occurred during the harvesting of salt grass. The reader will recall the important role played by salt as a sign of feminine culinary operations in the Kuba ritual (see p. 131). 2. The wound inflicted on the male genitals is perceived as an aesthetic value; a natural accident and a cultural project collaborate in its first realization. Occurring during a preculinary operation, circumcision is thus doubly situated at a point of articulation of nature and culture. In the myth, as in reality, it separates the son from the mother. The Ndembu add a cosmogonic dimension to this sociological element, which is invariable in Black Africa: from the beginning of the *ing'ung'u* dance that precedes the operation, each novice is perched on the shoulders of a male relative, a father or elder brother. The young circumcised men who have not been present at more than two *mukanda* rituals are also obliged to assume elevated positions when the drumming begins: they climb trees. If the young uncircumcised or newly circumcised men found themselves in contact with the earth at this time they would suffer from hemophilia or urinary incontinence.[57] Ndembu explain that the novices lie on the ground when the ritual wound is inflicted on them; in this context, the earth is the place of suffering and death. In contrast, "to be raised up means to be alive, to have strength."[58] It is immediately apparent that the ritual follows the same code as *mungonge*:

low / high
earth / sky
death / life

This code allows us to understand the remarkable significance of the sun in initiatory symbolism. Most published accounts, whether from the Ndembu, the Chokwe, the Mbunda, the Lunda, or the Lwena, assert that the novices salute the rising and setting of the sun with ritual songs.[59] Delille and Vrydagh, with nearly forty years between their reports, and writing respectively of the Lunda-Lwena[60] and the Mbunda,[61] add the additional and invaluable detail that the sight of the sun is strictly prohibited to the novices until their wounds have healed. According to Delille, the young Lunda and Lwena intone the hymn to the rising sun, as to the setting sun, with heads turned to the *east*.[62] But this must be a mistaken interpretation, contradicting the prohibition about the sun. Vrydagh spells it out exactly: the youths salute the sun, just before dawn, *by turning their backs to it*. They never look at the sun for fear that a white patch, *likenja*, appear on the penis. The ritual chant that greets the rising sun evokes the bird *ntumba kambungu* (*Saxicola torquata*), which noisily beats its wings at the first sign of dawn; among the Lwimbi this sparrow is believed to cause the sun to rise.[63] It should also be noted that the *Saxicola torquata* bears the three ritual colors, like the palm-nut-eating vulture *Gypohierax angolensis*, whose movements are imitated by the *mungonge* dancers (see p. 176); a red-orange patch on the breast enlivens the black and white plumage of the male bird.[64] The novices appear to mimic the behavior of *Saxicola torquata* because they sing "We are drawing the sun," meanwhile *striking sticks together*. The ritual meaning of this noise is obvious: it is a way of ending the reign of night. But in fact, night continues to reign for them during the whole period of their retreat. The wooden instruments they beat to put an end to this symbolic darkness have funereal connotations: women are told that the sticks are human bones.[65]

These remarkable facts, left without commentary by the authors, evidently relate to the code we have elucidated: the novices, condemned to initiatory death, are cut off from the sun. They are also separated from fire, being forbidden to approach it until their wounds have completely healed; this prohibition holds for the Ndembu,[66] the Mbunda,[67] and the Luvale.[68] In the *dark*, *cold* world to which the novices have been consigned, both terrestrial and celestial fire are denied (or suspended); they sleep naked and only their guardians are allowed to maintain the isolated fires around which they warm themselves as best they can during the night.[69] They depend on the outside world for their food. Terrestrial fire, which in theory is far away, is the sign of a simplified and impoverished cooking: not only must the novices observe specific alimentary prohibitions, but their food is without salt until the masked figures appear.[70]* Turner, who obtained this information among the Ndembu, says that the boys' mothers, who cook for their sons on a collective ritual fire, have to refrain also from salting their own food; it is further forbidden for them to have sexual relations with their husbands until the healing of the sons' ritual wounds. According to Turner there is a symbolic equivalence between blood and sperm (which are equally *salted*) on the one side, and between salt and sexual activity on the other. Salt being the metonymic sign of cooking in this context, cooking is once more found equated

*This event occurs at the culmination called *chikula* ("maturation") of the Ndembu ritual, when the novices' wounds have healed. (R.W.)

with sexuality. Both are prohibited during the period of seclusion. But only sexuality can be suspended in reality; the suspension is symbolically applied to food, by eliminating salt. The alimentary prohibitions can bear on particular species or on the method of cooking: deprived of salt, the Lwena novices are allowed only smoked meat, meat that has not been in direct contact with flames.[71] Many food prohibitions imposed during *mukanda* continue to be observed into middle age, when they are gradually relaxed. In contrast, deprivation of salt is not prolonged beyond the healing of the circumcision wounds among the young Ndembu and Chokwe.[72] This restricted cuisine also has a precultural character. Among the Mbunda, food is served to novices on leaves; they are unable to use proper receptacles until after the "night of the genet" that marks the partial lifting of prohibitions.[73]

New oppositions, which also figure in *mungonge*, thus enrich the symbolic code:

absence of sun	sun
alimentary deprivations	abundance of food

Let us go more deeply into the fire symbolism in this comparative perspective. Among the Ndembu, on the first evening of *mukanda* and at the very moment when the sun goes down, the master of ceremonies lights a ritual fire at the place where the novices' relatives are gathered.[74] This "fire of *mukanda*" burns *day and night* until the dormitory-lodge built by the youths is itself delivered to the flames. It is there that the mothers of the novices are obliged to prepare food for their secluded sons.[75] This permanent fire lit at sundown on the first evening of the retreat, this warm but distant source of life and nourishment, burns until *dawn* on the final day: in fact, the young men's sleeping hut is destroyed by fire at the moment when the *morning star* comes up.[76] This ritual fire lit at sunset thus takes the place of the sun for the duration of a prolonged night lasting several weeks. More precisely it is the nocturnal sun, Venus herself. The time that elapses between this twilight and this dawn is in all respects analogous to the night of *mungonge* to which the torch of Venus brings an end. Star of evening and morning, heralding respectively the disappearance and the resurrection of the sun, Venus thus presides *in the form of fire* over the two key rituals of Lunda civilization. In both cases the time of initiatory death and hunger is likened to the night. During the long ordeal of *mukanda*, the permanent fire of Venus, which is also cooking fire, protects the novices. In this perspective, Venus really appears as the celestial counterpart of domestic fire: this distant nocturnal fire, mediating between dusk and dawn, is at once a promise of nourishment and a guarantee of resurrection. In the same way the appearance of the torch of Venus in the Pende *mungonge* heralds the sun and ritual refreshment. But all through the *mukanda* initiatory ordeal, the Ndembu mothers serve but a frugal cuisine, comparable to the enfeebled sunlight maintained by Venus in the sky of the hyena-moon.

It is noteworthy that the term "fire" designated (through metonymy) the whole initiation ceremony among the Lunda.[77] The fire of *mukanda* where the mothers cook evidently lies outside the encampment: among the Ndembu it marks the limit that may not be crossed by uncircumcised youths, nor by women during menstruation.[78] But there is also a ritual fire inside the initiatory world. It is called *lwowa*, and round it the novices receive instruction from the elders.[79] In the whole Lunda culture area the term *lwowa* belongs to an esoteric vocabulary and may not be used in front of women.[80] White adds that the *lwowa* fire cannot be used to cook food and that it is forbidden to take an ember from it or to burn anything whatever on it.[81] Turner appears to confirm the existence of this prohibition among the Ndembu: the novices gather round the *lwowa* fire to sing and be merry ("stand by it to sing and cheer," Turner, 1967, p. 237).* It is clear that the mothers' fire and the *lwowa* fire form a system of oppositions among the Ndembu:

mukanda fire	*lwowa* fire
exterior	interior
cooking	noncooking

The first fire being associated with Venus, one could theoretically deduce that the second is a substitute for the sun. Indeed, its sole function, that of warming, resembles that of the sun. But the sun is in principle absent, because the novices turn their backs to it.

†The Ndembu, like the Lunda, know only a single fire, the *lwowa*. But it happens that this fire is duplicated in its turn. Among the Luvale

*This sentence has been added by de Heusch to the English edition. (R.W.)

†The following passages, up to the phrase ". . . and called *wutu*, as among the Chokwe" (on p.211), represent new research findings prepared by de Heusch for *The Drunken King*. The passages replace material on pp.254–256 of *Le roi ivre*. (R.W.)

and among the majority of the Luchazi groups, a second fire is maintained outside the encampment. It is called feminine ("the female elephant"), whereas the internal fire is masculine ("the male elephant"). Gluckman, describing this arrangement among the Wiko of Zambia,* says that the novices go naked in the cold of dawn and evening, remaining close to the "female-elephant fire" and turning their backs to the lodge. In their chants, they implore the help of the mothers, who are themselves gathered around a fire on the outskirts of the village. After the sun has set, the novices gather round the "male-elephant fire," inside the encampment, and intone other chants.[82] In every region there is thus a feminine fire to complement the masculine ritual fire. The Ndembu consider the former as the preeminent fire of *mukanda*: kept continually burning, it is forbidden to the novices and available to the food-providing mothers. The Wiko light the feminine fire near the enclosure. In this case it is accessible to the novices before dawn and after sundown, but is forbidden to the mothers; nevertheless, it is here that the two groups communicate with each other at a distance, through chanting.

Among the Chokwe and Mbunda, it is not the mothers but a sterile old woman who prepares food for the segregated young men.[83] So that she can carry out her task, the Chokwe build her a temporary hut in an enclosure near the village.[84] In other groups, an old woman acts merely as the keeper of the fire on which the mothers cook their sons' food.[85] In all cases this fire constitutes an essential culinary link between village and encampment. The sterility of the cook evidently underlines the abolition of sexual life. Masculine fire (*lwowa*) and feminine cooking fire are nonetheless closely related. The Chokwe insist that the masculine fire burn continually: if it happens to go out, it has to be reignited with an ember from the old woman's fire.[86] Although, according to Borgonjon, "everyone can eat what is cooked on the *lwowa* fire," there are important restrictions concerning it. No one may step over it, or eat food cooked directly over its flame; and its ashes must never be removed.[87] *Lwowa* fire and cooking fire form a clearly defined system of oppositions among the Chokwe. Far from burning continually like the *lwowa* fire, the cooking fire is extinguished after each cooking operation; but it has to be fueled throughout the

*"Wiko" is a collective term of Lozi origin used in Zambia to denote immigrants from the west, notably members of the Mbunda, Chokwe, Luchazi, and Luvale-Lwena groups, all of whom observe some version of *mukanda* initiation. (R.W.)

retreat from a single tree-trunk which is, as it were, all in one piece.[88]*

This ritual cooking fire thus appears to be a transformation of the *mukanda* fire, entrusted by the Ndembu to the mothers of the novices:

Ndembu	*Chokwe*
cooking done by mothers who are temporarily "sterile" (abstaining from sexual relations)	cooking done by a genuinely sterile "grandmother"
permanent ritual cooking fire	intermittent ritual cooking fire; single and permanent source of fuel

There is no positive evidence in the Chokwe ethnography of a relation between this intermittent cooking fire and Venus. Nevertheless it is worth noting a curious solar rite performed in front of the house of the old cook, the *nachifwa*, among the Chokwe of Zaïre. At the end of the initiation period the novices light a new fire between the village and the camp they have just abandoned. This fire takes the place of that kept by the *nachifwa*; the novices do their cooking on it.[89] Returning to the village, they pass with bowed heads the home of their old cook. A chicken is found tied to a post outside this house, and the novices stab it in passing with wooden knives; this episode suggests comparisons with the strange "hunt for the white chicken" that marks the end of the solar quest of initiation among the Kuba (see p. 123).[90] In the Chokwe lodges the disappearance of the sun is linked with a prohibition against the novices eating the yolks of eggs; if they disregard this prohibition, it is said that white patches will appear on their penes.[91] This is the same penalty risked by the newly circumcised Mbunda if they dare look at the sun (see p. 203). The young Chokwe males, who have to avoid looking at the setting sun during their seclusion,[92] end their subjection to a set of prohibitions of a solar character by passing, *with bowed heads*, a chicken which they quickly stab, then hurry on.

It is significant that this rite takes place in front of the *nachifwa*'s house. It is also pertinent to inquire if the fire she tends signifies the evening star, like the ritual cooking fire maintained by the Ndembu

*De Heusch employs the expression *d'un seul tenant*, normally used of a block of contiguous plots of land held by one person. (R.W.)

mothers. For does not the evening star accompany the setting sun, which the novices are forbidden to look upon, and is not Venus the wife of the sun according to the Chokwe? It is now easier to understand why the masculine *lwowa* fire, around which the young men gather, should be rekindled, if it happens to go out, from *nachifwa*'s distant cooking fire.

Support for this argument comes from an examination of the *mukanda* ritual practiced by a neighboring society to the Chokwe of Zaïre, the Yaka. These people also entrust to a single cook, called *ifika*, the job of preparing the novices' food.[93] In some areas this woman is called *ngudi kikumbi*. The word *kikumbi* is also applied to the ritual as a whole, and is the equivalent of the more general term *mukanda*; *kikumbi* also denotes "the house where the chief keeps his guardian fetishes."[94] Despite the absence of tonal marks, it seems plausible to relate this name to the little Venusian stork (*nkumb* or *kumbi*) which figures in a Lunda myth (M27). Yaka initiation explicitly commemorates Kola, the country of origin of the conquering Lunda who imposed their rule on the Yaka.* The ritual language of *mukanda* is, in fact, Lunda.[95]

Let us look more closely at the role of the cook, *ifika*. Just before the opening ceremonies of initiation, each candidate has to go into the forest and together they cut down a *mukamba* tree (*Chlorophora excelsa*). They take care not to let it touch the ground, seizing it as it falls and carrying it to the village, singing "We are going to Kola." They leave the trunk in front of the house of the *ifika* (where presumably it serves to make the cooking fire, like the single piece of timber described for the Chokwe). On this "fire of blood" many chickens will be cooked. The *mukamba* trunk is beaten like a drum at second cock-crow and at sunset, for two days. The initiatory master of ceremonies also sacrifices a fowl on the tree.[96]

This tree that may not touch the ground at the moment of its fall and which announces the beginning of initiation is surely invested with considerable cosmological significance. It established a relation between high and low, sky and earth, because before the tree is felled, the leading novice shoots an arrow which has to remain lodged in the

*Plancquaert says (1932:22, note 3) that "Kola" was the name given to those Yaka chiefs who were [supposedly] of Lunda origin. More commonly, "Kola" (or "Koola") is used to refer to both Lunda *and* Luba heartlands. See Thomas Q. Reefe, "Traditions of Genesis and the Luba diaspora," *History in Africa*, 1977, 4:188, 190. (R.W.)

trunk, "otherwise we go on searching."[97] The veteran initiates, who oversee the new circumcision ritual, beat the novices severely so as to impede the transport of the tree. Once installed in the village, the trunk, transformed into a drum, salutes the coming up and the going down of the sun. It is entrusted (apparently as fuel) to a food-providing woman whose bird-name evokes Venus. The stork rises high in the sky to pursue the setting sun and shows itself helpful to man in M27; in this myth it comes down to earth and dries up a lake to make it easier for people to fish.

In this vast cosmological fresco, in which the cock and the chicken also have a solar connotation, attention is drawn to the preliminary sacrifice on the *mukamba* tree and the plentiful consumption of poultry (this food being shared between the veterans and the candidates for circumcision).

Plancquaert states that the cocks are ritually killed during *mukanda* and that their bones are preserved in the bag in which the master of the circumcision ritual also keeps various protective magical ingredients.[98] Even more curious is the fact that the novices are entrusted during their retreat with a live cock and a hen, called respectively *kambuya* and *inenga*. They are severely punished if one of these creatures dies; in such a case the creature has to be replaced by another. After the ritual is over, the new initiates are forbidden to eat the flesh of these two birds, or of their offspring.[99] Plancquaert says nothing about a permanent ritual fire inside the lodge. Taking all the preceding observations into account, it seems possible that the solar (and Venusian) principle is represented inside the Yaka initiatory enclosure by this mysterious pair of fowls.

One custom in particular appears to be a transformation of the prohibitions respecting the sun that we have noted in neighboring societies. Before being allowed to eat their meal, prepared morning and evening by the *ifika* (under the sign of Venus), the novices have to present a first morsel to the cock and the chicken; not until this has been pecked at are the youths permitted to eat. Further, "if the cock begins to crow, they must momentarily interrupt their meal."[100]

The cock also figures in the ritual scene of the *mungonge* initiatory society, an institution that, like *mukanda*, the Yaka have adopted from the Lunda. It will be remembered that *mungonge* (called *ngongi* by the Yaka) appears throughout the Lunda culture area as a quest for the sun, undertaken beneath the sign of the morning star. Among the

Yaka, the master of the initiatory ritual gives the new initiates a cock, which they hang by its feet from a stick. He kills the creature with an arrow, the initiates eat it, and then they reappear in the village.[101]

This rite is evidently similar to the killing of the chicken effected by the new initiates [among the Chokwe of Zaïre] when they bring their ritual segregation to an end. The Yaka initiates find themselves at this stage in front of their cook's house, which was the starting point of their journey. At the same time their lodge and all their ritual equipment are put to flames. The new initiates close their eyes and stop up their ears, "for it is forbidden to see either the light or hear the crackling produced by the burning of their old refuge, under penalty of being stricken with sexual impotence."[102] We discuss below this fearful blaze, which everywhere accompanies the end of *mukanda*. Let us simply note here that it coincides with the return of the Yaka novices to the Venusian site of ritual cooking. Let it also be remembered that, among the Ndembu, the encampment is destroyed by fire at the moment when the morning star rises.

The cosmological system invoked in *mukanda* by the Yaka calls for further exploration. On the roof of the building where the novices live there are several objects they must not look at. Among the Suku, immediate neighbors of the Yaka, these mysterious objects include a little tube of raffia containing several ingredients, notably poison and a piece of wood of the kind that provides the red cosmetic *nkula*. We are acquainted with the fearsome properties of this color, associated with blood and war. It happens that the "fetish" containing *nkula* wood and poison is called "the rainbow of *mukanda*" (*kongolo ki mukanda*).[103]

This observation, which Plancquaert makes without comment, leads us to posit a new symbolic property of the *lwowa* fire. In the Lunda-Lwena lodges, the ashes of this masculine ritual fire are never raked out; they accumulate to form a pile several yards long and called *wutu*, as among the Chokwe.[104] Delille adds some information which is of the greatest value for our inquiry. It is in front of this heap of ashes that the Lunda and Lwena novices, seated cross-legged in rows, intone before and after each meal the *song of the rainbow and the rain*. While rotating their arms, they sing: "The rainbow (Nkongolo) has gone away, the rain falls, let's go!"[105]

What does this mean? Let us note firstly, with White, that the Lunda are like the Ndembu in having only one *lwowa* fire. It is by this fire that the Lunda-Lwena novices salute the rising and setting of the sun.[106] Now we have them evoking in this same place the succession of the seasons, using a code already familiar to us: the rainbow signifies the dry season. The cosmogonic change to which allusion is made (the return of the rain) is purely imaginary: the novices are manifesting their desire to get away as fast as they can from the enclosure where night and drought symbolically reign. This unexpected diversion confirms the code of M27, in which the bird of twilight heralds both night and drought. As we have already suggested, the coming of daylight is homologous, along the axis of short periodicity, with the return of the rain. This interpretation, while still hypothetical, has the advantage of being compatible with Lunda royal symbolism, which makes Mwata Yamvo master of the sun and the lightning. The cosmogonic myth of the Lunda, recorded by Roelandts in Kahemba territory (M26), is founded, it will be remembered, on the same dialectic: the rainbow serpent Tianza Ngombe reigns over terrestrial waters, while the thunder Nzashi is master of the firmament. The latter has authority over the rain and the sun. When Tianza Ngombe sends Nzashi to the sky, he describes his mission in these terms: "Go to the firmament, so you will be able to pour down the beneficent rain; and may the sun accompany you so he can warm the arms and legs of my children."[107] A nearly identical variant has been recorded by Lima among the Chokwe. This narrative says that the sun and the stars are the fires of Nzanji, the Thunder, whose urine is the rain.[108]

If cooking fire is really Venusian as our preceding analysis suggests, it would have the same origin as the lightning that draws celestial water in its wake. This beneficent fire is particularly evident in the Pende *mungonge*. In the Lunda region, in conformity with the cosmogonic myth, the *mungonge* brings in the rainbow in person (Yikongolu): the breath of this fearsome personage, whose body is entirely covered with red and white stripes, is mortal.[109] Further, the *mukanda* poses the rainbow in opposition to the rain. The code established earlier is thus confirmed, and in an enriched form.

sky		earth
day		night
Sun	Venus	Moon
Thunder		Rainbow Serpent
wet season		dry season
food	cooking fire	hunger

Beside Venus, already part of the *mungonge* ritual as the presence of sunlight through the night, a second mediating term between sky and earth makes its appearance: the cooking fire that is interposed between hunger (associated with night) and repletion; this fire is the diurnal and terrestrial aspect of Venus. The only contradiction in the system is that the moon is associated with the earth although its light, according to the Chokwe myth, comes from the fire of Thunder, like that of all the other heavenly bodies. The almost total absence of information relating to lunar mythology in the Lunda area prevents our seeing how to solve this puzzle. A tale recorded by Baumann, the Luba version of which (M5) we already know, does, however, describe the conflict between the sun and the moon; in a weakened form it reproduces the opposition between light and darkness.

M31, Chokwe: Quarrel of the Sun and the Moon (Baumann[110])

> The sun and the moon each claimed to be the only one to possess knowledge. The sun became angry and covered the face of the moon with mud, making it black. Since then the moon provides only a feeble light at night while the sun is brilliant.

Where the Genet Is Found Again

On the road back to the village, between the initiatory night and the day, an old acquaintance awaits us: the genet (*thimba*). Its mottled coat connoted the alternation between light and darkness in the Kuba myth of Woot (see p. 140). Here the animal gives its name to the night when the healing of the newly circumcised is celebrated among the Mbunda.[111] At twilight men pronounce the ritual formula, "The genet has climbed up the *munjongolo* tree" (*Diospyros batocana*).

Vrydagh's informants say that the genet symbolizes the new condition of the initiates because this animal does not climb trees until it is an adult. Further, the metaphor signifies that sexual relations are no longer prohibited for the novices' relatives in the village. The explanation given for this figurative expression is particularly suggestive: the genet brings back *warmth* to the village where people had been trying to keep life at a low temperature ("life was kept to its coolest") in order to facilitate the healing of the wounds inflicted on the young men. In this rhetorical code, warmth expresses sexual activity, and coolness, abstinence. Moreover, it is obvious that the first term belongs to the side of the sun. The genet is thus a mediator between the night (in which the novices are immersed) and the day. The night of rejoicing, inaugurated at twilight by the song of the genet, is not over until dawn.[112]

Among neighboring groups, one of the officiants climbs onto the lodge roof and utters the ritual cry: "The genet has climbed."[113]* They thus find themselves in an elevated position and associated with the sky, light, and life according to the code of *mungonge*, which we have seen to be very similar to that of *mukanda*. Again, the genet is evoked in the long introductory song of the master of ceremonies in the Pende *mungonge*: "The genet with the short tail leaves its offspring in the hollow of a tree."[114] This formula refers to a supposed characteristic of the animal. It is said that the genet will never lack descendants because it "always leaves one offspring in the safety of a hollow tree trunk."[115] The genet thus connotes the idea of survival, if not immortality, among the Pende, whereas for the Mbunda it expresses the resurrection of young men and sexual life. In one way or another, this cosmic animal is found to be situated unequivocally on the side of life and vitality. It occurs in the Chokwe ritual, in which it bears the name of *shimba* (translated by Borgonjon, probably incorrectly, as *civet*). The song consecrated to it follows faithfully the cosmogonic code that we elicited earlier from the epic of Woot: when the new initiates return to the village, they sing "The *shimba* is mottled!"[116] If the variegated coat of the animal has attracted the attention of the Chokwe it is because they see in it, like the mythical Kuba plunged into the darkness of an eclipse, a coat of light and darkness, apt to symbolize the alternation of the maleficent night and the beneficent day. The day after the "night of the genet," the Mbunda novices are no longer required to live in perpetual darkness, even though they continue to avoid the sun.[117]

Cooking, Cosmos, and Noise

The initiatory enclosure is completely isolated from the village and there is no communication between the domain of cooking and the

*At the request of Professor de Heusch, this sentence replaces one with a slightly different sense on p.259 of *Le roi ivre*. (R.W.)

domain of noncooking. No one is allowed to pass through the arch of branches (*mukeleko*) marking the limit of the encampment in all these groups. A portion of food brought from the village is left by the arch before the rest is given to the novices; if the bearer inadvertently walks under the arch the meal cannot take place.[118] We interpret this ritual as a metonymic figure: a part of the (theoretically prohibited) meal is sacrificed to save the rest. Vrydagh has recorded the same restrictions among the Mbunda, where no one may pass under the initiatory arch, the place where food is transferred from the village to the encampment; and part of the meal is abandoned there.[119]

Turner's published diagrams show the Ndembu constructing this arch halfway between the mothers' fire (exterior) and the novices' fire (interior), thus precisely marking their separation. The women are not allowed to cross this doorway where hang the clothes abandoned by the novices and which they will never wear again.[120] It is easy to understand that this dummy entrance, a place of nonpassage, suppresses all communication between the past and the future, childhood and manhood. But the arch also separates day and night, man and woman, the feminine fire of Venus that promises nourishment and life, and the solar masculine fire.[121]

According to a widely held belief which is also remembered by the Ndembu, the remains of meals mysteriously disappear from the encampment.[122] Among the Mbunda the novices sing loudly while a guardian goes round the enclosure several times carrying off these remains; finally he disappears into the lodge and throws the rubbish through the window (*ndambala*) to the west.[123]

The singing has to hide the noise made by the scraps in falling to the ground. It is interesting that the novices are not allowed to look toward the *ndambala* window; that is why, according to Vrydagh, they have to leave the lodge before dawn and return after sundown.[124] This new association between the alimentary cycle and the course of the sun is thought-provoking. Writing of the neighboring tribes,* White reports that the initiatory lodge is provided with a garbage hatch (*ndambi*) that may not be looked at. But he neglects to describe its location, and interprets the *ndambi* as the symbol of the novices' abandoned childhood.[125] One feels strongly that this is a partial explanation related to the sociological code, which is all that ever interests the functionalist-oriented British investigators. Delille for his

*The Lunda, the Chokwe, and the Luchazi. (R.W.)

part mentions the existence of the *ndambi* window among the Lwena.[126]

It is impossible not to be struck by the fact that the scraps of food disappearing to the west belong to the same symbolic category as the setting sun. The night is associated with absence of food and with hunger, while sunlight signifies the fullness of life, and repletion. Do not the Mbunda novices, when they salute the sun each morning, precisely complain of being hungry?[127] The forbidden *ndambala* window is an opening unto rotting (of food) and death (of men).

But why is it necessary to sing loudly when the remains of the meal are disposed of? This ritual attitude is only one element in a complex acoustic code, the function of which is literally to orchestrate the cosmogonic symbolism. Once again, the richest information comes from the Mbunda (Vrydagh). Expelled from the initiatory lodge before dawn, the novices beat sticks together (sticks of death, equated with bones), like the *ntumba kambungu* bird, who beats his wings rapidly "to draw the sun." This ritual noise therefore calls the brightness and warmth of the sun. But it also accompanies a request for food, formulated in these terms:

> "Grandmother, at the morning meal
> I eat, I have slept in hunger
> I quickly eat the morning meal"[128]

The grandmother invoked here is the old sterile cook who prepared a light porridge without salt, the obligatory breakfast. The sun, significantly associated with food, is, like cooking, the object of restrictions for the novices, who may not look at it directly. The beating instruments manipulated by them before sunrise therefore deserve to be considered "instruments of darkness" as in Lévi-Strauss's usage: in the Old World, as in America, noisemakers of various kinds salute both famine (real or institutionalized) and a change of season.[129] The reader of *Du miel aux cendres* [*From Honey to Ashes*] will recall the Lenten culinary restrictions the abolition of which is signaled by the pealing of Easter bells. These bells remain silent for the last days of Holy Week; European folklore attests to the substitution for them of various percussive instruments, whether inside or outside the church.[130] Lévi-Strauss notes in this context that the "instruments of darkness" accompany the last period of Lent, "the period in which the hardships of fasting were most acutely felt, since they had lasted longer."[131]* This is also the time when all lights are extinguished in church (and when formerly, if we can believe Frazer, all domestic fires were put out). The problem of the cosmic and alimentary references of the acoustic symbols becomes patent when we listen to the various sounds produced at certain moments by the *mukanda* actors, deprived as they are of salt and sun, plunged in the darkness of initiatory death.

1. The Mbunda novices beat together their ritual batons (*mingongi*) each morning in an agonized attempt to put an end to the darkness (by musically imitating the wingbeats of the *ntumba kambungu* bird that "draws" the sun), and to obtain a meager meal. They sing:

> Our sun has just appeared,
> Just appeared, we eat,
> Just appeared, the elders come to beat us.[132]

Indeed, they then receive kicks. We can now understand why the *ntumba kambungu* bird is called "the red liar":[133] the beating of its wings is supposed to bring daylight, but the camp remains plunged in darkness. We have earlier compared this deceptive bird to the palm-nut-eating vulture of the Pende *mungonge* that should have brought men the color white but could offer them only the color red, connoting war. The black and white plumage of this vulture (*Gypohierax angolensis*), like that of the sparrow evoked in the song of the newly circumcised, does include several red feathers (see p. 204). The *ntumba kambungu* (*Saxicola torquata*) of *mukanda*, and the mythical vulture of *mungonge*, are deceptive birds; messengers of light, they bring men only the blood of murder or circumcision.

A little before dusk, the Mbunda novices salute in the same lusty fashion the departure of the sun, which lies down "with the spirits of the dead." Vrydagh does not say whether the beating together of the ritual batons accompanies their singing on this occasion also, but on the other hand he does note the use of beating sticks during nocturnal songs.[134]

**From Honey to Ashes*, translated by John and Doreen Weightman, 1973:408. (R.W.)

2. Another instrument of darkness is heard on the morrow of the "night of the genet," announcing to the villagers that the novices are about to leave their enclosure and take their first bath.[135] This time one of the guardians beats a piece of bark with sticks. The resulting noise (*liula*) awakens the village at dawn; the encampment has remained silent all through the preceding day and the mothers are anxious because they have been told that their children have been eaten by a cannibal monster. At the sound of *liula* the young men make for the river, while their mothers, held back by the guardians to the best of their ability, strive to join their respective offspring. After the ritual bath and this clandestine contact with the feminine world, the novices are no longer confined to the encampment, although they have to live on the edge of the village for several weeks more. The most rigorous phase of the initiation is over.[136]

The *liula* call would seem to be a duller sound than that produced by the clashing of the *mingongi* sticks. It also has a different function: it is the first sign of life to emanate from the encampment after a day and a night of silence, corresponding to the veritable initiatory death of the novices. On other evenings the young men communicate at a distance with the mothers gathered within the confines of the villages, the mothers greeting with shouts of joy the distant singing to the rhythm of the *mingongi*. The *liula* reestablishes the interrupted communication. It announces the resurrection of the novices and seems to invite the mothers to join their sons by the river; Vrydagh tells us that some are bold enough to touch their children.[137] The two rhythms are respectively an invitation to *listen* (*mingongi*) and an invitation to *see* (*liula*). In both cases these instruments of darkness reestablish a more or less discreet conjunction between the separated mothers and sons.

3. The ritual orchestra of *mukanda* includes a third instrument among the Mbunda, the bull-roarer (*ndumba*), which, as in many other parts of the world, has a disjunctive function.[138] It is heard throbbing during the night on the outskirts of the village; at first the novices are frightened by this unusual sound, which they take for the fearsome voice of an ancestor; later they learn its true nature.[139] Use of the bull-roarer has been recorded among the Ndembu and the Chokwe; the noise it emits during initiation is likened to the roaring of a lion.[140] Turner saw the instrument used in the daytime among the Ndembu, whereas

Vrydagh reports only nocturnal use of it among the Mbunda.[141] However, the Ndembu bull-roarer was used behind the initiation lodge, away from prying eyes. It frightened the mothers, who took it for the voice of the monster that would eat their children.[142]

It is apparent that the function of the bull-roarer is opposed to that of the preceding instruments, and has to do with separating the sexes. During the threatening dance that precedes circumcision, the elders, deliberately imitating the gait of a lion, produce the same kind of noise as the bull-roarer by making their tongues vibrate between their lips; this continuous murmur is supposed to simulate the growls of the wild beast.[143] Moreover, men like to produce the same sound when they teach their young children to pronounce the word "father" (*tata*). They seek thereby to prevent the infant's naming the mother first, which would be a bad omen. Turner concludes this interesting language lesson by remarking that it is expected that a child will call his father and not his mother during circumcision.* From this concordant collection of facts it is possible to conclude that the ritual murmuring has the function of separating the sexes and creating a purely masculine society. It should be equated with the bull-roarer proper because it foreshadows the roaring of the lion, with which this instrument is explicitly identified.

Bull-roarer and percussive instruments are therefore opposed within a ritual schema, the existence of which Lévi-Strauss has demonstrated among the Amerindians.[144] The acoustic facts can be ordered in the following manner:

Clashing beaters: (*mingongi*)	instruments of the beyond (equivalent to bones) maintaining communication at a distance with the mothers, who are invited to listen and to reply noisily.
Beaters on bark: (*liula*)	break the silence marking the "death" of the novices, reestablish clandestine contact with the mothers.
Bull-roarer:	voice of the monster that separates the novices from their mothers or "eats" them.

The bull-roarer thus silences the novices who manipulate the *min-*

*When he cries out from the pain of the operation. (R.W.)

gongi, instruments of darkness. Can we develop this contrast and attribute cosmogonic references to the acoustic code? The *mingongi* and the *liula* resound in the initiatory night, trying without success to restore the day, cooking, and communication with women, while the continuous throbbing of the bull-roarer delivers the young men to night and death; it also inverts the thematic of cooking insofar as the novices are thought to serve as (uncooked) food for an imaginary cannibal monster or a lion.

Let us compare this problematic with the acoustic code of Kuba initiation previously outlined: we shall find that it hardly differs from that just discovered among the Mbunda. One of the foundation myths of the institution (M11) makes the bull-roarer a disjunctive instrument: it separates the mother and the son. An acoustic equivalent of the bull-roarer, the friction drum, resounds in the initiatory tunnel where the novices ritually die to be reborn in a cold universe, comparable to that in which the Mbunda novices find themselves. The noise of the friction drum is likened to the cry of the leopard, which in the myth (M10) awakens Woot at the moment when the messenger of Mweel reaches him, at a time when night reigns over the world. In all three cases the bull-roarer (or its equivalent) is situated on the side of death and/or of night. The Kuba also know an "instrument of darkness" of the second type: a beater with a discontinuous sound. This is the *ngoontsh* root with which the novices beat the ground when they cross the village as ghosts after their initiatory death (see p. 111). The dance they perform then explicitly symbolizes complete separation from the village; the novices use the *ngoontsh* root to beat any women who approach them.[145] It is nonetheless remarkable that this instrument, the phallic character of which we have earlier emphasized, is used by the novices as a means of discreet communication with their mothers.

Several days later they again appear one morning in the village to sing and dance in the public square; when they are tired they withdraw from the village and proceed to beat the ground with the *ngoontsh* root according to a certain rhythm; the mothers then bring food to a place at some distance from the novices.[146] In the course of the dance of separation, the beating of the *ngoontsh* root clearly takes on the same function of a call for food: here also, the mothers offer nourishment to their children, who are held to be undertaking a long and dangerous journey toward the east, during the initiatory night.[147] To the discreet conjunction provoked by the beaters there is opposed, in the same context, the disjunctive friction drum beaten by the instructors: Vansina says explicitly that this instrument (equivalent to the bull-roarer) "covered the march" of the novices, discouraging those (the mothers) who would follow them. It will be recalled also that during the initiatory retreat the novices are separated from feminine cuisine: they are forbidden to eat vegetables. In contrast they are fed by their fathers, who steal chickens from their wives for the benefit of their secluded sons.

The *ngoontsh* beaters, like the *mingongi* sticks among the Mbunda, fulfill a positive function that is contrary to that of the bull-roarer: they provoke a delivery of feminine food while keeping men separate from the nourishing females. This percussive call also occurs in myth (M10). When the first envoy of Mweel, the dog Bondo, presents himself to Woot, he comes up against a rock the wall of which he strikes to announce himself; the dog solicits the return of sunlight. The same kind of discontinuous noise emphasizes physical separation in both cases while initiating a dialogue with the goal of procuring nourishment (ritual) or sunlight (myth). Our analysis of the *mukanda* ritual has already familiarized us with this double connotation. However, the dog Bondo should have abstained from eating the meat sent by Woot in order that the sun should shine again. Once again the price paid for the sun's return is an alimentary deprivation. This alternation of days and nights is precisely coded by the genet skin covering Woot's gift.

Do we also find among the Kuba the cosmogonic dialectic of the bull-roarer and the percussive instruments? Seemingly, yes. This equivalent of the bull-roarer that is the friction drum (or the leopard's cry in the myth) salutes the substitution of night for the alternating reign of light and darkness, whereas the sound of the *ngoontsh* instrument (a beater) accompanies the quest for the sun in the symbolic night. The opposition between the two instruments of darkness is even enriched by a new dimension among the Kuba. The bull-roarer or the friction drum is held to belong to the natural domain because the throbbing noise it emits is identified with the cry of the leopard, whereas the *ngoontsh* root represents the weaver's baton, preeminent symbol of culture.

Friction drum	Ngoontsh *root*
fabricated object symbolizing natural violence	natural object symbolizing the cultural order
continuous sound	discontinuous sound
cry of the man-devouring leopard	quest for nourishment
death	life

4. The Ndembu introduce a fourth element into the acoustic code of initiation: drums. These instruments provide rhythmic backing for the dance of the circumcisers on the first evening, when the ritual fire has been lit at dusk. Those to be circumcised then climb hastily onto their fathers' shoulders and close their ears.[148] Turner offers no explanation for this prohibition on hearing. The dangerous noise (on this occasion) of the drum is evidently situated on the side of earth and night, in opposition to the sky and light, in conformity with the general code (see p. 212). In this ritual context, it announces, like the bull-roarer, the transition from the alternation of day and night to the exclusive reign of the latter. There is an equivalent sound signal in the Lunda *mungonge*, but in this case the light of Venus shines forth in the twilight from the very drum that inaugurates the fearful night of initiation: a burning ember is introduced into the instrument, together with some dry grass. As they beat the drum, the drummers revive the ember, which will serve to ignite the big fire said to be "stolen from the village."[149] This event, which terrifies those round about, coincides with the dance in which the initiates imitate the twilight birds of M27, birds we have shown to connote the evening star (see p. 190). By this artifice, the fire engendered by the rolling of the drum is directly associated with Venus. Crine-Mavar's description, however, does not indicate whether the neophytes have to stop their ears during this noise, like the Ndembu novices in the first case.

5. An old tradition among the Mbunda places a prohibition on a barely perceptible noise during the initiatory retreat: the faint sound of food scraps falling to the ground after being thrown through the west window of the initiatory lodge. It will be recalled that this noise was the point of departure for the present discussion. A common characteristic between this case and the previous prohibition enables these two negative attitudes to noise to be combined, for both are related to the disappearance of the sun, a metaphor of death. When the

initiates-to-be hasten to an elevated position and *stop up their ears* when the circumcision drums roll, it is to escape from the night-shrouded world. This dangerous noise (equivalent to the throbbing of the bull-roarer) should no more be heard than the faint sound made by the falling remains of food cast toward the setting sun, associated with the dead. But in the latter case the threat is countered in an active rather than a passive way, by loud singing.[150] The prime activity of the Mbunda novices after sundown is indeed singing, accompanied by the clashing of *mingongi* sticks. Like these instruments of darkness, the song sets up communication at a distance with the mothers. "Not a night goes by," says Vrydagh, "without the initiates singing, because this is their only means of letting their mothers know they are well."[151] At the end of each refrain, the women respond from the village with piercing cries. This vocal and instrumental *nocturne* thus has the purpose of combating the state of dereliction in which the novices find themselves. Songs and beaters protest against the disjunction of man and woman, of earth and sun, created by the bull-roarer (or by the circumcision drum that is dangerous to hear).

6. It is time to distinguish these cries of joy (the recurrent response of the Mbunda women to their sons' nocturnal songs) from the demented clamor of the novices themselves; at the end of initiation as the young Ndembu fled the burning encampment, "Everyone was madly shouting."[152] This ultimate episode takes place at dawn, after the rising of the morning star. With their cries the novices exhort one another to turn their eyes away from the flames and to hide. They fling themselves on the ground and people cover them with reed mats. A new kind of sound is brought into play in this final episode: the parents of the new initiates slap their children with the palms of their hands, while others clap their hands together. It will be noted that the lowly position of the initiates on this occasion contrasts with their elevated position at the beginning of the ritual, when they climbed on their fathers' shoulders:

beginning:	*end:*
novices in elevated position	novices in low position
forbidden to hear the drum	forbidden to see the fire

The behavior of the novices when they throw themselves to the ground when the encampment is delivered to the flames suggests that the return of the sun calls for a precaution that is symmetrical with and converse to the precaution observed at the beginning of the ritual when a night lasting for several months descended on the world. "Novices who looked at the flames would be 'burned' by leprosy, which leaves white marks on the skin."[153*] Leprosy is therefore a solar malady, a product of an excessive conjunction of earth and sun; we can better understand now why it is so often associated in Central Africa with incest, that other type of dangerous and inauspicious conjunction.

In the initial position, the drum is an instrument of death, like the bull-roarer. In the final position, the new initiates are themselves beaten like drums to ward off a converse danger from the preceding one: the burning power of this sun of life coming back to the earth after the long night in the camp.

The ensemble of these occasions for noise contrasts with the silence that the secluded Ndembu and Lunda-Lwena novices must observe when they eat.[154] In their case, a single word is enough to put an end to a meal. It will be recalled that, in the Yaka lodges, the meal is interrupted if the cock *kambuya* starts to crow (see p. 210). It is necessary to recall here that the novices' food has been cooked on the symbolic fire of Venus and that that planet is a mediator between sky and earth, day and night. From this, one could conclude that the silence imposed during meals is one of the required conditions for the restoration of a harmonious space-time, compromised by the disjunction of the luminous sky and the darkened earth.

It would seem then that the final shouts avoid the danger of an excessive conjunction of sun and earth, whereas the ritual silence establishes them under the sign of Venus. We are now able to reconstitute the whole Ndembu acoustic code:

bull-roarer	disjoins earth and sun, and separates the sexes
mingongi *beaters and songs*	combat the total disjunction of earth and sun, of man and woman

*This "quotation" is less than accurate. What Turner says is: "The penalty for seeing *ng'ula* burn, if one is uninitiated or young, is madness or leprosy. The stripes of flame will produce, it is thought, stripes of leprosy." (Turner 1967:256). (R.W.)

demented shouts and use of the novices as drums	remove the danger of a burning conjunction of earth and sun at the end of the initiatory night
silence	introduces the mediation of Venus

Let us compare these findings with the other acoustic codes. It would be hazardous to equate the *joyful shouts* of the Kuba novices saluting the return of the sun and the departure of lightning at the end of initiation (see p. 135) with the *terrified cries* of the Ndembu novices faced with the (solar) burning of their encampment ("Hide yourselves! Burning already!"[155]). In this context one should note that the Kuba and Lunda cosmogonic codes are radically opposed. In the first case the conjunction of sun and earth introduces a beneficent dry season; in the second, the reappearance of the sun accompanies the return of the beneficent rain to a world condemned to night and drought. That is probably why the Ndembu ritual so strongly emphasizes the necessity of keeping a proper distance from this sun of life that has the power of burning up the world.

In contrast, the Lunda acoustic code (insofar as we have deciphered it among the Ndembu) presents great affinities to the Luba code, in which noise appears in the form of the *charivari*, with the same disjunctive function: this ritual din conjures the burning conjunction of sky and earth that the rainbow tries to bring about under the sign of drought. As for silence, it becomes a general rule of good manners governing meals among the Luba, and is even extended to all culinary operations. There is reason to believe that this reserved attitude, as among the Ndembu, is placed under the sign of Venus, at least at the royal court. Indeed, we earlier put forward the hypothesis that the two wives concerned with the king's cooking represented respectively the morning and evening stars (see p. 51).* The food of the Luba divine king would therefore be cooked on a Venusian fire like that of the newly circumcised in the Lunda culture region. This fire, which de-

*This correspondence, although certainly plausible, is not in fact made explicit by de Heusch until its formulation on this page. What is established earlier is: the Moon, like Mbidi Kiluwe, has two wives (p. 51); the Moon's wives are the morning and evening stars (two manifestations of Venus); the term *kibanga* appears to apply both to Venus and to the raffia headdress worn by the two wives responsible for the cuisine of a Luba king (pp. 14 and 51). (R.W.)

mands silence, is doubly a mediator between sky and earth, for it was brought by the very spirit of rain and lightning.

		LUBA	LUNDA
	ritual silence	mediation of Venus between sky and earth (cooking fire)	mediation of Venus between sun and earth (fire of *mukanda*)
Uproar	ritual cries		disjunction of sun and earth (introduction of the wet season)
	charivari	disjunction of sky and earth (introduction of the wet season)	

But lexical transformations also confirm that Lunda mythology occupies a medial position, at a pivotal point between the Luba and Kuba symbolic systems:

Luba	*Lunda*	*Kuba*
moon and rain	sun and rain	sun and drought
maleficent dry season	maleficent dry season	beneficent dry season
sun little marked	beneficent sun	beneficent sun
maleficent rainbow	maleficent rainbow	rainbow unmarked
beneficent moon	maleficent moon	moon little marked

It is important to note that the opposition between a maleficent dry season and a beneficent wet season is considerably weakened in the Lunda system, where the cosmogonic myth makes neutral use of the dualist scheme, limiting itself to emphasizing the eminent value of sunlight and rain, both ruled by Lightning. The Chokwe variant even insists on the original supremacy of the rainbow serpent, master of terrestrial waters and the dry season; let us not forget that Lueji, from whom Chibinda Ilunga obtained his power, is a descendant of this divinity. In contrast the Luba mythical scene is dominated by the epic combat of the deleterious rainbow and the beneficial rain. These stylistic variations are at least as important as the purely structural ones.

One remark, relating to methodology: the Luba terms of the comparison do not belong to the series of symbols proper to the initiation of young men, which has not been considered here. The reason for this omission is that the dearth of information about this institution, which resembles the Lunda in including circumcision, precludes our further exploration of the mythical universe in the direction of ritual. Van Avermaet thinks, not without reason, that young men's initiation (*mukanda*) is of foreign origin, probably emanating from the Lunda region.[156] In both cases the novices salute the sun, morning and evening. Theeuws remarks in this context that on these occasions they utter a cry that normally accompanies the reappearance of the moon.[157] The published evidence[158] does not allow us to decide in what measure this solar symbolism is integrated with the lunar symbolism which dominates the ritual scene among the Luba.

We have found that *mungonge* and *mukanda* belong to the same symbolic configuration under the sign of the fire of Venus. This unity is evident among the Lunda where the master circumciser (Mbindi) is also the chief of the *mungonge* society.[159] Among the Pende (and probably elsewhere) it is necessary to undergo "the death of circumcision" to "die" in *mungonge*.[160] A Ndembu informant says in cryptic language that the ritual scenes of *mungonge* and *mukanda* take place in the same mystic landscape characterized by three rivers (white, black, and red)[161]; he thus reveals the unity and continuity of the esoteric teachings the symbolism of which we have earlier touched upon in connection with the color code (see p. 175). It would seem that the religious character of *mungonge* is more pronounced than that of *mukanda*, and White is probably correct in emphasizing that the second ritual is felt by those concerned as a purely symbolic death whereas *mungonge* initiation is held to plunge the novices really into the land of the dead (Kalunga); this sinister place, he adds, is never referred to in explanations of the puberty ritual.[162] This gloss is no doubt worthy of consideration, but the exploratory work of the preceding pages makes it appear highly unlikely that creation myths are not evoked during *mukanda*.

Circumcision and *mungonge* initiation form a ritual configuration with an essentially solar character. However, the third stage of initiation defies all interpretation in the existing state of our knowledge.[163] It would seem to relate to a complementary mythical cycle about which we know virtually nothing and which is concerned with smoke and honey: apparently, initiatory death occurs by suffocation in a doorless hut with a sacred basket of honey hanging from the ceiling.[164]

Myth and Historical Events

The foundation myth of the Lunda empire is completely intermeshed with a symbolic system that in certain respects constitutes a transformation of the Luba foundation myth. In relation to the first narrative (M1), the second (M20) is characterized by a change of style: what was an epic among the Luba becomes a love story among the Lunda. But in both cases the function remains the same: it is a matter of showing how an original culture, in some way incomplete or crude, welcomed divine kingship from outside. Notwithstanding our initial declaration of principle concerning the ethnohistorical use of such narratives, we can no longer ignore what seems to lie behind the fable: the arrival of Chibinda Ilunga probably represents the more or less peaceful incursion into Lunda country of a group of Luba emigrants, bearers of new political institutions. There is no reason to question the historical interpretation proposed by Vansina:

> A little before 1600, a daughter Rweej (Lueji) became chief of the land and married Kibinda (Chibinda) Ilunga, a Luba-Katanga, son of Kalala Ilunga, founder of the second Luba empire. The installation of Chibinda Ilunga and his numerous following in the chiefdom caused many disturbances. Many Lunda groups left the country and founded the Imbangala, Lwena, and Chokwe chiefdoms and kingdoms. Some members of Kibinda's following left him, discontented at not receiving more elevated positions; they founded the Bemba state.[165]

The first of these events is already familiar: Vansina is referring here to the exile of Chinguli and Chiniama; this episode is the subject of a historical controversy to which we must briefly allude. One of Chinguli's successors founded the chiefdom of Kasanji on the western bank of the Kwango and made contact with the first Portuguese merchants; the governor of Luanda received a Lunda chief who took the title of Jaga and was given firearms. De Carvalho thinks that Chinguli is the sole hero of this long adventure.[166] Vansina believes, more plausibly, that there were two waves of immigration into northern Angola. The first wave, led by Chinguli and later by Kasanji, settled for a time on the plateau that gives rise to the Kasai and Kwango rivers. The settlers were soon dislodged by new Lunda emigrants, who created the Chokwe and Songo chiefdoms. Kasanji, Chinguli's nephew, took up the great journey to the west and reached the ocean. In 1610 he took an oath of allegiance to the Portuguese of Luanda. He took part with his Imbangala followers in the wars waged by the Portuguese against Ngola, king of Ndongo.[167] Birmingham has pushed back the whole Lunda chronology in establishing 1575 as the approximate date of the first contacts between the Imbangala chiefs and the Portuguese. He goes on to deduce that the foundation of the Lunda state by the Luba chief Chibinda Ilunga should be dated to the first quarter of the sixteenth century and not to the beginning of the seventeenth.[168]

The appearance of Chibinda also led to an event of the first importance in quite another direction: the creation of the Bemba state in Zambia. From the Bemba foundation epic, it is possible to deduce that a group of Luba aristocrats at the Lunda court where Chibinda had just taken power decided, following various disagreements, to seek their fortunes elsewhere. This time these migrants directed their steps toward the east. The narrative of their adventures forms a new myth, which takes its place in the preceding ensemble; once more history molds itself in the categories of symbolic thought.

M32, Bemba: The Origins of the Bemba Kingdom (Labrecque[169])

In the Lunda country there reigned a queen mother, Mumbi Mukasa, the niece of God. She had fallen from the sky with ears as big as an elephant's. She married Mukulumpe and by him had four children, including Chiti Mukutwi. This person was none other than the future Bemba king Chiti Mukulu. From a first marriage, Mukulumpe had had two children, of whom the eldest became heir to the throne. The sons of Mumbi Mukasa conceived the fanciful notion of building a tall tower by mobilizing all the workers in the capital. When the edifice had reached a certain height, it collapsed, killing many people. Then Mukulumpe became furious. He decided to put to death the three sons responsible: Katongo, Nkole, and Chiti. He put out the eyes of the first, and the other two were barely able to escape. The king had a trap constructed on their path, a ditch bristling with spears and hidden from sight. The blind Katongo, warned of the danger threatening his two brothers, sent messengers after them who began to shout in all directions. On his side, the father sent envoys to his sons, assuring them of his pardon if they returned in the middle of the night. But the fugitives had heard the warning broadcast by the messengers of Katongo. They made a detour and arrived safe and sound in the capital at the dead of night. They awoke their father, who ordered them to appear before him the next morning. To humiliate his sons, he ordered them to sweep the square of the royal village. Mukulumpe's anger subsided.

But some months later the young princes committed other offences, possibly adultery with a young wife of their father's. This time they were condemned to sweep the royal cemetery. Chiti and Nkole refused to obey and fled with a band of followers. They were pursued by the people of the royal court, armed with sticks. The fugitives resisted the attack and killed the royal envoys charged with administering a correction. Beside himself, Mukulumpe sent his wife Mumbi Mukasa back to heaven. She had hardly got home when she died. Shattered by so many disasters, the king decided to bring together his rebellious sons. He showered presents on them and told them to go and seek their fortunes elsewhere.

Chiti, Nkole, and their half brother Kasembe, a son of their father's first marriage, journeyed toward the east, accompanied by a large number of aristocrats (belonging to the same totemic clan of the crocodile*) and slaves. A white man (or a Portuguese half-caste), accompanied by a dog, guided them. This stranger, called Luchele, was a diviner of repute; he left the imprint of his feet on a number of rocks in the country. Chiti led the migration. The head [hair] of Nkole was filled with various kinds of seeds. They crossed the Luapula River and founded a great village called "extension of the race." They spent some time there. It was then that Chiti regretted that his sister Chilufya-Mulenga had not accompanied him to assure the royal succession, in conformity with matrilineal descent. Mukulumpe kept his daughter imprisoned in a hut without either door or window. This jail was surrounded by a cordon of bells (to give the alarm). The young daughter had just come of marriageable age. Chiti selected five men of royal blood and ordered them to rescue his sister during the night. After several days' march, they arrived at the father's village during a pitch-dark night. The prison of the princess was a few paces from the royal residence. They managed to remove the alarm apparatus without attracting attention. They lifted up

*The crocodile clan (*Bena Ing'andu*) is the royal clan of the Bemba. (R.W.)

the roof and slid a ladder inside. Gently, they awoke the princess, who agreed to follow them. On the way back, they rested for several days on the banks of the Luapula. The prince Kapasa sent two of his companions to inform Chiti of the success of their mission. During the night Kapasa lay with Chilufya-Mulenga, who was his classificatory sister. Six months later the pregnant princess confessed the name of her incestuous seducer. Chiti flew into a great rage; he expelled Kapasa from the royal clan and gave him a degrading totem (the female genitalia). Kapasa, covered with shame, left the group with his close relatives.

Before pushing further eastward, Luchele consulted the oracle to find out whether the land they were heading for was fertile. The ancestors' response was favorable and the Bemba people went on their way under Chiti, while Kasembe founded a small kingdom along the Luapula River. After some weary months, the caravan reached the country of the Nsenga chief, Mwase. Chiti made a pact of friendship with him. One day Chilimbulu, Mwase's wife, decided to seduce the noble stranger by sending him a message in unequivocal terms: she impressed the splendid tattoos on her breast onto a ball of red powder made from the *nkula* tree and caused this declaration of love to be taken to Chiti. The latter exclaimed: "How beautiful this woman must be!" Chilimbulu's messengers confirmed him in this opinion. She met Chiti in great secrecy near a stream and they lived there together for three days, without the husband's knowledge. But the husband became suspicious and went to visit his friend's camp. Catching Chiti in the act of adultery, Mwase mortally wounded him in the arm with a poisoned arrow.

Nkole succeeded Chiti. He had his brother's corpse mummified by means of lenses[170] which caught the rays of the sun. This ritual took several months. Then Nkole ordered the caravan to turn back (toward the west). He founded another two villages, then decided to avenge his brother's death. He organized a military expedition against the regicide's people and killed them all. The corpse of Chilimbulu was cut into pieces. But the skin of her belly, ornamented with tattoos, was dried and carefully preserved as a fertility charm. Since then, the king's senior wife covers her loins with this skin when she begins to sow sorghum. The dismembered remains of Chilimbulu and her husband were placed in enormous water-filled jars and kept at Nkole's village. The caravan continued westward. It was necessary to perform the funeral ceremonies for Chiti. To obtain a cowhide in which to wrap his broth-

> er's mummified body, Nkole made war on the Fipa cattle-keepers. Luchele Nganga, the white diviner, reappeared. He built a round hut and covered it with a shield of iron rods for a roof, with grass on top. The mummy of Chiti lay in this sanctuary for several months. A magician was charged with burning what remained of Chilimbulu and her husband on an enormous funeral pyre. The smoke was so thick that it suffocated Nkole and he became gravely ill. The day of the solemn funeral of Chiti, he felt his own end to be near. He had a second grave dug. He ordered that the tomb of Chiti should be "at the base of the termite mound" and his should be "at the top," because he was the elder. It was thus that the second king was buried beside the first, "in an all-white termite mound."
>
> Their uterine nephew, barely six years old, succeeded to the kingship. He was the son of Chilufya-Mulenga, the incestuous sister. He led the migration further west until two dignitaries accidentally discovered the place of permanent settlement. The first dignitary (called "Little Dog") was dumb, but had the gift of detecting animals by their smell. One evening he guided the hunters along the trail of a warthog, which they soon killed. The second dignitary noticed a strong putrid odor: he discovered the carcass of a crocodile on a rock. This animal, it will be recalled, is the totem of the royal clan. The place was judged propitious for the building of the royal village.

The narrative continues with the history of the Bemba kings up to the twentieth sovereign, without loss of continuity between myth and history. But the miraculous tone fades.

An enigmatic synthesis of complicated historical traditions and mythical schemas, this text presents great problems of interpretation. Let us begin by drawing out some familiar threads from this tangled skein.

From the very beginning the cosmogonic code is tightly bound up with the kinship code. A celestial mother marries an earthly prince. The Bemba epic is a mirror image of the Luba-Lunda sacred union of the prince from above and the terrestrial princess. The elephant's ears of the celestial princess recall the hunter status of the masculine partner as he appears in the Luba-Lunda context; but this time it is the woman (object of the hunt insofar as this is a metaphor of fecundity) and not the hunter who is marked from this point of view. Mumbi Mukasa is at least partly animal (it will be recalled that we were earlier led to compare Lueji to a wounded game animal). The thematic inversion continues on other levels. Mumbi Mukasa, daughter from above, is prolific whereas Lueji, the chthonic princess, is sterile. In both cases the sacred union of sky and earth is the source of disasters: sooner or later it causes a massive exodus. But it is the sons of the princess who go into exile in the Bemba epic, her brothers in the Lunda epic. The symbolic numerology nevertheless remains unchanged: corresponding to the two brothers, Chiniama and Chinguli, who conduct a migration *toward the west*, there are the two sons, Chiti and Nkole, the first Bemba kings, who venture into unknown country *toward the east*. The other two sons of Mumbi Mukasa are really no more than assistants, and the historical destiny of Kasembe, the half brother, separates him from the rest.

The disjunction of Lueji and her brothers finds its counterpart in M32. Chiti and Nkole are at once separated from their mother (who is sent back to heaven) and from their sister, Chilufya-Mulenga. But the Bemba princes manage to carry Chilufya-Mulenga off, for it is a question of founding matrilineality, whereas the Lunda epic restores patrilineality. It is not surprising to rediscover the familial code of Kuba mythology in M32: the social conjunction of brother and sister is reestablished by way of incest.

It is through just such a play of mirrors that we can make out the passage between Kuba and Bemba mythology. Chiti sends the prince Kapasa to his sister, whereas Mweel sends various emissaries to her brother Woot in an attempt to make him return. One of these envoys, the woodworm Bombo, finds Woot asleep (M10); in the same way Chilufya-Mulenga is sleeping in M32 when Kapasa and his companions manage to join her after taking great precautions. They have to be careful to make no noise, whereas Bombo knocks on the rock separating him from Woot to make himself known.

Let us compare M32 and M10 closely. Woot leaves his sister after committing incest, plunging the village he has left into darkness. Chiti's sister lives, after her brother's departure, in an artificially induced perpetual night, imprisoned by her father in a hut without apertures. But conversely to what happens in the Kuba myth, incest occurs after this miniature eclipse and not before. M32 takes care to point out, moreover, that Kapasa and his companions arrive in Chilufya-Mulenga's village during a pitch-black night.

One also finds in M32 the theme of the excessive conjunction of mother and son, the kernel of another Kuba myth, M11. The ascent to heaven projected by Chiti and his brothers when they build the tower could be interpreted as an Oedipal quest for the celestial mother; as in M11, it provokes the anger of the outraged father. Darkness is associated in two different ways with this abortive attempt at maternal incest. After the collapse of the tower, the father inflicts on one of his sons the punishment that Oedipus imposed on himself: he puts his eyes out. In addition, the father requires his other sons to come to him *in the middle of the night.*

The familial problematic is also articulated with the thematic of the matrilineal Luba-Hemba (M8), in which the sons enter into conflict with the primordial father. But this time it is the father (Mukulumpe) who entertains the somber design of killing his sons. In spite of this inversion, the Bemba myth, like the Luba-Hemba (M8) and Kuba (M9) myths, justifies the transition from patrilineal to matrilineal systems by the disjunction of the father and his sons. We have seen that the conjunction of father and daughter is the correlative *mythème* to this critical situation. We find it again in M32: Chiti's sister is jealously kept a prisoner by a cruel father. But we have also seen that this sterile relationship cannot lead to the matrilineal system without being denied in its turn in favor of a moderate conjunction of brother and sister. The Bemba epic confirms this analysis precisely, since Chiti is obliged, to ensure matrilineal dynastic continuity, to remove Chilufya-Mulenga from their common father. Finally, we know that a second obstacle occurs to the effective realization of the matrilineal order: the excessive (incestuous) conjunction of brother and sister. The Bemba scenario is exemplary. The prince Kapasa, who has been charged with the removal of Chilufya-Mulenga, seduces her. Chiti thereupon flies into a great rage. By banishing the guilty one from the royal clan, he clearly proclaims the fundamental law of matrilineal society which unites brother and sister in a socioeconomic association devoid of erotic ambiguity.

This familial crisis can be read in other ways. The violent conflict between the father and his sons is expressed in the building of a tower, of which the mythical purport is now familiar to us. The failure of this project heralds the future exodus, while causing numerous deaths in the present. The dispersion of people and the resultant cultural diversity are once again associated with the disjunction of sky and earth, that is, with the introduction of discontinuity into the world. The union of sky and earth conversely connotes incest because the rebel princes approach the maternal domain in building the tower. This initial crisis is resolved by sending the mother to heaven. On the cosmogonic level, one could interpret this *mythème* as a more radical formulation of the disjunction of high and low, connoted earlier by the collapse of the tower. This time the mother herself dies, the sons leave the father, the peoples disperse.

From this moment, the myth takes on a new spatial orientation. The vertical axis of the narrative disappears. Or rather, the quest for the sky (and the mother) that marked the first episode is succeeded by the search for a new land situated to the east. The man who guides this migration is a white magician called Luchele. Far from being a Portuguese half-caste, as Labrecque supposes, this personage is purely and simply a solar hero. According to Doke, the name Luchele, which is sometimes applied to God among the Lamba, is closely related to the term designating the dawn.[171] The quality of whiteness applied to Luchele is therefore explained without needing the intervention of an external historical element. This person appears several times during the Bemba epic: first, at the beginning of the exodus; then during the march, when it is necessary to find out whether to venture further eastward. He left the Bemba when they forded the great Chambeshi River, and retraced his steps; and he met his companions again when they had turned around and were moving westward. He then finally disappeared toward the east, promising to return. Luchele thus performed a triple movement that could be schematized in the following way:

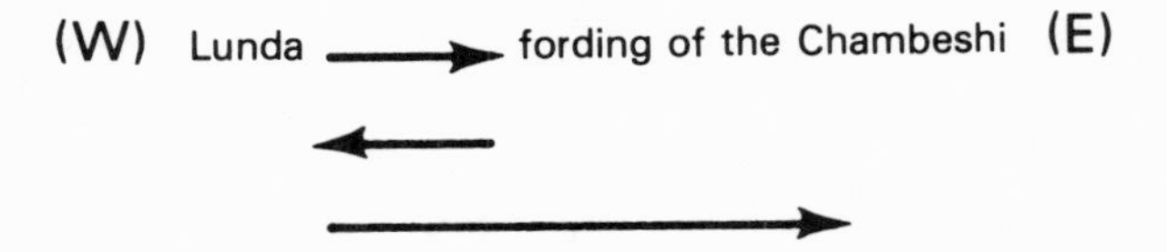

The general movement, oriented from west to east, immediately evokes the headlong flight of the solar hero Woot. Like Woot moreover (M10), Luchele has left the trace of his feet on the rocks; both finally disappear toward the east. In moving toward the unknown land whence the dawn comes, the ancestors of the Bemba enact a solar quest similar to that undertaken by the ancestors of the Kuba. The episode in which Luchele retraces his steps is analogous to the symbolic return of Woot who sends Mweel the birds of light to put an end to the great darkness. This return toward the west, connoting the apparent movement of the sun, is only briefly mentioned in M32: the narrative does say, however, that Luchele is accompanied by other members of the royal family when he reappears. By this token, Luchele is certainly the guide to the auspicious land located in the east. One characteristic detail allows no further doubt that Luchele participates in the solar nature of Woot. A dog is associated with the hero in both the Kuba and the Bemba myths: the animal is Mweel's emissary to Woot in M10, the faithful companion of Luchele in M32. At the end of the narrative, when Luchele has finally disappeared eastward and the Bemba pursue their course in the opposite direction, Luchele's dog reappears under a curious disguise: a dumb man, oddly called *Little Dog* because of his keen sense of smell, guides a group of Bemba hunters to a warthog; this successful hunt is an augury that the long march, first from west to east, then from east to west, is at an end. Finally, the Lala decisively confirm our argument, for they have a myth which explicitly portrays Luchele as the hero who brings sunlight to men, arousing the jealousy of his elder brother.[172]

Still other indications suggest that the historical topography of M32 is also a mythical cosmography. The first migratory phase ends at an extreme easterly point where the Bemba mummify the corpse of their first king by capturing the rays of the sun. In so doing they symbolically realize the conjunction of sky and earth that Chiti had tried in vain to achieve during his lifetime by building a tower. From thence it is clear that the east is analogous to the sky in virtue of a rotation through ninety degrees of the initially vertical cosmogonic axis. It is also noteworthy that to rejoin Chiti in the country of the east, his sister Chilufya-Mulenga, a prisoner in a hut without door or window, has first to scale a ladder introduced through the roof by her brother's emissaries; in a sense, they make her climb to heaven.

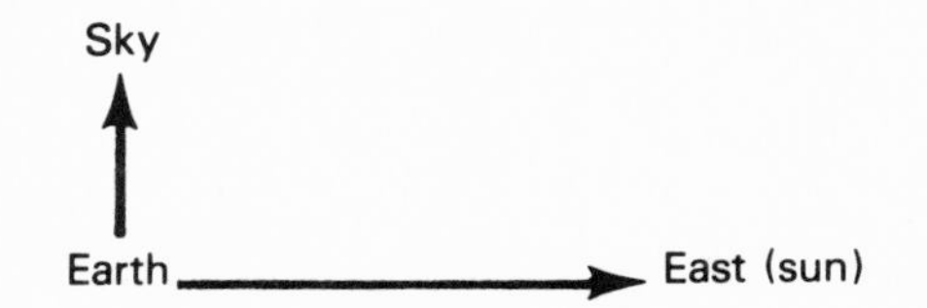

This transformation provides the key to the Lunda variant (Kazembe region) of the myth of the cosmic tower, in which the king derisively compels a certain Lubunda to build an enormous edifice to capture the sun (see p. 199). This personage doubly deserves comparison with the solar Luchele of M32. Like him, Lubunda leaves the court of Mwata Yamvo after the collapse of the tower; he is also a skilled ironsmith, like Luchele, who covers the funerary hut containing Chiti's mummified corpse with an iron roof. The anthropo-cosmogonic code elicited earlier receives verification here, because it is at the extreme point of the eastward march (i.e., toward the sun) that the founder of the Bemba royal line becomes effectively immortal through the action of this heavenly body. The imperishable mummy is nothing other than the place where earth and sun meet, in complete contrast with the decomposing carcass of the crocodile that marks the terrestrial site of the royal capital. The myth also opposes the royal mummy to the dismembered corpse of Chilimbulu, Chiti's mistress. Delivered to multiplicity, the corpse of Chilimbulu rots in the water, whereas her lover's body, its unity intact, is brought into contact with celestial fire and promised a kind of eternity, comparable to that assured by the funerary rites to another solar sovereign, the king of the Lunda.

The macabre funerary rite undergone by the mutilated corpse of Chilimbulu leads us to consider the cosmogonic significance of the contrasting intervention of water and fire. The lethal smoke given off by the rotting remains of Chilimbulu and her husband when they are burned is reminiscent of the fearsome smoke of Nkongolo which threatens the wet season among the Luba (see p. 38). Do not the enormous jars in which the remains of Chilimbulu are macerated before this cremation connote the wet season, introduced, as in the Holoholo myth (M7), by a military expedition?

Two "dry" episodes set off this dramatic scene of the jars. Chiti's mummification by a solar technique precedes it, and the cremation of the decomposed remains of Chilimbulu succeeds it. The killing of Chiti clearly corresponds to the beginning of the dry season: the myth says that the mummification went on for several months and it is hard to see how this technical operation could have been carried out during the rains. The celestial fire to which Chiti's corpse is submitted therefore connotes drought, just as the water in the jars containing the rotting remains of Chilimbulu and her husband marks the presence of rain. Terrestrial fire and the smoke of the funeral pyre interrupt the wet season in their turn. The three successive deaths which punctuate the narrative correspond to three cosmogonic moments in a cyclical structure with the last term taking us back to the first.

death of Chiti (mummification):	beginning of the dry season
death of Chilimbulu (remains placed in a jar):	beginning of the wet season
death of Nkole (suffocation):	interruption of the wet season

The poisonous smoke of the funeral pyre that causes the death of Nkole therefore has the same cosmogonic function as the lethal smoke given off by the termite mound sheltering Nkongolo the Rainbow in Luba mythology: both combat the rain. But the originality of M32 in relation to M1 is that the heroes of the Bemba epic, who are colorless during their lifetimes, assume their cosmogonic functions only after their deaths. All the situations of M1 are negated. Theoretically Chiti, the founder of Bemba kingship, should be situated like Kalala Ilunga, the founder of Luba kingship, on the side of the rain; but in fact M32 employs the negative of this image and Chiti's corpse submitted to the sun becomes the very symbol of drought. In the same way, it is through her death that Chilimbulu connotes the wet season.

mummified corpse of Chiti:	dry season
dismembered and putrifying corpse of Chilimbulu:	wet season

Each of these two cosmogonic figures, associated respectively with fire and water, possesses a double. While Nkole, suffocated by the smoke of the funeral pyre, is a replica of Chiti (whom he succeeds), the crocodile, totemic symbol of the royal clan, recalls Chilimbulu: Chilimbulu is a terrestrial being whose corpse is abnormally plunged into water, while the crocodile, an aquatic animal, putrifies out of its natural element.

These doubles are in no way redundant. Chiti and Nkole are complementary opposites in several respects. The first leads the caravan toward the east, the second toward the west. Chiti is not associated with violent action but is something of a jurist: he establishes matrilineal succession and banishes the incestuous Kapasa. But morally his conduct is shabby: he does not hesitate to commit adultery at a friend's expense. In contrast, Nkole is a warrior, savagely avenging his brother's death by massacring the people of Chilimbulu. He is the hero of agriculture, his head [hair] a kind of granary containing the seeds of cultivated plants.

In death, Chiti and Nkole take over different parts of the space symbolized by their last resting place, a termite mound. Nkole as the elder is lodged at the top of the mound, while the younger Chiti is assigned the lower portion. This high and dry place of the myth (its white color attesting its association with the sun) symbolizes the universe in a more complex manner than in the Luba myth, in which this natural funerary monument shelters only the head of the first king, Nkongolo. Chiti, mummified by *celestial fire* (the sun), occupies a low position in the cosmic termite mound, while Nkole, suffocated by the *terrestrial fire* of the nauseating pyre, occupies the high part. The division of fire between the two heroes is more complex than this, however. Celestial fire, strangely brought close by lenses, is used like a terrestrial fire. Conversely, by cooking putrified human flesh, meat doubly unfit for consumption, Nkole denies the culinary function of terrestrial fire. To the beneficent use of the sun to "cook" a man so as to preserve him intact, there corresponds symmetrically the bad use of cooking fire to consume the rotting remains of a dismembered woman. The first fire preserves, the second destroys. To understand this symbolism, it is necessary to know that cooking is paradoxically, in the eyes of the Bemba, a permanent source of danger. The domestic hearth, a dominant symbol of the social order, is incompatible with sexual activity: any person who does not ritually wash after copulation and who approaches a fire will contaminate the food cooked there; children who took part in such a meal would be endangered.[173] The polluting power of adultery, the mortal sin of Chiti, is particularly dangerous for the fire. One can understand how the dismembered body of the adulteress, when brought into direct contact with the flames, gives off a particularly pernicious smoke. It is probably to escape from this evil, and even to reverse its effects, that the corpse of Chiti, the accomplice and victim of adultery, is burned by the rays of the sun, the purifying celestial fire. This solar cooking at a distance is the inverse counterpart of the monstrous cuisine to which Nkole delivers the corpse of the seductress.

Together in the same termite mound, Chiti and Nkole complement each other in a mausoleum which is the natural counterpart of the cosmic tower they tried vainly to build in order to become immortal like the sun. Sky and earth are joined in the corpses of the two first kings: the one who lies below (near the earth) has been in contact with the beneficent sun, and the one who lies above (near the sky) has submitted to the power of a maleficent terrestrial fire.

corpse of Chiti	*corpse of Nkole*
younger	elder
base of the termite mound	top of the termite mound
beneficent celestial fire	maleficent terrestrial fire

If one takes account of the whole configuration of oppositional pairs, it can be seen that the cosmogonic correspondences inscribed in the foundation epic of the Bemba state form a great funerary hymn dedicated to the life of the cosmos.

dry season (fire)	corpse of Chiti: celestial fire (sun)
	corpse of Nkole: terrestrial fire (pyre)
wet season (water)	corpse of Chilimbulu: celestial water (jar)
	carcass of crocodile: terrestrial water (river)

But what has become in this myth of the Luba figure of the Rainbow, the master of the dry season? It has undergone the same transformation as in the Lunda foundation epic (M20): Nkongolo has taken on the appearance of a seductive woman, Chilimbulu. The fatal passion she inspires in Chiti is the direct cause of the onset of the dry season and her own death liberates the wet season. One detail in particular reveals that the Bemba seductress is the transformation of Nkongolo: their respective corpses are mutilated and cut into two or more pieces, precisely to allow the setting up of the seasonal dialectic. In this respect, the *dried* skin from the belly of the Bemba heroine is the equivalent of the head of Nkongolo buried in the dry earth of the termite mound; likewise, the decapitated corpse of the Luba king, interred under a river, is the equivalent of Chilimbulu's remains cast into a water-filled jar. It will also be noted that the Bemba seductress imprints the marks of her tattoos on a red ball of cosmetic, the very color of which relates to Nkongolo.

If Chilimbulu is really the feminine counterpart of Nkongolo, one should be able to establish a series of symbolic equivalences between her and Lueji, the heroine of the Lunda epic. We find that both take the initiative in seducing a foreign hero; and both are without children, the erotic function eclipsing the procreative one. This last parallel throws light on the mysterious circumstances of Chiti's death. Mwase, the wronged husband, surprises him in the company of his wife in the middle of the night; he does not bother to bend his bow but plunges a poisoned arrow into the left arm of Chiti, who soon dies from this wound. The hero dies tragically, treated like a *game animal*, whereas Chibinda Ilunga, his homologue in the Lunda epic, is defined as a *hunter*.

Luba epic (M1)	*Lunda epic (M20)*	*Bemba epic (M32)*
hunter-hero	hunter-hero	hero treated like a game animal
fecund, seductive woman	sterile, seductive woman	seductive woman, a source of death

The adulterous seductress who provokes the death of the hero in M32 systematically inverts, as one would expect, the qualities of the beneficent seductress of M1:* legitimate wife and source of life, the latter participates in the wet season, whereas Chilimbulu, the childless mistress, participates in drought.

The unusual circumstances of the deaths of Chiti and Nkole pose a new semantic problem. Observing that the nauseous smoke from the funeral pyre lit by Nkole could be considered as a particular form of poison, one concludes that the two kings died in the same way and for the same cosmogonic reason:

death of Chiti:	poison (of an arrow)	introduction of the dry season
death of Nkole:	smoke (poisoned by rotting flesh)	

*De Heusch is evidently referring to Bulanda, the mother of the hero Kalala Ilunga, rather than to Bulanda's co-wife Mabela. (R.W.)

The slight difference which nevertheless exists between these two signifiers corresponds to a difference of signifieds: it invites us to inscribe the cosmogonic code of the myth in a circular model, which is also that of cyclical time. The poisoning of the king Chiti marks the beginning of the dry season; the poisoned smoke given off by the pyre lit on the orders of the king Nkole marks the end of the wet season.

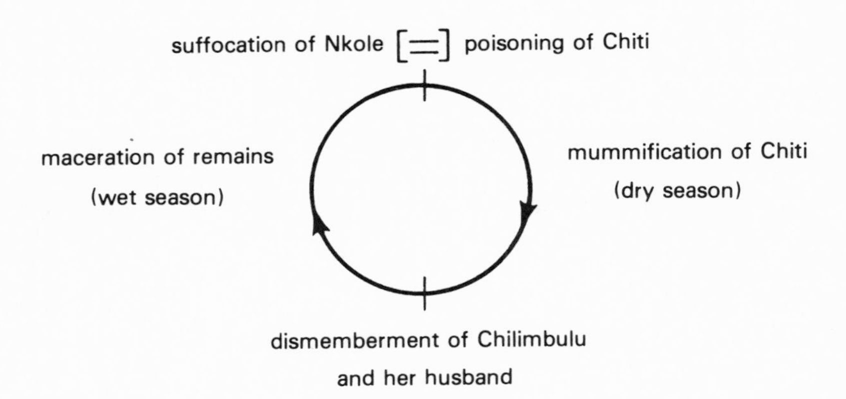

In the structural interval separating the death of Nkole from the death of Chiti, before the circle closes on itself, the totemic figure establishes itself with all its meaning. The crocodile which emerges from the water, its natural domain, to die on a dry and elevated rock and so determine the site of the first settled royal capital—this creature also establishes a mediation between the two sovereigns, while assuming the dialectical transition from wet to dry.

There is no indication of a minor dry season within the wet, as in the Holoholo myth. That is because the rains are virtually continuous in Bemba country; there is sometimes a brief remission at the end of January, but precipitation soon recommences and remains copious until March–April. The harvest takes place in the first months of the dry season: "Bemba cultivation," says Audrey Richards, "is entirely dependent on this type of rainfall and is limited in most cases to the production of one crop a year."[174]

We can now resolve the philosophic puzzle posed by the duality of Chiti and Nkole, forever joined in the cosmic termite mound at the same point of articulation of the wet and dry seasons. The mummification of Chiti's corpse is a victory over decay, connoted by the remains of Chilimbulu decomposing in the water. The Bemba evidently accord a high value, like the Lunda, to the beneficent action of the sun, agent and witness of the immortality of kings. By desiccating the royal corpse, men bring together, as we have seen, the earth and the sun. However, the myths of neighboring peoples tell us that this operation ends mortal life at the same time as it suspends cosmic time. If the conjunction of the earth and the burning sky assures the mystic survival of the sovereign, the situation also entails a grave cosmogonic risk, threatening the world with permanent drought. The dismemberment of Chilimbulu's corpse should therefore be interpreted as a rite of conjuration, under the dual sign of the *discontinuous* and the *wet*. This seemingly barbaric act does no more than invert the principles brought into play by the mummification of Chiti. This mummification appears in the singular form of a *cooking* that is slow and *continuous*, preserving the unity and permanence of the body. In contrast, the brutal dismemberment of Chilimbulu's corpse, then the sinister decomposition of her remains, reintroduce to the world the principle of discontinuity in the double form of decay and succession of the seasons: the rain brings an end to the perilous eternity of drought. By inverting in all respects the funerary rite employed to preserve Chiti's body intact, Nkole actively assumes the dialectic of time in his capacity as hero of agriculture.

The double intervention of poison in this philosophic tragedy is altogether remarkable. The poisoning of Chiti has two contradictory consequences (mummification of the victim on one side, dismemberment of the female seductress on the other), bringing into play the principles of both continuity and discontinuity. As for the suffocation of Nkole, it causes the master of the wet season, the hero of discontinuity, to pass over to the side of perpetual drought: his corpse joins the mummy of Chiti in the termite mound, his elevated position in this microcosm of a tomb indicating that he is, in death, in direct contact with the sun.

This problematic of poison, in which continuity and discontinuity are anticipated, presents curious affinities with Amerindian theory. Let us recall the terms: ". . . in the natives' conception of poison of vegetable origin," writes Lévi-Strauss, "the interval between nature and culture, although present as it is in all other contexts, is reduced to a minimum. Consequently, poison, whether used for fishing or hunting, can be defined as *maximum continuity which brings about maximum discontinuity* . . ."[175]* (our emphasis). It would seem that the Bemba, whose mythical thought is dominated by historical concerns, are little preoccupied with the passage from nature to culture. The problematic of continuity and discontinuity takes up the whole cosmogonic dimension of the myth. But Amerindian thought here suggests a link between poison and the phenomenal world, since the power of primitive *continuity*, expressed in the first term, is also found in the rainbow.[176] Now, we have seen that the seductress of M32, whose adulterous passion summons up the husband's poison, is but a transformation of this natural phenomenon, which has to be literally taken to pieces in order to establish a discontinuous space-time. Paraphrasing Lévi-Strauss, one could say that Chilimbulu is a "poisoning" Iseult† of the social order. But the fatal desire that she shamelessly arouses in Chiti is indispensable to the cosmic order and to fertility: the skin of her belly, imprinted with the erotic charm of the tattoo, has become one of the major symbols of the ritual of sowing. The poison of love, a philter of death, is supreme ruler of the universe.

The origin of poison, called "the destroyer of the world," is one of the main themes of the creation myth of the Lala, a neighboring people to the Bemba.[177] This narrative (M33) relates the more directly to our discussion for the appearance in it of a familiar personage, Luchele, the solar guide of the Bemba.

> Luchele, the youngest son of God, brings the light of the sun to men. His envious elder brother Kashindika asks their father to give him poison. God refuses, and Kashindika decides to take it by force. He successively brings about the deaths of his brother's wife and his own wife. It was after these events that Luchele decided to emigrate to the east.

The interest of this myth lies in its clear opposition of the sun, the source of life, and poison, the source of death. It is evidently in virtue of the same logic that the body of the poisoned Chiti is exposed to the rays of the sun, which constitute a kind of structural antidote.

**The Raw and the Cooked* (translated by John and Doreen Weightman), Jonathan Cape, London, 1969:279. (R.W.)

†In the medieval legend of Tristan and Iseult (or Iseut) the two protagonists were led to drink a magic philter together, igniting in them an irresistible and eternal love that resulted in the death of Tristan. (R.W.)

As in many other myths, but with a particular elegance, the Bemba epic establishes a necessary homology between the destiny of man, condemned to finitude, and cosmic harmony. The cyclical rhythm of the universe is tragically opposed to the human dream of eternity, which expresses itself in a compelling manner in Central Africa in the fantasy of the Tower of Babel. This contradiction permits only an illusory resolution, of a religious kind: to assure, through a symbolic conjunction of the royal corpse and the sun, the survival of a power guaranteeing the permanence of the body social, in spite of the deaths of individuals. The ancient Egyptians arrived at the same result, on one side identifying the vital force of the king with solar radiation and, on the other, mummifying his mortal remains.

The ultimate conjunction of sky and earth, realized by Nkole in concentrating the rays of the sun on his brother's body to save it from destruction, relates to the initial episode of the cosmic tower, which has the same meaning: to create a continuous universe where man would be immortal and human society one. The majority of the peoples claiming Luba-Lunda origin explain their migrations and the resulting ethnic diversity by the collapse of a tower constructed by the son of a great chief. It was thus that the Crocodile clan took the road to Bemba country and the Goat clan took power in Lamba and Aushi country.[178] M32 says that the ancestors of neighboring peoples left the Bemba caravan peacefully at various times. Linguistic diversity therefore corresponds on the cultural plane to cosmogonic discontinuity, as Kuba mythology has already taught us. The extension in space of cultural diversity is the direct consequence of the temporal dialectic. The ordering of our world implies the condemnation of incest, the blocking of the incestuous conjunction of sky and earth, but also the renunciation of immortality. In bringing together the sun and the corpse of Chiti, Nkole nevertheless reintroduces this pathetic hope, necessary for the survival of his people, into the midst of kingship. There is reason to believe that the ceremonial fire of royalty, which burns continually at the capital and which a delicate ritual safeguards from all pollution,[179] relates to this grandiose illusion, just as the fire of Venus keeps a day-and-night guard over the encampment of the circumcised in the Lunda area.

The Bemba symbolic system participates in the three intellectual universes that we have explored earlier, those of the Luba, the Lunda, and the Kuba. It resembles them also in taking account of the pleasure principle in a traveler-king who seems a trifle decadent by comparison with the brave warrior- or hunter-heroes occupying the center of the Luba-Lunda mythical scene, where a moralizing story seeks to explain the acquisition of a superior civilization.

These structural affinities are at least partially of historical origin. This is clearly spelled out in the genealogies of the heroes. The Bemba aristocracy hives off from the Luba following which accompanied the prince Chibinda Ilunga at the Lunda court. More mysterious is Kuba participation in this mythological fresco, the secret unity of which we have demonstrated. One should not lose sight of the fact that until the beginning of this century the Kuba maintained a veritable international commerce through the intertribal market system described by Vansina. Before European colonization, Katanga provided the Kuba with salt and copper, while the Kuba exported to this region ivory, cosmetic wood, fish, mats, raffia cloth, and embroidery.[180] It is obvious that these commercial relations with the Luba world could not have existed before the formation of the Kuba kingdom. The Bushong and other tribes of the central Kuba group left the Atlantic coast in the sixteenth century, probably after fighting against the Portuguese.[181]

The migratory period ended with the beginning of the following century, but a strong central power was not established before the middle of the seventeenth century. It is certain that important cultural exchanges took place between the Kuba kingdom and the Lunda, who were at this time expanding vigorously westward. It would be hard to explain otherwise how a royal myth as important as M9 (the Kuba myth of the origin of matrilineality and young men's initiation) should be completely identical with the first part of the foundation myth of the Lunda state (M20). The Pende, who themselves borrowed the *mungonge* ritual from the Lunda, could well have served as intermediaries, particularly since a Kuba tradition recorded by Torday tells of direct contacts. The king Shamba Bolongongo (Shyaam, according to Vansina) is supposed to have introduced weaving to his people after observing the technique among the Pende.[182] Whatever reservations we may have about this report as it stands, it at least indicates that at the time when the Kuba kingdom was becoming strongly organized, it was open to ideas as well as goods from outside. Vansina moreover asserts that before seizing power, the great reformer Shyaam (who was a usurper) lived in Kwango, from whence he brought many cultural items; Vansina even considers that the ideology of divine kingship that Shyaam imposed could have been of Lunda or Kongo origin.[183] Lunda emigrants did indeed form small states in the Kwango region in the seventeenth century.

It was probably during this epoch that a common mythological system developed in the Congolese savanna. Osmosis between divergent traditions was made easier because they probably all originated in a common ideological heritage handed down from proto-Bantu society. Far from denying history, structural analysis can sometimes offer it insights of great value. Such analysis has shown that highly dissimilar societies share a common conception of man and the universe and constitute a single civilization that has spread far and wide to the south of the great equatorial forest. Maintained by strong political structures, this civilization covers Katanga, Zambia, and part of Angola. It established trading relations with the civilization of the Atlantic coast, of which the Kongo kingdom was the political center at the end of the fifteenth century. That kingdom was unfortunate enough to become the bridgehead of Portuguese colonial expansion at that time. The cultural disintegration of Kongo society which followed the tragic impact of European mercantile and missionary agents leaves scant hope of reconstituting its traditional symbolic ideas in their entirety. The only myth emanating from this region that we have used (M3) nevertheless fits in well enough with the system of transformations we have outlined. Other aspects that are less easily reducible to this ensemble will detain us on the next stage of this long journey.

The Congolese myths are exchanged like merchandise. But they have, properly speaking, no value. They are not the products of labor, and they defy all attempts at appropriation, whether private or collective. No copyright attaches to their telling, retelling, and transformation. They even elude the ideological function that the kings invariably try to force on them. They are borne along by the slack tides of history, but they dance with the rays of the sun and laugh with the rain, knowing no other master than themselves.

Notes

Introduction

1. The interested reader is referred to our previous book, *Pourquoi l'épouser?*
2. Shaw, 1969, p.226.
3. Hiernaux, 1968, p.507. The Machili site has been given a Carbon 14 dating of A.D. 96 (± 212), but this estimate should be treated with reserve.
4. We are particularly grateful to Marie-Louise Bastin and Michel Museur.
5. Frazer, 1919, vol. II.
6. Engels, *L'Origine de la famille, de la propriété privée et de l'État*, French translation, Paris, 1946.

CHAPTER ONE: *Kingly Manners*

1. Vansina, 1965, pp.55–56.
2. Vansina, 1955, p.162.
3. Verhulpen, 1936, p.97.
4. *Ibid.*, p.89.
5. Vansina, 1966, p.162.
6. Vansina, 1965, p.59.
7. *Ibid.*, p.68.
8. Labrecque, 1933, p.633.
9. Labrecque, 1949, p.12.
10. Nenquin, 1963, p.200; Hiernaux, Maquet, and de Buyst, 1968.
11. Vansina, 1965, p.9.
12. Colle, 1913, pp.353–359.
13. Donohugh and Berry, 1932, pp.182–359; Verhulpen, 1936, pp.92–93, 97; Van der Noot, 1936, pp.141–142; Burton, 1961, pp.3–11; Van Malderen, 1940, pp.205–206; Makonga, 1948, No. 10, pp.304–316; Orjo de Marchovelette, 1950, pp.354–359; Sendwe, 1954, pp.113–116; Theeuws, 1954, pp.15–17, 1962, pp.202–209, 1964, pp.5–8.
14. The author uses the spelling "Kongolo."
15. In fact Mijibu, who is called a *vidye* (spirit), is a medium.
16. This is a game of counters played with the fruits (*masoko*) of the

musoko vine; testicles are called by the same name as these fruits (Van Avermaet, 1954, p.623, on *mu-soko*).

17. The verb *mona* means "to see" (Van Avermaet, 1954, p.409). It thus seems that the expression describes the place as a witness of Nkongolo's disappearance.

18. *Mu-nza* = barbs (of arrows), Van Avermaet, 1954, p.469.
19. Burton, 1961, pp.3–12.
20. Verhulpen, 1936, pp.92–94, 97.
21. Colle, 1913, pp.353–358.
22. Sendwe, 1954, p.113.
23. Burton, 1961, p.206.
24. Theeuws, 1962, p.206.
25. Colle, 1913, p.354.
26. Sendwe, 1954, p.91.
27. Lévi-Strauss, 1966.
28. Theeuws, 1954, pp.14–16.
29. Sendwe, 1954, pp.113–116.
30. Studstill, 1969, p.55.
31. Van Avermaet, 1954, on *ki·nà* (excavation, hole, and also *os vaginae mulieris quae labia interna non ampliavit* [*sic*], p.193.
32. *Ibid.*, on *ì·kana*, p.226.
33. *Ibid.*, on *ki·nà*, pp.193, 423.
34. Sendwe, 1955, p.72.
35. Van Avermaet, 1954, on *bw-inà*, p.193.
36. Van Malderen, 1940, p.199.
37. *Ibid.*, p.206.
38. Van Avermaet, 1954, p.479, on *-onga*.
39. Sendwe, 1954, pp.113–116.
40. Colle, 1913, II, p.519.
41. Van Avermaet, 1954, p.392.
42. Theeuws, 1962, pp.27 ff.
43. Burton, 1961, pp.11–12.
44. Van Avermaet, 1954, p.644, on *-sula*.
45. Burton, 1961, p.12.
46. Van Malderen, 1940, p.206.
47. Burton, 1961, p.12.
48. Verhulpen, 1936, p.183; Sendwe, 1955, p.84.
49. de Heusch, 1958.
50. Burton, 1961, p.21; Van Avermaet, 1954, pp.372, 471; Sendwe, 1955, p.84; Verhulpen, 1936, p.183.
51. Theeuws, 1962, p.206.
52. Burton, 1961, p.11.
53. *Ibid.*, pp.19–20.
54. Verbeke, 1937, p.54.
55. Theeuws, 1954, pp.18–19.
56. Theeuws, 1964, p.8.
57. Burton, 1961, p.20.
58. Verhulpen, 1936, p.94.
59. Lucas, 1966, p.86.
60. Theeuws, 1954, p.16.
61. Theeuws, 1960, p.163.

CHAPTER TWO: *The Rainbow and the Lightning*

1. Turner, 1967, pp.152–153, 288.
2. Tempels, 1949, p.28.
3. Theeuws, 1954.
4. Colle, 1913, p.353; Verhulpen, 1936, p.92.
5. Van Avermaet, 1954, p.283, on *n-kongolo.*
6. Verhulpen, 1936, p.92.
7. Theeuws, 1962, p.158.
8. Wauters, 1949, p.237.
9. Theeuws, 1964, p.5.
10. Van Avermaet, 1954, p.622, on *-so·ka* (burn, set fire to).
11. Theeuws, 1964, p.5.
12. Burton, 1961, p.43.
13. Verhulpen, 1936, p.94.
14. Colle, 1913, II, p.715.
15. Van Malderen, 1940, p.199.
16. Nolleveaux, 1949.
17. Colle, 1913, pp. 718, 419–421.
18. Theeuws, 1962, p.302.
19. Makonga, 1948, p.312.
20. Theeuws, 1964, p.6.
21. Van Malderen, 1940, p.205.
22. Studstill, 1969, pp.90–91.
23. Sendwe, 1954, p.104.
24. Van Avermaet, 1954, pp.296, 810, on *n-kuba* and *n-zadji.*
25. *Ibid.*, p.810, on *n-zadji.*
26. Feytaud, 1949, p.44.
27. Bittremieux, 1936, pp.244–265.
28. *Ibid.*, p.172.
29. *Ibid.*, p.173.
30. Doutreloux, 1967, p.219.
31. Nicolaï, 1961, p.29.
32. Roumeguère-Eberhardt, 1963, pp.14–15.
33. Stayt, 1931, p.333.
34. Roumeguère-Eberhardt, 1963, p.17.
35. Colle, 1913, p.421.
36. Bittremieux, 1936.
37. Roumeguère-Eberhardt, 1963, p.91.
38. *Ibid.*, p.57.
39. Burton, 1961, p.19; Verhulpen, 1936, p.94.
40. Makonga, 1948, p.308.
41. Theeuws, 1962, p.301.
42. Studstill, 1969, p.68, quoting de Bouveignes, 1933, p.228.
43. Tempels, 1936, pp.131–132.
44. Theeuws, 1962, p.301.
45. Van Avermaet, 1954, p.51, on *lu-bangà.*
46. Theeuws, 1962, p.301.
47. Tempels, 1936, pp.131–132.

48. Cf. an Amerindian myth, *Taulipang*, "the two wives of the moon," in Lévi-Strauss, 1968, pp.34–35.
49. Theeuws, 1962, p.304.
50. Nolleveaux, 1949.
51. Bittremieux, 1936, p.241.
52. Colle, 1913, p.718.
53. Feytaud, 1949, pp.83, 87.
54. Colle, 1913, p.421.
55. Theeuws, 1962, p.158.
56. Denolf, 1954, pp.481–482.
57. Van Avermaet, 1954, p.283, on *n-kongolo.*
58. White, 1948, p.34.
59. Theeuws, 1962, p.158.
60. Burton, 1961, p.96.
61. *Ibid.*, p.49.
62. Theeuws, 1962, p.304.
63. *Ibid.*, p.305.
64. Lévi-Strauss, 1964, p.253.
65. *Ibid.*, p.300.
66. Boone, 1961, p.51; Coupez, 1955, pp.9–10.
67. Schmitz, 1912, pp.261–266.
68. Therefore, for the Holoholo, on the left bank of the river, corresponding to the domain of Nkongolo according to M1.
69. Van Avermaet, 1954, p.140, on *kwêzi* (lunation).
70. Kalala Ilunga in M1 is both one and the other, without contradiction.
71. On the relations between the Bantu magician and the ideology of shamanism, see de Heusch, 1971a, p.277.
72. Lévi-Strauss, 1964, pp.252–253.
73. Van Avermaet, 1954, p.618, on *bushipo*, the dry season.
74. Lévi-Strauss, 1968, p.298.
75. Grévisse, 1946–1947, p.74.
76. Dumézil, 1948.
77. Smith, 1970.
78. Lucas, 1966, p.87; d'Hertevelt and Coupez, 1964, p.49.
79. Smith and Sperber, 1971.

CHAPTER THREE: *The Outraged Father*

1. Mbidi Kiluwe.
2. Colle, 1913, I, p.324.
3. Sendwe, 1954, p.113.
4. Theeuws, 1962, p.207.
5. de Heusch, 1966.
6. Grévisse, 1946–1947, pp.68–69.
7. Marchal, 1936, pp.7–28.
8. Bourgeois, 1965, p.28, quoting Doke, 1931, p.31.
9. Bourgeois, 1965, p.28.
10. Whiteley, 1951, p.60.

11. Bourgeois, 1965, p.26.
12. Whiteley, 1951, p.60; Bourgeois, 1965, p.26.
13. Whiteley, 1951, p.56; Bourgeois, 1965, p.28.
14. Vansina, 1955, p.144.
15. *Ibid.*, pp. 144–145.
16. Denolf, 1933, pp.237–246, and 1954, pp.134, 465–468. See also Torday and Joyce, 1911, pp.247–248, and Vansina, 1963, pp.94–95.
17. Denolf, 1933, p.246.
18. Torday, 1925, p.248.
19. Torday and Joyce, 1911, pp.246–248.
20. Vansina, 1964, p.17.
21. Torday and Joyce, 1911, pp.240–241.
22. de Heusch, 1958.
23. Vansina, 1963, pp.93–95, 100–101.
24. Nyimilong is an incestuous soon of Woot and Mweel (cf. Vansina and Jacobs, 1956, p.11).
25. Torday and Joyce, 1911, p.21.
26. Vansina, 1956, pp.257–300.
27. Vansina, 1964, pp.28–29.
28. de Heusch, 1971a, p.23.
29. Frazer, 1919, I, p.362.
30. Vansina, 1963, p.93.
31. *Ibid.*
32. *Ibid.*, p.362.
33. Torday and Joyce, 1911, p.235.
34. Vansina, in Oliver, 1961, Chapter XII. See also Vansina, 1963.
35. Vansina and Jacobs, 1956.
36. Vansina, 1963, p.32.
37. Torday, 1925, pp.127–128 and Torday and Joyce, 1911, pp.21–23.
38. Vansina, 1955, p.145.
39. Achten, 1929, pp.192–193.
40. On the symbolism of palm wine, see Chapter 5.
41. Torday, 1925, pp.106–107.
42. Lévi-Strauss, 1964, p.326.
43. Vansina, 1963, pp.111–112, 365; Denolf, 1954, pp.134, 280.
44. Vansina, 1963, p.111.
45. *Ibid.*, p.365.
46. *Ibid.*, p.373.

CHAPTER FOUR: *The People of the Sun*

1. Vansina, 1955, p.142.
2. *Ibid.*, p.151.
3. *Ibid.*, p.148.
4. *Ibid.*, pp.138–153.
5. Or a sister; or even, failing that, a wife.
6. Vansina, 1955, p.152.
7. *Ibid.*, pp.145–146.
8. de Heusch, 1971b.

9. Vansina, 1955, p.151.
10. *Ibid.*
11. *Ibid.*, pp.140, 148.
12. *Ibid.*, p.142. Vansina does not say whether this "adultery of initiation" allows infringement of the prohibition on intraclan incest.
13. *Ibid.*, p.148.
14. *Ibid.*, pp.150–151.
15. *Ibid.*, p.147.
16. *Ibid.*
17. *Ibid.*, pp.145, 726–727.
18. *Ibid.*, p.151.
19. *Ibid.*, p.148.
20. *Ibid.*
21. *Ibid.*, p.142.
22. *Ibid.*, p.147.
23. *Ibid.*, p.148.
24. *Ibid.*
25. *Ibid.*, p.150.
26. de Heusch, 1971a, pp.104 ff.
27. Vansina, 1955, p.150.
28. *Ibid.*
29. Vansina, 1964, p.90.
30. Vansina, 1955, p.150.
31. *Ibid.*
32. *Ibid.*
33. Vansina, 1963, p.362.
34. Vansina, 1955, p.149.
35. Vansina, 1958, p.732.
36. Vansina, 1963, p.93.
37. Vansina, 1958, p.732.
38. Vansina, 1963, p.82.
39. Torday and Joyce, 1911, p.20, and 1925, pp.124–125.
40. Vansina, 1955, p.147.
41. Torday and Joyce, 1911, p.20.
42. Ibid., p.21. According to Vansina (1958, p.727), Woot also installed the clan system.
43. Torday and Joyce, 1911, p.21.
44. *Ibid.*
45. Vansina, 1964, p.200.
46. Vansina, 1958, p.730.
47. Torday and Joyce, 1911, pp.236–237.
48. *Ibid.*, pp.235–236.
49. *Ibid.*
50. Vansina, 1955, p.149.
51. *Ibid.*, p.150.
52. Vansina, 1958, p.732.
53. Vansina, 1955, p.149.
54. *Ibid.*, p.139.
55. *Ibid.*, p.150.
56. Lévi-Strauss, 1964, p.299.

57. *Ibid.*, pp.292–293.
58. *Ibid.*, p.300.
59. We are referring here to the first three volumes of the *Mythologiques.*
60. Vansina observes that the concept of *paam*, "the violence of outraged royal authority," also evokes burning fire, the reddening appearance of the westering sun, and the fury of the leopard (Vansina, 1964, p.104).
61. Torday and Joyce, 1911, p. 250.
62. Vansina, 1964, p.109.
63. Achten, 1929, p.192.
64. Bouillon, 1953, p.578.
65. Schouteden, 1948, p.136.
66. Sendwe, 1954, p.114.
67. Bouillon, 1953, p.576.
68. Schouteden, 1948, p.140.
69. Vansina, 1964, p.102.
70. de Heusch, 1971a, pp.70–71.
71. Vansina, 1964, p.100.
72. *Ibid.*
73. *Ibid.*, p.99.
74. *Ibid.*
75. *Ibid.*

CHAPTER FIVE: *Palm Wine, the Blood of Women, and the Blood of Beasts*

1. Crine-Mavar, 1963, p.81.
2. Duysters, 1958, pp.81–86.
3. The term *pombe* is ambiguous; another authority, Van den Byvang, translates it more precisely as "palm wine" (see below).
4. Pogge, 1880, pp.224–226.
5. de Carvalho, 1890, pp.58–76.
6. Van den Byvang, 1937, pp.429–435; the text was collected in 1926.
7. Struyf, 1948, pp.373–375.
8. Labrecque, 1949.
9. Biebuyck, 1957, p.803.
10. Turner, 1968, p.58.
11. Biebuyck, 1957, pp.791, 796, 803.
12. Bastin, 1966, p.15, quoting de Carvalho, 1890.
13. Turner, 1967, p.41.
14. Bastin, 1966, appendix, p.xxxv.
15. Struyf, 1948, p.358.
16. Turner, 1967, p.42.
17. *Ibid.*, p.288.
18. Turner, 1962b, p.133.
19. Lévi-Strauss, 1968, p.177.
20. Theeuws, 1962, pp.222–223.
21. Formerly, the ficus was an object of veneration in some regions (it furnished bark-cloth). See Van Avermaet, 1954, p.779, on *m-umo.*
22. de Brandt, 1921, p.257.

23. Struyf, 1948, p.359.
24. Duysters, 1958, p.84.
25. Labrecque, 1949, p.12.
26. Bastin, 1961, p.101.
27. Vansina, 1965, p.22.
28. Biebuyck, 1957, p.789.
29. *Ibid.*
30. *Ibid.*, pp.804–805.
31. Lévi-Strauss, 1966, p.139.
32. *Ibid.*, p.157.
33. Turner, 1962b, pp.149–150.
34. Turner, 1967, p.42.
35. *Ibid.*, p.70.
36. de Carvalho, 1890, p.353, cited in Lucas, 1968, p.65.
37. Turner, 1962b, p.150.
38. Lévi-Strauss, 1968, p.330.
39. Turner, 1962b, p.150.
40. *Ibid.*, p.152.
41. Turner, 1967, Chapter III.
42. *Ibid.*, p.77.
43. *Ibid.*, p.78.
44. *Ibid.*, p.80.
45. *Ibid.*, p.81.
46. Turner, 1962b, p.150.
47. Turner, 1967, pp.77–78.
48. *Ibid.*, p.80.
49. *Ibid.*, p.78.
50. *Ibid.*, p.41.
51. Turner, 1962b, p.149.
52. Turner, 1967, p.70.
53. *Ibid.*, p.73.
54. *Ibid.*
55. Turner, 1962b, p.131.
56. *Ibid.*, p.135, and 1967, p.73.
57. Turner, 1967, p.73.
58. *Ibid.*, pp.63–64.
59. Sendwe, 1955, pp.74–75.
60. de Sousberghe, 1956, pp.22–23.
61. *Ibid.*, p.23.
62. Vansina, 1964, p.13.
63. Vansina, 1956, p.914.
64. Torday and Joyce, 1911, pp.235–236.
65. Lévi-Strauss, 1966.
66. de Carvalho, 1890, p.229; Pogge, 1880, p.231.
67. Cited by Baumann, 1926a, p.153.
68. de Heusch, 1958, p.122; de Sousberghe, 1963, p.62.
69. Vansina, 1965, pp. 20–21.
70. Denolf, 1954, p.823.
71. Turner, 1926b, p.140.
72. Bastin, 1961, pp.102–103.

73. Crine-Mavar, 1963, p.101.
74. *Ibid.*
75. Biebuyck, 1957, p.803.
76. Bastin, 1966, p.16, quoting de Carvalho, 1890, p.223.
77. Lucas, 1968, p.53.
78. Bastin, 1961, pp.114, 117–118.
79. Baumann, 1935, p.159.
80. Crine-Mavar, 1963, p.167.
81. Roelandts, manuscript copied at Kikwit by de Sousberghe. Bastin has reproduced this important text (1966, appendix, p. xvi).
82. Baumann, 1935, p.159.
83. Biebuyck, 1957, p.798.
84. Crine-Mavar, 1963, p.167.
85. Lucas, 1968, pp.61–65, quoting oral statements by Jeroom Gubbels and Arno Stevens.
86. Biebuyck, 1957, p.799.
87. *Ibid.*, p.798.
88. Bastin, 1961, I, p.102.
89. *Ibid.*, p.100.
90. *Ibid.*, III, p.274.

CHAPTER SIX: *Animals with Eyes of Night*

1. Crine-Mavar, 1963, p.101.
2. Turner, 1953 and 1967; White, 1954; Baumann, 1935; Delille, 1944; dos Santos, 1962; Plancquaert, 1930.
3. Crine-Mavar, 1963, p.95.
4. Turner, 1953, pp.28–29.
5. White, 1954, pp.114–115.
6. de Sousberghe, 1956.
7. *Ibid.*, pp.49–53.
8. *Ibid.*, p.6.
9. *Ibid.*, pp.21–22.
10. *Ibid.*, p.33.
11. *Ibid.*
12. *Ibid.*
13. *Ibid.*, p.30.
14. *Ibid.*, p.36.
15. *Ibid.*, p.29.
16. Cordemans, manuscript study, Kikwit archives, cited by de Sousberghe, 1956, p.30.
17. White, 1954, p.110; dos Santos, 1962, p.146.
18. This document, copied by de Sousberghe, has been kindly made available by him.
19. An example of this headdress is to be found in the Dundo Museum, Angola.
20. de Sousberghe, 1956, p.24.
21. Horton, 1953, p.165.
22. Crine-Mavar, 1963, p.84.

23. de Sousberghe, 1956, p.7.
24. *Ibid.*, p.7, quoting Plancquaert, 1930, pp.21, 25.
25. Crine-Mavar, 1963, p.95.
26. *Ibid.*, p.96.
27. *Ibid.*
28. de Sousberghe, 1956, pp.43–44.
29. Plancquaert, 1930, p.44.
30. de Sousberghe, 1956, p.14 (quoting Cordemans).
31. *Ibid.*, p.50.
32. *Ibid.*, p.42.
33. *Ibid.*, p.23.
34. White, 1954, p.112.
35. Turner, 1967, p.42.
36. de Sousberghe, 1956, p.23.
37. *Ibid.*, pp.40, 61.
38. *Ibid.*, p.41.
39. *Ibid.*, pp.50–52.
40. *Ibid.*, pp.52–53.
41. Turner, 1953, p.33.
42. Baumann, 1935, p.120.
43. *Ibid.*, p.159.
44. McCulloch, 1951, p.61.
45. Roumeguère-Eberhardt, 1963, p.56.
46. Bastin, 1961, p.212.
47. Cunnison, 1959, p.151.
48. Unpublished manuscript.
49. de Sousberghe, 1958, p.1336.
50. Grévisse, 1946–1947, p.74.
51. *Ibid.*
52. de Sousberghe, 1958, p.1337.
53. Labrecque, 1933.
54. Grévisse, 1946–1947, pp.72–73.
55. Delille, 1944, p.50; White, 1953, p.42.
56. Turner, 1967, pp.152–153.
57. *Ibid.*, p.207.
58. *Ibid.*, p.209.
59. *Ibid.*, pp.247–248; Vrydagh, 1969, p.57; Borgonjon, 1945, 2, p.59; Delille, 1930, p.857.
60. Delille, 1930, p.857.
61. Vrydagh, 1969, p.57.
62. Delille, 1930, p.857.
63. Vrydagh, 1969, pp.57–58; Tucker, 1949, p.57.
64. Vrydagh, 1969, pp.58–59.
65. *Ibid.*, p.58.
66. Turner, 1967, p.239.
67. Vrydagh, 1969, p.58.
68. White, 1953, p.50.
69. Vrydagh, 1969, p.58.
70. Turner, 1967, pp.234–235.
71. Delille, 1930, p.853.

72. Turner, 1967, p.234; Borgonjon, 1945, p.59.
73. Vrydagh, 1969, pp.62, 73.
74. Turner, 1967, p.207.
75. *Ibid.*
76. *Ibid.*, p.256.
77. Turner, 1953, p.19.
78. Turner, 1967, p.209.
79. *Ibid.*, p.230.
80. White, 1953, p.48.
81. *Ibid.*
82. Gluckman, 1949, p.148.
83. Bastin, 1961, vol. I, p.128; Borgonjon, 1945, p.61; Vrydagh, 1969, p.60.
84. Bastin, 1961, vol. I, pp.52, 128.
85. White, 1953, p.46.
86. Borgonjon, 1945, p.22.
87. *Ibid.*, p.22.
88. *Ibid.*, p.61.
89. wa Sesemba, 1974, p.86.
90. *Ibid.*, p.71.
91. *Ibid.*, p.62.
92. *Ibid.*, p.82.
93. Plancquaert, 1930, p.61.
94. *Ibid.*, p.57.
95. *Ibid.*, p.60.
96. *Ibid.*, pp.70–71.
97. *Ibid.*, p.70.
98. *Ibid.*, p.75.
99. *Ibid.*, p.87.
100. *Ibid.*
101. *Ibid.*, p.44.
102. *Ibid.*, p.113.
103. *Ibid.*, p.84.
104. Delille, 1930, p.857; Borgonjon, 1945, p.22.
105. Delille, 1930, p.857.
106. *Ibid.*
107. Roelandts, 1936 (unpublished), cited by Bastin, 1966, p.xvi.
108. Lima, 1969, p.38.
109. White, 1954, p.111.
110. Baumann, 1935, p.232.
111. Vrydagh, 1969, pp.71–72.
112. *Ibid.*, p.72.
113. White, 1953, p.51.
114. de Sousberghe, 1956, p.33.
115. *Ibid.*, p.31.
116. Borgonjon, 1945, p.70.
117. Vrydagh, 1969, pp.66–67.
118. White, 1953, p.48.
119. Vrydagh, 1959, p.57.
120. Turner, 1967, p.213 and diagrams 7, 8.

121. Turner, who admits the fragmentary nature of his description, does not say whether the bearers of food are forbidden to pass under the arch that marks the beginning of the path (leading to the novices' fire).
122. Vrydagh, 1969, p.62; White, 1953, p.48; Turner, 1967, p.238.
123. Vrydagh, 1969, p.62.
124. *Ibid.*
125. White, 1953, p.48.
126. Delille, 1930, p.856.
127. Vrydagh, 1969, p.59.
128. *Ibid.*
129. Lévi-Strauss, 1966, fourth part.
130. *Ibid.*, pp. 348–349.
131. *Ibid.*, p.352.
132. Vrydagh, 1969, p.59.
133. *Ibid.*, p.58.
134. *Ibid.*, p.67.
135. *Ibid.*, p.72.
136. *Ibid.*, pp.72–73.
137. *Ibid.*, p.67.
138. Lévi-Strauss, 1966, pp.354–363.
139. Vrydagh, 1969, p.69.
140. Turner, 1967, p.230; Borgonjon, 1945, p.67.
141. Turner, 1967, pp.224, 230.
142. *Ibid.*, p.231.
143. *Ibid.*, p.193.
144. Lévi-Strauss, 1966, pp.361–363.
145. Vansina, 1955, p.148.
146. *Ibid.*, p.143.
147. *Ibid.*, p.142.
148. Turner, 1967, p.207.
149. Crine-Mavar, 1963, p.95.
150. Vrydagh, 1969, p.62.
151. *Ibid.*, p.67.
152. Turner, 1967, p.256.
153. *Ibid.*
154. *Ibid.*, p.247; Delille, 1930, p.856.
155. Turner, 1967, p.256.
156. Van Avermaet, 1954, p.227.
157. Theeuws, 1960, p.140.
158. *Ibid.*, pp.136–145; Sendwe, 1954, pp.93–97.
159. Turner, 1953, p.29.
160. de Sousberghe, 1956, p.4.
161. Turner, 1967, p.249.
162. White, 1961, p.33.
163. de Sousberghe, 1956, pp.54–60.
164. *Ibid.*, p.60.
165. Vansina, 1966, p.175.
166. de Carvalho, 1890, pp. 76–83.
167. Vansina, 1965, pp. 189–193.
168. Birmingham, 1965.

169. Labrecque, 1933.
170. Labrecque writes of "burning lenses," perhaps referring to mirrors of Portuguese origin.
171. Doke, 1931, p.226, cited by Bourgeois, 1965, p.27.
172. Munday, 1942, p.50.
173. Douglas, 1969, pp. 154–156, quoting Richards, 1956.
174. Richards, 1951, pp.32–33.
175. Lévi-Strauss, 1964, p.205.
176. *Ibid.*, p.286.
177. Munday, 1942, pp.50–51.
178. Munday, 1961, p.8.
179. Whiteley, 1951, p.26.
180. Vansina, 1964, p.23.
181. Vansina, 1963, p.365.
182. Torday and Joyce, 1911, p.26.
183. Vansina, 1961, pp.86–87.

Bibliography

Achten, L. 1929. "Over de geschiedenis der Bakuba," *Congo*, I, 2, 189–205.

Bastin, Marie-Louise. 1961. *Art décoratif tshokwe*, Lisbon.

———. 1966. *Tshibinda Ilunga: Héros civilisateur*, Brussels (roneotyped).

Baumann, H. 1926a. "Vaterrecht und Mutterrecht in Afrika," *Zeitschrift für Ethnologie*, 58, 62–161.

———. 1926b. "Die Mannbarkeitsfeiern bei den Tshokwe (N.O. Angola Westafrika) und ihren Nachbarn," *Baesslerarchiv*, XV, I, 1–54.

———. 1935. *Lunda, bei Bauern und Jägern in Inner-Angola*, Berlin.

Biebuyck, Daniel. 1957. "Fondements de l'organisation politique des Lunda du Mwaantayaav en territoire de Kapanga," *Zaïre*, XI, 8, 787–817.

Birmingham, D. 1965. "The date and significance of the Imbangala invasion of Angola," *Journal of African History*, VI, 2, 143–152.

Bittremieux, Léo. 1936. *La société secrète des Bakhimba au Mayombe*, Brussels.

Boone, Olga. 1961. *Carte ethnique du Congo: Quart sud-est*, Annales du Musée royal de l'Afrique centrale, Tervuren.

Borgonjon, P. Joh. 1945. "De Besnijdenis bij de Tutshiokwe," *Aequatoria*, VIII, 1, 13–25; 2, 59–74.

Bouillon, A. 1953. "Les mammifères dans le folklore luba," *Zaïre*, VII, 6, 563–601.

Bourgeois, E. 1965. "La Promotion d'un pays en voie de développement, problème délicat et difficile," *Mémoires du CEPSI*, 24, Elisabethville [Lubumbashi].

de Bouveignes, O. 1933. *Un fruit dans la haie*, Brussels.

de Brandt, L. 1921. "Het heelal van de Muluba," *Congo*, I, 2, 249–261.

Burton, W. F. P. 1961. *Luba Religion and Magic in Custom and Belief*, Annales du Musée royal de l'Afrique centrale, Tervuren.

de Carvalho, H. A. Dias. 1890. *Etnografia e historia tradicional dos povos da Lunda*, Lisbon.

Colle, R. P. 1913. *Les Baluba*, 2 vols., Brussels.

Coupez, André. 1955. *Esquisse de la langue holoholo*, Annales du Musée royal de l'Afrique centrale, Tervuren.

Crine-Mavar, B. 1963. "Un aspect du symbolisme luunda: L'association funéraire des Acudyaang," in L. de Sousberghe, B. Crine-Mavar, A. Doutreloux, and J. de Loose, *Miscellanea Ethnographica*, Annales du Musée royal de l'Afrique centrale, Tervuren.

Cunnison, I. 1959. *The Luapula Peoples of Northern Rhodesia*, Manchester.

Delille, A. 1944. "Over de Mukanda en Zemba bij de Tshokwe," *Aequatoria*, VII, 2, 49–55.

Delille, P. A. 1930. "Besnijdenis bij de Aluunda's en Aluena's in de streek ten Zuiden van Belgisch Kongo (grensstreek Belgisch Kongo-Angola)," *Anthropos*, XXV, 5–6, 851–858.

Denolf, P. 1933. "De Oto-legenden," *Congo*, I, 2, 237–246.

———. 1954. *Aan de rand van de Dibese*, Brussels.

Doke, C. M. 1931. *The Lamba of Northern Rhodesia*, London.

Donohugh, Agnes and Berry, Priscilla. 1932. "A Luba tribe in Katanga: Custom and folklore," *Africa*, V, 2, 176–183.

Douglas, Mary. 1969. *Purity and Danger: An Analysis of Concepts of Pollution and Taboo*, London.

Doutreloux, Albert. 1967. *L'ombre des fétiches: Société et culture yombe*, Louvain and Paris.

Dumézil, Georges. 1948. *Mitra-Varuna: Essai sur deux représentations indo-européennes de la souveraineté*, Paris.

Duysters, L. 1958. "Histoire des Aluunda." *Problèmes d'Afrique centrale*, 40, 79–98.

Feytaud, Jean. 1949. *Le Peuple des termites*, Paris.

Frazer, James George. 1919. *Folk-lore in the Old Testament: Studies in Comparative Religion, Legend and Law*, 3 vols., London.

Gluckman, Max. 1949. "The roles of the sexes in Wiko circumcision ceremonies," in M. Fortes (ed.), *Social Structure*, Oxford.

Grévisse, F. 1946–1947. "Les traditions historiques des Basanga et de leurs voisins," *Bulletin du CEPSI*, 2, 50–84.

Hambly, Wilfrid D. 1934. *The Ovimbundu of Angola*, Field Museum of Natural History, Publication 329, Anthropological Series XXI, 2, Chicago.

d'Hertevelt, M., and Coupez, A. 1964. *La Royauté sacrée de l'ancien Rwanda*, Musée royal de l'Afrique centrale, Tervuren.

de Heusch, Luc. 1958. *Essai sur le symbolisme de l'inceste royal en Afrique*, Brussels.

———. 1966. *Le Rwanda et la civilisation interlacustre: Études d'anthropologie historique et structurale*, Brussels.

———. 1971a. *Pourquoi l'épouser? et autres essais*, Paris.

———. 1971b. Preface to *De la souillure [Purity and Danger]*, by Mary Douglas, Paris.

Hiernaux, Jean. 1968. "Bantu expansion: The evidence from physical anthropology confronted with linguistic and archaeological evidence," *Journal of African History*, IX, 4, 505–515.

Hiernaux, Jean, Maquet, Emma, and de Buyst, Josse. 1968. "Excavations at Sanga, 1958: A first millennium civilization on the Upper Lualaba," *South African Journal of Science*, 64, 2, 113–117.

Horton, A. E. 1953. *A Dictionary of Luvale*, Rahn Brothers, El Monte, California.

Labrecque, Ed. 1933. "La tribu des Babemba. I: Les origines des Babemba," *Anthropos*, XVIII, 5–6, 633–648.

———. 1949. "Histoire des Mwata-Kazembe," *Lovania*, 16, 9–33; 17, 21–48.

Lévi-Strauss, Claude, 1964. *Le Cru et le cuit, Mythologiques I*, Paris.

———. 1966. *Du miel au cendres, Mythologiques II*, Paris.

———. 1968. *L'origine des manières de table, Mythologiques III*, Paris.

Lima, Mesquitela. 1967. *Os Akixi (Mascarados) do Nordeste de Angola*, Lisbon.

———. 1969. *Fonctions sociologiques des figurines de culte hamba dans la société et dans la culture tshokwe (Angola)*, doctoral thesis, École Pratique des Hautes Études, Paris.

Lucas, Stephen Andrew. 1966. "L'État traditionnel luba." *Problèmes sociaux congolais*, 74, 83–97.

———. 1968. *Baluba et Aruund: Étude comparative des structures sociopolitiques*, doctoral thesis, École Pratique des Hautes Études, Paris.

McCulloch, Merran. 1951. *The Southern Lunda and Related Peoples*, Ethnographic Survey of Africa, International African Institute, London.

Makonga, Bonaventure. 1948. "Samba-a-kya-Buta," *Bulletin des juridictions indigènes et du droit coutumier congolais*, 10, 304–316; 11, 321–345.

Marchal, R. 1936. "Histoire des Balamba," *Artes Africanae*, 3 and 4, 7–28.

Munday, J. T. 1942. "The Creation Myth amongst the Lala of Northern Rhodesia," *African Studies*, I, 1, 47–53.

———. 1961. "Kankomba," *Rhodes-Livingstone Communications*, 22, XIII–XX, 1–40.

Nenquin, J. 1963. *Excavations at Sanga, 1957: The Protohistoric Necropolis*, Annales du Musée royal de l'Afrique centrale, Tervuren.

Nicolaï, Henri. 1961. *Luozi: Géographie régionale d'un pays du Bas-Congo*, Brussels.

Nolleveaux, J. 1949. "La cosmogonie des Bazela," *Aequatoria*, XII, 4, 121–128.

Oliver, R. (ed.). 1961. *The Dawn of African History*, London.

d'Orjo de Marchovelette, E. 1950. "Historique de la chefferie Kabongo," *Bulletin des juridictions indigènes et du droit coutumier congolais*, 12, 354–368.

Plancquaert, M. 1930. *Les Sociétés secrètes chez les Bayaka*, Louvain.

———. 1932. *Les Jaga et les Bayaka du Kwango*, Brussels.

Pogge, P. 1880. *Im Reiche des Muata Yamvo: Beiträge zur Entdeckungsgeschichte Afrika's*, Drittes Heft, Berlin.

Richards, Audrey I. 1951. *Land, Labour and Diet in Northern Rhodesia*, London (2nd edition).

———. 1956. *Chisungu: Girls' Initiation Ceremony among the Bemba of Northern Rhodesia*, London.

Roumeguère-Eberhardt, Jacqueline. 1963. *Pensée et société africaines:*

Essais sur une dialectique de complémentarité antagoniste chez les Bantu du Sud-Est, Cahiers de l'Homme, Paris.

dos Santos, Eduardo. 1962. *Sobre a religião dos Quiocos*, Junta de Investigaçoes do Ultramar Estudo, Ensaios documentos 96, Lisbon.

Schmitz, R. 1912. *Les Baholoholo*, Brussels.

Schouteden, H. 1948. *Faune du Congo belge et du Ruanda-Urundi. I: Mammifères*, Annales du Musée du Congo belge, Tervuren.

Sendwe, Jason. 1954. "Traditions et coutumes ancestrales chez les Baluba Shankadji: I," *Bulletin du CEPSI*, 24, 87–120.

———. 1955. "Traditions et coutumes ancestrales des Baluba Shankadji: II," *Bulletin du CEPSI*, 31, 57–84.

wa Sesemba, Nange Kudita. 1974. "Un rite d'initiation chez les Tshokwe: Mukanda ou Tshamvula," *Cahiers des religions africaines*, VIII, 15, pp.55–108.

Shaw, Thurstan. 1969. "On radiocarbon chronology of the Iron Age in Sub-Saharan Africa," *Current Anthropology*. April–June, 226–229.

Smith, Pierre. 1970. "La forge de l'intelligence," *L'Homme*, X, 2, 5–21.

Smith, Pierre, and Sperber, Dan. 1971. "Mythologiques de Georges Dumézil," *Annales*, XXVI, 3–4, 559–586.

de Sousberghe, L. 1955. *Structures de parenté et d'alliance d'après les formules Pende (ba-Pende, Congo belge)*, Brussels.

———. 1956. *Les danses rituelles mungonge et kela des ba-Pende (Congo belge)*, Brussels.

———. 1958. "Découverte de 'tours' construites par les Pende sur le Haut-Kwango," *Bulletin des séances de l'Académie royale des Sciences coloniales*, Brussels, IV, 7, 1334–1345.

———. 1963. "Les Pende: Aspects des structures sociales et politiques," in de Sousberghe, L., Crine-Mavar, B., Doutreloux, A., and de Loose, J., *Miscellanea Ethnographica*, Annales du Musée royal de l'Afrique centrale, Tervuren.

Stayt, H. A. 1931. *The Bavenda*, London.

Struyf, Y. 1948. "Kahemba: Envahisseurs Badjok et conquérants Balunda," *Zaïre*, II, 4, 351–390.

Studstill, John, 1969. *Trois héros luba: Étude d'une épopée congolaise*, Diploma of *l'École Pratique des Hautes Études*, Paris.

Tempels, P. 1949. *La Philosophie bantoue*, Paris.

Theeuws, Th. 1954. "Textes luba," *Bulletin du CEPSI*, 27, 1–153.

———. 1960. "Naître et mourir dans le rituel luba," *Zaïre*, XIV, 2–3, 115–173.

———. 1962. *De Luba-mens*, Annales du Musée royal de l'Afrique centrale, Tervuren.

———. 1964. "Outline of Luba culture," *Cahiers économiques et sociaux*, II, 1, 3–39.

Torday, E., 1925. *On the Trail of the Bushongo*, London.

Torday, E., and Joyce, M. A. 1911. *Notes ethnographiques sur les peuples communément appelés Bakuba, ainsi que sur les peuplades apparentées—Les Bushongo*, Annales du Musée du Congo belge, Tervuren.

Tucker, J. T. 1949. "Initiation ceremonies for Luimbi boys," *Africa*, XIX, 1, 53–60.

Turner, V. W. 1953. *Lunda Rites and Ceremonies*, Rhodes-Livingstone Occasional Papers 10, Livingstone.

———. 1962a. *Chihamba the White Spirit: A Ritual Drama of the Ndembu*, Rhodes-Livingstone Papers, 33, Manchester.

———. 1962b. "Ndembu circumcision ritual," in *Essays on the Ritual of Social Relations*, ed. M. Gluckman, Manchester.

———. 1967. *The Forest of Symbols: Aspects of Ndembu Ritual*, Ithaca, New York.

———. 1968. *The Drums of Affliction: A Study of Religious Processes among the Ndembu of Zambia*, Oxford.

Van Avermaet, E. (in collaboration with Benoît Mbuya), 1954. *Dictionnaire kiluba-français*, Annales du Musée royal du Congo belge, Tervuren.

Van den Byvang. 1937. "Notice historique sur les Balunda," *Congo*, I, 4, 426–438; 5, 548–562; II, 2, 193–208.

Van der Noot, A. 1936. "Quelques éléments historiques sur l'empire luba," *Bulletin des juridictions indigènes et du droit coutumier congolais*, IV, 7, 141–149.

Van Malderen, A. 1940. "Contribution à l'histoire et à l'ethnologie des indigènes du Katanga," *Bulletin des juridictions indigènes et du droit coutumier congolais*, 7, 198–206; 8, 227–239.

Vansina, Jan. 1955. "Initiation rituals of the Bushong," *Africa*, XXV, 2, 138–153.

———. 1956. "Le régime foncier dans la société kuba," *Zaïre*, X, 9, 899–926.

———. 1958. "Les croyances religieuses des Kuba," *Zaïre*, XII, 7, 725–758.

———. 1961. "South of the Congo," in *The Dawn of African History*, ed. R. Oliver, London.

———. 1963. *Geschiedenis van de Kuba von ongeveer 1500 tot 1904*, Annales du Musée royal de l'Afrique centrale, Tervuren.

———. 1964. *Le royaume kuba*, Annales du Musée royal de l'Afrique centrale, Tervuren.

———. 1965. *Les anciens royaumes de la savane*, Université Lovanium, Institut de Recherches économiques et sociales, Kinshasa.

———. 1966. *Introduction à l'ethnographie du Congo*, Éditions universitaires du Congo, Brussels.

Vansina, Jan, and Jacobs, John. 1956. "Nshoong atoot: Het koninklijk epos der Bushoong," *Kongo-Overzee*, XXII, 1, 1–39.

Verbeke, F. 1937. "Crimes et superstitions indigènes: Le bulopwe et le kutomboka par le sang humain chez les Baluba-Shankaji," *Bulletin des juridictions indigènes et du droit coutumier congolais*, V, 2, 52–61.

Verhulpen, E. 1936. *Baluba et Balubaïsés du Katanga*, Anvers.

Vrydagh, Paul-André. 1969, *Mbunda and Old Mbunda Makisi Masks and Dances*, Doctoral thesis, Free University of Brussels.

Wauters, C. 1949. *L'Ésotérie des noirs dévoilée*, Brussels.

White, C. M. N. 1948. "The Supreme Being in the lives of the Balovale tribes," *African Studies*, VII, I, 29–35.

———. 1953. "Notes on the circumcision rites of the Balovale tribes," *African Studies*, XII, 2, 41–56.

———. 1954. "Notes on the Mungongi ritual of the Balovale tribes," *African Studies*, XIII, 3–4, 108–116.
———. 1961. *Elements in Luvale Beliefs and Rituals*, The Rhodes-Livingstone Papers, 32, Manchester.
Whiteley, Wilfred. 1951. *Bemba and Related Peoples of Northern Rhodesia*, Ethnographic Survey of Africa, International African Institute, London.

List of Myths

CHAPTER FOUR

CHAPTER FIVE

CHAPTER SIX